M000115005

Consumption-Based Forecasting and Planning

Wiley and SAS Business Series

The Wiley and SAS Business Series presents books that help senior level managers with their critical management decisions.

Titles in the Wiley and SAS Business Series include:

The Analytic Hospitality Executive: Implementing Data Analytics in Hotels and Casinos by Kelly A. McGuire

Analytics: The Agile Way by Phil Simon

The Analytics Lifecycle Toolkit: A Practical Guide for an Effective Analytics Capability by Gregory S. Nelson

Anti-Money Laundering Transaction Monitoring Systems Implementation: Finding Anomalies by Derek Chau and Maarten van Dijck Nemcsik

Artificial Intelligence for Marketing: Practical Applications by Jim Sterne

Business Analytics for Managers: Taking Business Intelligence Beyond Reporting (Second Edition) by Gert H. N. Laursen and Jesper Thorlund

Business Forecasting: The Emerging Role of Artificial Intelligence and Machine Learning by Michael Gilliland, Len Tashman, and Udo Sglavo

The Cloud-Based Demand-Driven Supply Chain by Vinit Sharma

Consumption-Based Forecasting and Planning: Predicting Changing Demand Patterns in the New Digital Economy by Charles W. Chase

Credit Risk Analytics: Measurement Techniques, Applications, and Examples in SAS by Bart Baesen, Daniel Roesch, and Harald Scheule

Demand-Driven Inventory Optimization and Replenishment: Creating a More Efficient Supply Chain (Second Edition) by Robert A. Davis

Economic Modeling in the Post Great Recession Era: Incomplete Data, Imperfect Markets by John Silvia, Azhar Iqbal, and Sarah Watt House

Enhance Oil & Gas Exploration with Data-Driven Geophysical and Petrophysical Models by Keith Holdaway and Duncan Irving

Fraud Analytics Using Descriptive, Predictive, and Social Network Techniques: A Guide to Data Science for Fraud Detection by Bart Baesens, Veronique Van Vlasselaer, and Wouter Verbeke

For more information on any of the above titles, please visit www.wiley.com.

Consumption-Based Forecasting and Planning

Predicting Changing Demand Patterns in the New Digital Economy

Charles W. Chase

WILEY

Copyright © 2021 by SAS Institute Inc. All rights reserved.

Published by John Wiley & Sons, Inc., Hoboken, New Jersey.

Published simultaneously in Canada.

No part of this publication may be reproduced, stored in a retrieval system, or transmitted in any form or by any means, electronic, mechanical, photocopying, recording, scanning, or otherwise, except as permitted under Section 107 or 108 of the 1976 United States Copyright Act, without either the prior written permission of the Publisher, or authorization through payment of the appropriate per-copy fee to the Copyright Clearance Center, Inc., 222 Rosewood Drive, Danvers, MA 01923, (978) 750-8400, fax (978) 750-4470, or on the web at www.copyright.com. Requests to the Publisher for permission should be addressed to the Permissions Department, John Wiley & Sons, Inc., 111 River Street, Hoboken, NJ 07030, (201) 748-6011, fax (201) 748-6008, or online at http://www.wiley.com/go/permission.

Limit of Liability/Disclaimer of Warranty: While the publisher and author have used their best efforts in preparing this book, they make no representations or warranties with respect to the accuracy or completeness of the contents of this book and specifically disclaim any implied warranties of merchantability or fitness for a particular purpose. No warranty may be created or extended by sales representatives or written sales materials. The advice and strategies contained herein may not be suitable for your situation. You should consult with a professional where appropriate. Neither the publisher nor author shall be liable for any loss of profit or any other commercial damages, including but not limited to special, incidental, consequential, or other damages.

For general information on our other products and services or for technical support, please contact our Customer Care Department within the United States at (800) 762-2974, outside the United States at (317) 572-3993 or fax (317) 572-4002.

Wiley also publishes its books in a variety of electronic formats. Some content that appears in print may not be available in electronic formats. For more information about Wiley products, visit our web site at www.wiley.com.

Library of Congress Cataloging-in-Publication Data

Names: Chase, Charles, author. | John Wiley & Sons, publisher.
Title: Consumption-based forecasting and planning : predicting changing demand patterns in the new digital economy / Charles W. Chase.
Other titles: Wiley and SAS business series
Description: Hoboken, New Jersey : John Wiley & Sons, Inc., [2021] | Series: Wiley and SAS business series | Includes index.
Identifiers: LCCN 2021020635 (print) | LCCN 2021020636 (ebook) | ISBN 9781119809869 (cloth) | ISBN 9781119809883 (adobe pdf) | ISBN 9781119809876 (epub)
Subjects: LCSH: Business forecasting. | Business logistics. | Demand (Economic theory).
Classification: LCC HD30.27 .C473 2021 (print) | LCC HD30.27 (ebook) | DDC 658.4/0355—dc23
LC record available at https://lccn.loc.gov/2021020635
LC ebook record available at https://lccn.loc.gov/2021020636

Cover image: © Radoslav Zilinsky/Getty Images
Cover design: Wiley

Set in Meridien LT Std 10/14pt, Straive, Chennai

SKY10027745_062221

Contents

Foreword

I have the honor of writing the foreword to Charles Chase's new book *Consumption-Based Forecasting and Planning: Predicting Shifting Demand Patterns in the New Digital Economy*. I have known Mr. Chase ("Charlie") for roughly 35 years. Charlie and I have common interests in business forecasting and market analytics. In addition, Charlie and I are close friends, and he and his wife Cheryl are adopted members of my immediate family.

The purpose of a foreword is to confer credibility to the author(s) and to provide context and background of the book in question. Let's start with credibility. Charles Chase is unquestionably a leader in forecasting/ modeling and advanced marketing analytics. Currently employed at SAS Institute, Inc., he is the author of *Next Generation Demand Management: People, Process, Analytics, and Technology; Demand-Driven Forecasting: A Structured Approach to Forecasting*; and coauthor of *Bricks Matter: The Role of Supply Chains in Building Market-Driven Differentiation*. Each of these books is required reading in my Business Forecasting PhD-level class at Texas A&M University. Moreover, Charlie has served as president of the International Association of Business Forecasting and currently writes a quarterly column in the *Journal of Business Forecasting* entitled "Innovations in Business Forecasting."

Concerning the context of his new pithy tome, the book is divided into seven chapters: (1) The Digital Economy and Unexpected Disruptions; (2) A Wake-up Call for Demand Management; (3) Why Data and Analytics Are Important; (4) Consumption-Based Forecasting and Planning; (5) AI/Machine Learning Is Disrupting Demand Forecasting; (6) Intelligent Automation Is Disrupting Demand Planning; and (7) The Future Is Cloud Analytics and Analytics at the Edge. Targeting principally business executives, the main objective is to describe how the new digital economy and the disruption attributed to COVID-19 have changed the way companies deploy demand forecasting. As such, this book is very timely. Further, Chase argues for repositioning demand planning downstream in the supply chain closer to customers (ultimately consumers) to maximize sales. While not necessarily a novel concept, the emphasis on this repositioning is important operationally to firms, especially those engaged in the consumer-packaged goods industry. Additionally, the case is made for applying predictive analytics and machine learning to available data sources to ameliorate modeling efforts associated with customer demand patterns. Improvements in the ability to model demand lead to efficiencies, the reduction of costs and hence advances in the bottom line. Finally, a unique contribution of the book is the introduction of cloud analytic solutions and edge analytics, what Chase calls the future of demand forecasting and planning. On all fronts, Chase provides information on various key topics not presently evident in the extant literature.

Data are the lifeblood of the digital economy providing business insights and supporting real-time delivery of critical information to enable decision making. Massive amounts of data are routinely collected from sensors and devices operating in real-time from remote locations operating globally. As supply chain executives face the new digital economy, Chase argues that the appropriate vision for data and analytics is to harness relevant information not only to make better decisions but also to react faster to disruptions like the unprecedented COVID-19 pandemic. Chase states that "Intelligent automation supported by machine learning is changing the game, particularly for demand forecasting and planning." Chase makes clear that "when shaping business plans and strategy, consumption-based forecasting and planning can serve as a great counterweight to gut feelings and biases."

Given that demand forecasting and planning generally have been designated as the areas that likely will deliver the most benefits from predictive analytics, it is not unreasonable to assume that cloud computing would also be the preferred technology platform. As this technology continues to grow, Chase points out that there will be incessant debate surrounding the best approaches to utilizing cloud computing due to the demand for advanced analytics skills. Analytics at the edge is a technology-based approach to data collection and analysis where automated-analytical calculations are performed using sensors, network switches, or other devices instead of utilizing centralized data repositories.

In agreement with Chase, the virtual flood of data is changing the way businesses handle data storage, processing, and analytics.

The traditional computing paradigm built on centralized data warehouses with conventional Internet connectivity is not well suited for dealing with huge volumes of data. Bandwidth limitations and unpredictable system disruptions all contribute to network bottlenecks. Chase notes that companies are responding to these data challenges related to the new digital economy by deploying edge computing applications. Chase opines that the cloud is a key component for a successful digital transformation. Further, he observes that open-source cloud solutions now allow companies to monitor consumer demand on a daily and/or weekly basis providing real-time updates regarding ever-changing consumer demand patterns based on current market conditions.

Not surprisingly, Chase astutely provides a concise and cogent blueprint for how business executives should deal with the digital economy and unexpected disruptions. Indeed, his contribution provides a wake-up call for demand management. Without question, Chase illustrates why data and analytics are important, challenging business operations to embrace consumption-based forecasting and planning. Additionally, Chase notes that artificial intelligence, machine learning, and automation are vital capabilities in the digital economy. This pronouncement is not only important to the business community but also to the academic community as well. Finally, Chase accurately surmises that applications of cloud analytics and analytics at the edge will grow in the future as businesses continue to grapple in a time-sensitive manner with the ever-present challenges of demand forecasting and planning. Simply put, business executives who read carefully and take copious notes of the concepts set forth in this book will have a decided advantage in coping with the full potential of the digital economy.

Dr. Oral "Jug" Capps, Jr.
Executive Professor and Regents Professor
Co-Director of the Agribusiness, Food, and Consumer
Economics Research Center
Department of Agricultural Economics
Texas A&M University
Also Managing Partner and Co-Founder, Forecasting and
Business Analytics, LLC
College Station, Texas
March 30, 2021

Preface

Retail and consumer goods executives know that when shaping business plans forecasts serve to temper and balance gut feelings and judgmental bias. Yet, most will admit that their forecasts are still disgracefully inaccurate. There are signs, however, based on early adoption of applying intelligent automation supported by machine learning and traditional predictive analytics that are changing the playing field, particularly for demand forecasting and planning. For example, a large global consumer goods company reduced its global days of finished goods inventory by 1.2 days after improving their overall forecast accuracy from 70% to 81% on average across their product portfolio. That corresponded to a 50 basis points improvement in overall customer service levels. So, you don't need to move the needle that much to gain significant improvements in overall supply chain performance.

The past year of the pandemic has highlighted that companies don't respond quickly to shifting consumer demand patterns, as well as other market disruptions. Companies were already facing many new challenges because of the new digital economy. The unforeseen disruption of COVID-19 worsened the economic uncertainty and market volatility. This perfect supply chain storm has become even more important for commercial teams to explore predictive analytics and automation. Those teams will need new systems to turbocharge their demand forecasting and planning capabilities to capture those shifting consumer demand patterns that are taking place as consumers move through the four phases of the pandemic—preliminary, outbreak, stabilization, and recovery. They will need efficient ways to generate and disseminate real-time consumer demand forecasts that reflect rapidly shifting market conditions. Likewise, it will be imperative for analysts and demand planning teams to embrace automated digital applications and dashboards to allow data to be refreshed frequently and incorporate multiple scenarios.

WHY IS THIS IMPORTANT?

We all know that not all forecasts will be 100% accurate, 100% of the time. That's also reflective of best-made plans and strategic initiatives. No statistical formula can predict the surge, outcome, or exact length of a black swan event like COVID-19—or can it? There's no data available for an unforeseen disruption—or is there? Nor will analytics generate optimal forecasts every time, maybe not when using traditional time series methods. In the wake of COVID-19, for example, retailers and consumer goods companies had to reset their traditional algorithms and data sets in an attempt to understand the effects of multiple phases of self-isolation, lockdowns, and reopenings over the past 10 months in an attempt to understand shifting consumption patterns.

The COVID-19 pandemic has disrupted the usual demand forecasting and planning processes. Consumer demand patterns for different products and services have shifted from the norm, given the uneven spread of the virus, and continuing economic and health uncertainties. Traditional statistical models that rely heavily only on shipments (supply) historical data alone were unable to capture the effects of the crisis for both current demand and into the next normal. However, some early adopter demand planning teams were using predictive analytics and were able to stress-test their demand forecasts and create "What If" scenarios. The technology allowed them to drill down on the impact of the crisis across specific product categories using different parameters. For instance, one consumer goods company used a combination of precrisis data, postcrisis assumptions across specific business drivers, and consumer-behavior research to model the shifting consumer demand patterns for their products across categories under various scenarios. One early finding showed that the next 1–8 weeks compound annual growth rate in the "pasta goods" category changed from a single-digit growth percent in a business-as-usual setting to a double-digit percent increase based on the scenarios. The behavior was linked to POS (point-of-sale), Google trends, epidemiological, stringency index, and regional economic data. By contrast, non-essential products were not influenced as much by the current situation, as demand remained unchanged across all scenarios and assumptions.

Once opportunities have been identified and benefits targeted, organizations implementing predictive analytics and machine learning on a large-scale basis must invest in the following core requirements:

- **Clean, quality, accessible data.** Perhaps more than other functional groups, the demand planning organization implementing or scaling up a predictive analytics process must ensure the reliability and accuracy of data. When business information isn't adequately sourced, aggregated, reconciled, or secured, demand analysts and planners spend more time on redundant tasks that don't add value. Business leaders must work with IT and the business to set the governance rules for data usage, what good data looks like, who owns the data, and who can access the data.

- **Organizational training, protocols, and structure.** Demand Planning, IT, and business leaders must ensure that employees at all levels are trained to understand the systems required to collect, access, and maintain the data. It doesn't matter how clean or how easy it is to access the data if the demand planning function doesn't have the right operational and organizational training and structure to implement predictive analytics programs. It needs supporting processes and protocols to gather insights from the data, share those insights, and develop action plans in unison across all the other functions.

- **Cultural challenges.** The executive team will also need to focus on corporate cultural challenges; for example, by highlighting "lighthouse cases" that might inspire other parts of the business to use predictive analytics. The company and demand planning team will most likely need to hire data scientists and data-visualization specialists. They will need to retrain internal demand planners to work with data scientists, as well. Otherwise, execution will stall, and in many cases, fail.

- **Process and model sustainability.** Analytics and machine learning models are never 100% stable over time, so they need to be adjusted continually, which strengthens the case for in-house competences. It is worth assembling a small hybrid group of data scientists and demand planners with strong business acumen to work together on special projects that make the case for deeper investments in analytics talent.

- **The importance of having a strategic vision.** The SVP supply chain, or CAO (Chief Analytics Officer), of companies must have a clear vision of how they will use new technologies. In my experience, CAOs are well positioned to provide that vision and to lead the widespread adoption of advanced analytics. They have most of the necessary data in hand, as well as the traditional quantitative expertise to assess the real value to be gained from analytics programs. Project teams and senior leaders may suspect that their companies could streamline processes or export products more efficiently. For example, the CAO can put these ideas in the proper context.

At investor days or in quarterly earnings reports, C-suite leaders tend to talk about analytics programs in broad terms. For instance, how they will change the industry, how the company will work with customers differently, or how digitization will affect the financials. In doing so, they can help fulfill the repeated request, from both senior management and the board, that they serve not only as traditional transaction managers but also as key strategy partners and as value managers. Of course, CAOs cannot lead digital transformations all alone; they should serve as global collaborators, encouraging everyone, including leaders in IT, sales, and marketing, to own the process. CAOs on the cutting edge of advanced analytics are positioning themselves not just as forward-thinking analytics leaders but also as valued business partners to other leaders in their companies. Those who aren't will need to think about how analytics programs could change the way they work, and then lead by example.

TRACKING SHIFTING CONSUMER DEMAND PATTERNS

Without a doubt, consumer behavior has changed several dimensions across product categories, channel selection, shopper trip frequency, brand preferences, and omnichannel consumption. These shifts, combined with projections for virus containment and economic recovery, are critical for retail and consumer goods strategies. Leading retail and consumer goods companies are using traditional predictive analytics and machine learning algorithms with multiple sources of insights including point-of-sale data, primary consumer research, social media, and online search trends to understand how consumer demand could evolve during and after the crisis at a granular level (SKU/Ship-to-location).

Leading executives are planning to rapidly adapt their sales and marketing plans to reflect changing consumption patterns as well as consumer sentiment. The overall consumer outlook seems to vary depending on the stage of the pandemic response, causing executives to adjust the intensity of their marketing, including ad copy and calls to action, and to stay in sync with the evolving situation. Changing consumer demand patterns for essential purchases and non-essentials is leading retail and consumer goods companies to consider shifting marketing spending in channels such as digital and social media. All these actions are beneficial due to real-time testing and measurement. Just because the crisis is unprecedented does not mean rapid analytic testing should be abandoned. Many companies are using it surgically to gather data regarding the effectiveness of ongoing marketing efforts and adjust promotional campaigns accordingly given the resulting insights.

Consumer goods companies can maximize the impact of their new demand plans by collaborating with key customers (retailers) to refine, deploy, and revamp commercial plans. Flexibility and compassion have been found to be important elements in this collaboration. The pandemic has changed the retail landscape, especially for smaller retail outlets that have been hit the hardest. Making daily calls and adjusting payment terms as needed are setting the right tone. Changes in sales techniques are being considered to adapt, as well. Companies are considering providing additional support and technologies to their sales force to improve virtual-selling techniques. Similarly, companies are reallocating field sales and brokerage resources to the channels, key customers, and geographies that are experiencing the highest demand. Retail and consumer goods companies who successfully execute these strategies will have a clear view of how the market will unfold and positioned to come out of the COVID-19 crisis ahead of their competitors. By contrast, those companies who wait until after the crisis to act on these opportunities will find themselves lagging their counterparts.

To be successful in the rapidly changing digital economy, companies need to properly tackle digital transformation. This is not possible if it's not part of their business agenda. The speed of digitalization will only continue to increase as consumers of demand forecasts throughout the business ecosystem mandate answers in real time. As more and more companies reinvent the way they do business, the efficiency of the digital economy will see its full potential.

This book describes the organizational, operational, and leadership requirements necessary to use predictive analytics and AI/machine learning technologies to generate more accurate consumption-based forecasts and demand plans. Some leading-edge companies are already well on their way in the digital journey, providing several case studies. Their stories and approaches will be a testament to the effectiveness of predictive analytics and machine learning providing a path forward for others.

Acknowledgments

Over the course of my career, I have had many chance meetings with others, several of whom have had a significant impact on my life, career, and this book. More than a few of those chance meetings lead to personal friendships that have spanned several decades.

First and foremost, I want to thank Dr. Oral Capps, executive professor and Regents Professor, department of Agricultural Economics at Texas A&M University, who has been a mentor and a best friend—not to mention being one of the smartest people that I have ever known. Dr. Chaman Jain, founder of the Institute of Business Forecasting (IBF), and chief editor of the *Journal of Business Forecasting (JBF)*, who has given me a platform to write, speak, and share my experiences with others—to pay it forward.

A special thank-you to Albert Guffanti, VP/Group Publisher of Retail Information Systems (RIS News) and Consumer Goods Technology (CGT) at Ensemble IQ for allowing me to share several analytics research studies and reports that his team has created over the past six years. Also, I thank him for his support in providing another social media platform for me to publish and share my experiences and knowledge, to continue paying it forward.

For the past 18 years I have had the privilege of working at SAS Institute Inc., where I have been humbled by the sheer number of extremely smart people. Without their curiosity, passion, and innovative spirit, this book would not have been written. They have provided a steady flow of groundbreaking work in the field of statistical forecasting and machine learning that is reflected in this book. They include Roger Baldridge, James Ochiai-Brown, Brittany Bullard, Jessica Curtis, Sherrine Eid, Michael Gilliland, Sudeshna Guhaneogi, Pasi Helenius, Adam Hillman, Matteo Landrò, Valentina Larina, Kedar Prabhudesai, Varunraj Valsaraj, Dan Woo, and many others for their amazing work.

Most of all, I want to thank the best chance meeting of my life, my wife and best friend, Cheryl, for keeping the faith all these years and supporting my career. Without her support and encouragement, I would not have been able to write this book.

Charles Chase
Executive Industry Consultant and Trusted Advisor
Global Retail/Consumer Goods Practice
SAS Institute, Inc.

About the Author

Charles Chase is Executive Industry Consultant with SAS Global Retail/Consumer Goods Industry Practice. As executive industry consultant, Charles Chase is a thought leader and trusted adviser for delivering analytics-driven solutions to improve SAS customers supply chain efficiencies. Chase has more than 20 years of experience in the consumer goods industry, and is an expert in demand forecasting and planning, market response modeling, econometrics, and supply chain management.

Prior to working as executive industry consultant, Chase led the strategic marketing activities in support of the launch of SAS® Forecast Server, which won the Trend-Setting Product of the Year award for 2005 by KM World magazine. Chase launched SAS Demand-Driven Planning and Optimization Solution in 2008, which is used by over 100 large corporations globally. He has also been involved in the re-engineering, design, and implementation of three forecasting/ marketing intelligence process/systems. His employment history includes the MENNEN Company, Johnson & Johnson, Consumer Products, Reckitt & Benckiser, the Polaroid Corporation, Coca Cola, Wyeth-Ayerst Pharmaceuticals, and Heineken USA.

Chase's authority in the area of forecasting/modeling and advanced marketing analytics is further exemplified by his prior posts as president of the International Association of Business Forecasting, associate editor of the *Journal of Business Forecasting*, and chairperson of the Institute of Business Forecasting (IBF) Best Practices Conferences. He currently writes a quarterly column in the *Journal of Business Forecasting*. He also served as a member of the Practitioner Advisory Board for *Foresight: The International Journal of Applied Forecasting*.

He has been an invited guest lecturer at several well-known universities including the Fuqua School of Business, Duke University; the Sloan School of Management, MIT; North Carolina State University;

Northeastern University; Agricultural School of Economics, Texas A&M; Institute of Retail Management, Templeton College, University of Oxford; William & Mary University; Wake Forest University; and Virginia Commonwealth University.

CHAPTER 1

The Digital Economy and Unexpected Disruptions

We are experiencing unprecedented and unpredictable times where disruption has been felt globally by many companies, particularly retailers and consumer goods companies. The digital economy has had an impact on almost every aspect of our lives from banking and shopping to communication and learning. This incredible progress driven by digital technologies is affecting the world we live in by improving our lives, but also creating new challenges. The most successful organizations get ahead of an unpredictable future by being prepared for the unknown. There have been significant developments in the evolution of various disruptive technologies over the past two decades and this development brings new opportunities, both in terms of cost savings and overall value creation. The benefits of IoT, big data, advanced analytics, AI/machine learning, cloud computing, and other advanced technologies collectively can make an impact that companies can leverage to digitize their supply chains to address business challenges.

The world is changing at an accelerated pace and companies are seeing that the biggest benefits of digitization come from the ability to move faster, adapt quickly to disruptions, anticipate changes, and automatically execute information faster by managing large volumes of data more effectively—all resulting in speed of innovation and execution of those changes. As a result, companies are looking for real-time data collection across multiple media platforms that will provide actionable insights from the data to advanced analytics with easy-to-use user interfaces (UI). Additionally, these companies hope to remotely gather relevant information affecting day-to-day operations to monitor performance, make the right decisions at the right time, and improve the velocity of supply chain execution. Digital transformation will help companies establish that foundation by becoming more agile and flexible.

The consensus is that the overarching impact of digital transformation strategies and objectives will have significantly more influence than just cost savings. Companies are facing increased consumer demand for reasonably priced, high-quality products and cannot afford quality-related disruptions with their products and services. Visual depiction of a demand plan, graphical depictions of performance indicators, and better visibility of KPIs through dynamic searches and interactive dashboards and reports will enable seamless data discovery and visualization. Users need to easily compare multiple scenarios and visualize them fully for improved performance.

DISRUPTIONS DRIVING COMPLEX CONSUMER DYNAMICS

Over the past decade, consumers have been gaining power and control over the purchasing process. Unprecedented amounts of information and new digital technologies have enabled more consumer control, and now, instead of being in control, marketers have found themselves losing control. In the past several years, however, there's been a shift. Even as consumers continue to exert unprecedented control of purchasing decisions, power is swinging back toward marketers, with the help from technology and analytics that play a new and larger role in the decision-making process.

Consumers are turning increasingly to technology to help them make decisions. This has been enabled by four key disruptions.

1. **Automated consumer engagement.** A shift from active engagement to "automated engagement" where technology takes over tasks from information gathering to actual execution.

2. **Digital technologies.** An expanding IoT which embeds sensors almost anywhere to generate smart data regarding consumer preferences triggering actions offered by marketers.

3. **Predictive analytics.** Improved predictive analytics or "anticipatory" technology driven by artificial intelligence (AI) and machine learning (ML) that can accurately anticipate what consumers want or need before they even know it—based not just on past behavior but on real-time information and availability of alternatives that could alter consumer choices.

4. **Faster, more powerful cloud computing.** The availability of faster and more powerful on-demand availability of computer system resources, especially data storage (cloud storage) and computing power, without direct active management by the user. Cloud-based demand forecasting and planning solutions that crunches petabytes of data, filters it through super-sophisticated models, and helps analysts and planners gain previously unheard-of efficiencies in creating more accurate demand plans.

Instead of merely empowering consumers, technology is making decisions and acting for them. Analytics technology will be doing more and more of the work for companies by automating activities around demand forecasting and planning in real time.

It's no longer merely about *predicting* what consumers want. It's about *anticipating*—which includes the ability to adapt marketing offers and messages to alternatives based on data from hundreds of possible sources. By anticipating, we gain a greater chance of influencing outcomes. Consumer's phones or smartwatches can deliver recommendations and offers where to go, how to get there, and what to buy based on what they are about to do, not just what they've done in the past. Anticipation is about the short-term future, or even a specific day and time. Analytics provides marketers with the ability to create contextual engagements with their customers by delivering personalized, real-time responses.

Technology is helping both marketers and customers take the next evolutionary step. Instead of merely empowering customers, it's making decisions and acting for them. Analytics technology will be doing more and more of the work for companies by automating activities around research and making actual purchases.

IMPACT OF THE DIGITAL ECONOMY

The new digital economy has affected all aspects of business, including supply chains. The Internet of Things (IoT), with its network of devices embedded with sensors, is now connecting the consumer from the point of purchase to the factory. Technologies such as RFID, GPS, event stream processing (ESP), and advanced analytics and machine learning are combining to help companies to transform their existing supply chain networks into more flexible, open, agile, and collaborative digital-driven models. Digital supply chains enable business process automation, organizational flexibility, and digital management of corporate assets.

Crossing the "Digital Divide" requires a holistic approach to digital transformation of the supply chain that includes new skills and corporate behaviors. New capabilities are also required such as digitally connected processes, predictive analytics to sense demand using pattern recognition, and scalable technologies with the capability to process "big" data using in-memory processing and cloud computing.

WHAT DOES ALL THIS MEAN?

The gradual replacement of human judgment across the supply chain. Companies will use advanced analytics to optimize complex cross-functional trade-offs to facilitate value across the supply chain directly from the consumer back to the supplier. This new digital supply chain network allows companies to match the long tail of demand, supply, and production capabilities to create the ultimate customer/consumer fit and fulfillment.

Digitization will affect all supply chain IT systems including seamless integration across organizations, as well as real-time synchronization of data, global standardization of workflows, and rising demands of cybersecurity. This requires companies to evolve in order to best support areas such as automated data gathering, short-term tactical demand and supply planning, procurement, and execution. The challenges inherent in digital transformation are:

- **Continual connectivity.** We live in an always-on, always available world where customers/consumers expect to access information and execute any task from any device.
- **Organizational speed.** Those companies who recognize market change and opportunities will profit the most from digital transformation.
- **Deluge of information.** Information is being collected by companies from multiple channels, devices, and forms at incredible speeds with minimal latency.

Those companies who understand how to capture, store, and process this information will uncover business value and experience the most benefits.

Digital transformation crosses many facets of a company's business including collaboration platforms, cloud, mobile, social media, big data, and most of all, predictive analytics. Digital transformation hinges on big data and advanced analytics. The analytics process needs to be tied to distinct digital architectures that include data integration and management, robust visualization and advanced statistical models for discovery and prediction, as well as continuous delivery of insights as events unfold, which is vital to digital transformation.

According to the 2020 Consumer Goods Technology (CGT) Retail and Consumer Goods Analytics Study, retailers and consumer goods suppliers for the first time agree on the top three areas of focus over the next year (mainly as a result of the coronavirus pandemic). Those three areas are:

1. Demand Forecasting (57% retail and 67% CG, respectively);
2. Consumer Insights (43% and 50%); and
3. Inventory Planning (40% and 30%).

In addition, roughly one-third of retailers chose pricing as a top-of-mind area of focus followed by personalization and logistics optimization. Consumer goods companies felt that assortment planning followed by marketing mix optimization completed their top areas of focus for the next year. (See Figure 1.1.)

The myriad forces affecting the relationship between demand and supply are set to expand their influence as a result of the "automated consumer engagement" and the recent disruptions. The ability to collect real-time consumer demand through digital devices will force companies to digitize their supply chains. Finding ways to be better prepared means implementing a corporate culture and structure that

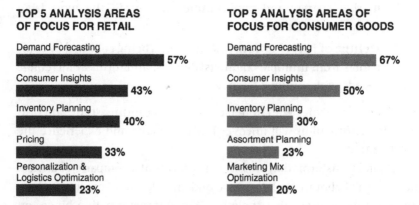

Figure 1.1 Top 5 Analysis Areas of Focus
Source: Tim Denman and Alarice Rajagopal, "Retail and Consumer Good Analytics Study 2020," *Consumer Goods Technology*, March 2020.

brings together organizations and, most of all, data from different sources. The analytics and technology capability are now available, so organizational changes and skills must transition to the next generation demand management with a renewed focus on people, process, analytics, and technology.[1] However, it also requires ongoing change management to not only gain adoption, but to sustain the new (normal) corporate culture.

There is a more fluid distribution of goods today because customer purchase behavior has changed the way products are created and sold. The rise of omnichannel and new purchasing processes such as Amazon.com make inventory management more unpredictable. The influence of external factors, such as social media, Twitter, and mobile devices, makes it more challenging for distributors and retailers to plan deliveries and stock orders. Regardless, next-day or even same-day delivery is an expectation that consumer goods companies' supply chain processes are tasked to provide. These factors are making demand more volatile, and as a result, manufacturers can no longer operate using inventory buffer stock to protect against demand volatility, as it can too easily result in lost profit.

SHIFTING TO A CONSUMER-CENTRIC APPROACH

The definition of "fast" for consumers today is dramatically different to the "fast" of five or ten years ago. Consumers are demanding more and expect it quicker than ever before. This is being driven by millennials and other generational groups that want instant response and same-day delivery. Consumer demand is no longer driven by supply availability. A supply (push) strategy is no longer viable in today's digital world. Companies must shift their operational models by listening to demand and responding to the consumer (consumption) in order to remain successful.

Sales and marketing tactics must be more focused on automated consumer engagement. Unstructured data and social media are having a more prevalent impact than ever before on the entire purchase process, which must be factored into the demand management process. This is the result of the openness and availability of consumer feedback that social media influences and delivers. Feedback via social media is both an asset and a liability for retailers, distributors, and consumer goods companies. Although feedback provides insight into sentiment and provides opportunity for brand exposure, it adds additional complexity to how consumption can be influenced. This also means demand can be influenced across multiple channels and often with very immediate consequences. Demand is also changing as consumers want to consume products in new ways. Subscription lifestyles and shared economies due to the on-demand world have had an impact on how companies need to plan, design, and create products for an indecisive generation of consumers. The consumer experience must remain at the forefront of retailer and consumer goods companies' priorities. Flexibility, efficiency, and a consumer-centric approach is the key to their success.

Transitioning to the digital economy requires a complete assessment of current processes, leading to a detailed road map to move from the current state to a future state. The focus must be on investment in training people to improve their analytical skills to sense demand, to understand those factors that influence the demand signals that matter, and to act on the insights. This fundamental shift is required to maintain a leading edge in our new digitized world. As a result, the birth of short- and long-term consumption-based forecasting and planning will be more anticipatory, rather than prescriptive.

As the retail and consumer goods industries continue to invest their energy and resources into the ongoing disruption (pandemic), they are emerging with a renewed focus on analytics. Both retailers and consumer goods executives have clearly allocated a large portion of their IT budgets to the pursuit of analytics. Those numbers will only continue to rise into the future. According to the Consumer Goods Technology 2020 Retail and Consumer Goods Analytics Study, 60% of consumer goods companies allocated less than 10% of their total IT spend to analytics. By 2021, however, over 52% of consumer goods executives predict more than 10% of their IT budgets will be spent on analytics. As impressive as that may be, other consumer goods leaders (nearly 7%) are even more bullish, anticipating even higher IT investment in analytics, representing as much as a quarter of total IT spend over the next three years.

The analytics marketplace continues to evolve as personalization and replenishment become ever more significant to maintain competitive advantage. Signs indicate both retailers and consumer goods companies are enthusiastically exploring these next-generation technology solutions. The focus is now on how to leverage these new tools to gain advantage over their competitors by investing in new capabilities such as artificial intelligence and machine learning, supported by cloud-ready solutions that carry the potential to supercharge analytics programs. These new machine learning algorithms not only uncover data patterns faster, but sometimes even learn how to create their own algorithms to further fine-tune the results. That makes them the perfect match for high-volume, rapid response functions that can quickly uncover changing consumer demand patterns. Signs indicate both retailers and consumer goods companies are enthusiastically exploring these next-generation solutions. The key is how to leverage these new tools to gain competitive advantage. We will explore this in more detail in the following chapters with real examples and case studies.

Worldwide challenges due to the coronavirus pandemic, however, have exposed unforeseen gaps in consumer goods companies' ability to effectively predict and plan demand, as consumers rapidly shift their buying patterns. Retailers and consumer goods companies need to be able to react seamlessly in real time to manage unanticipated demand disruptions. Although the industry has responded in a rapid frenzy to shore up supply chains and alter operations on the fly to ensure product is where it needs to be and when, doing so requires making costly changes in order to meet consumer exceptions. As the industry has entered recovery mode, more mature retailers and consumer goods companies have had to invest in their analytic capabilities with increased vigor to ensure a seamless transition from basic analytics to more consumer-centric, data-driven predictive analytics. Retailer and consumer goods leaders are now realizing the importance of investing in today to guarantee they are prepared for tomorrow.

THE ANALYTICS GAP

Although many retailers and consumer goods companies have a solid understanding of basic analytics, they are still lagging in investigative

**DEMAND
FORECASTING
MATURITY**

	CG	Retail
Basic (After the Fact)	54%	28%
Investigative Analytics	18%	17%
Predictive Analytics	11%	7%

Figure 1.2 Retail and Consumer Goods Companies Analytics Maturity
Source: Tim Denman and Alarice Rajagopal, "Retail and Consumer Good Analytics Study 2020," *Consumer Goods Technology*, March 2020.

and predictive analytics. It appears that retailers have put more emphasis on investigative analytics than have consumer goods companies. However, both will need to invest more aggressively in both investigative and predictive analytics to meet today's consumer expectations. (See Figure 1.2.)

The ability to understand, predict, and ideally shape consumer behavior lies at the heart of today's heightened interest in analytics. Consumer goods companies have been working at the limits of the data analytics opportunity for a long time, leveraging point-of-sale (POS) and syndicated scanner data to convince retail partners to collaborate on analysis influenced by consumer programs to drive sales for their shared benefit. Some retailers have slowly warmed up to this approach, but a large number have remained resistant to share their data, or have charged fees to do so, hindering progress. This is not surprising given the decades of experience and maturity gained by consumer goods companies, who are now forcing retailers to play catch-up with their analytics capabilities.

You can't do analytics correctly if your data is not at an expected level of quality, making it difficult to integrate with all the new omnichannel customer engagement options (mobile, social, and online) that are available to consumers. Data management is the core foundation of getting things right.

WHY PREDICTIVE AND ANTICIPATORY ANALYTICS?

Today, vast amounts of structured and unstructured data are being collected on a minute-by-minute basis through devices embedded almost everywhere as a result of IoT. That information could be integrated together to form some highly accurate conclusions about your business. Therefore, providing the ability to predict shifting consumer demand patterns using predictive analytics, which leverages data mining, statistical algorithms, advanced modeling, and machine learning techniques. Using predictive analytics, companies can identify the likelihood of future outcomes based on historical data, as well as causal factors like price, sales promotions, in-store merchandising, Google trends, economic information, stringency index, and COVID-19 epidemiological data. While the practice of using predictive analytics is getting more attention among retail and consumer goods companies, especially for demand forecasting and planning, its use is still lagging in comparison to the other industries. Although predictive analytics was not designed to definitively predict the future, it is far more advanced than current basic (after the fact) analytics that only models patterns associated with trend and seasonality.

What if trend and seasonality have been disrupted by an unanticipated event like a global pandemic? Your historical trend and seasonality patterns are now no longer good predictors of the future. You must find real-time leading indicators other than trend and seasonality that can explain the changing consumer behavioral patterns affecting demand for your products. This requires more advanced analytics that can take advantage of such additional data as daily POS data, weekly syndicated scanner data (Nielsen; Information Resources Inc. IRI]), Google trends, stringency indices, epidemiological data, economic data, and others.

As an alternative, predictive analytics can tell you what might happen given the same set of circumstances if all things hold true. Although predictive analytic models are still probabilistic in nature, they are generally very good at predicting future demand, as compared to basic trend and seasonal methods that only utilize past historical demand. It's easy to find a model that fits the past demand history well, but a challenge to find a model that correctly identifies those demand patterns that will continue into the future. In other words, you can't always rely on past historical trends and seasonality alone. You must account for factors that may arise due to unforeseen disruptions to truly make accurate predictions. A common criticism of predictive analytics is that markets and people are always changing, so static historical trends are too simplistic to describe how something will or will not happen with any level of certainty.

As technology continues to improve, so does our ability to collect and process data at an exponential rate, making it possible to perform "anticipatory" analytics. While still a new concept, anticipatory analytics is gaining awareness as a viable methodology across many disciplines. Anticipatory analytics is enabling companies to forecast future behaviors quicker than traditional predictive analytics by identifying changes in demand acceleration and deceleration. It addresses business challenges and places the burden on the decision makers to take action to reach a discrete outcome.

DIFFERENCE BETWEEN PREDICTIVE AND ANTICIPATORY ANALYTICS

Predictive analytic models range from a simple linear model to more complex algorithms affiliated with traditional causal models, such as ARIMA, ARIMAX, dynamic regression, and machine learning models (Neural Networks, Gradient Boosting, Random Forest, and others). Predictive models tend to be very accurate when past patterns continue in the future. They tend not to be as accurate in identifying inflection points, or a real-time disruption that may alter the future outcome. Anticipatory models build on the foundation of predictive models that allow you to identify and adjust predictions based on inflection points, business turning points, or an abrupt change in direction due to a real-time disruption.

Predictive models based on Artificial Intelligence (AI) are enabling more accurate forecasting by analyzing patterns not only of historical data, but also those factors that influence consumer demand. AI uses data mining, statistical modeling, and machine learning (ML) to uncover patterns in large data sets to predict future outcomes. For example, a retailer or consumer goods company can use machine learning to determine the likelihood that specific items will be out of stock and when, or the likelihood that a consumer will buy an alternative brand of paper towels if the production of a national brand suddenly halts due to a disruption. It also could analyze consumer goods suppliers to determine which ones will prove most reliable in an emergency.

Anticipatory analytics helps to identify the future needs of a business before the obvious signals occur. The goal of anticipatory analytics is to understand all the potential outcomes that could occur in the future in addition to those that occurred in the past. Anticipatory models are more advanced machine learning models, such as cognitive learning, that can learn and process information in real time.

Utilizing the right mixture of data, processing tools, and technology like "event stream processing" and cloud computing, anticipating alternative future outcomes can be achieved in real time. Key enablers of anticipatory analytics are faster data management and the ability to process vast amounts of information in real time. Another enabler is the ability to merge the past and present by seamlessly combining data and behavioral trends such as real-time data inquiries, purchase behavior, social media, and economic data to provide a holistic view of future consumer demand patterns.[2] Anticipatory analytics evaluates real-time data signals at the edge of the network to predict the future faster than traditional predictive analytics.

Anticipatory analytics is certainly an appealing opportunity for demand forecasting, but it is not meant to replace predictive analytics, which has not been fully utilized by most companies over the past 30 years. The one thing we have learned from the current COVID-19 crisis is that traditional (basic) analytics using simple methods that can only model trend and seasonality no longer work in the digital economy, particularly when the trends and seasonality have been disrupted. Predictive models that incorporate other factors, such as POS, price, sales promotions, in-store merchandising, epidemiolocal, stringency indices, economic and other data sources need to be utilized before attempting more sophisticated methods like anticipatory models. Both approaches are valuable and can work individually and/or together.

It is important to evaluate each business situation where predictive analytics can be best applied and where anticipatory analytics may be a more appropriate approach to solve the business problem. One approach is not necessarily superior to the other; it is about which methodology can be best utilized to solve each specific business problem. Traditional response modeling and other predicative analytic practices will always be important options, as more companies focus on analytics to facilitate growth. Also, companies will have to invest in data scientists in order to successfully leverage both predictive and anticipatory analytics to gain competitive advantage.

THE DATA GAP

It's no secret that retailers and consumer goods companies historically have not agreed when it comes to data sharing. According to the Consumer Goods 2020 Retailer and Consumer Goods Analytics Study, 36% of retail partners are sharing POS transaction data on a weekly basis, and 25% report promotions performance on a weekly basis with no set cadence. However, many retailers openly admit that they don't share much data at all. The highest among the data that they are not sharing includes online customer behavior data (80% of retailers) followed by loyalty or other related customer data.

What's even more interesting, for the data that is being shared, consumer goods companies say that 35% of retailers are charging for it. However, 73% of retailers indicate that they are not charging consumer goods companies for the data because they are not sharing enough data to justify it. That said, retailers and consumer goods companies are in alignment that they are still working in silos, but are making progress toward a shared data model, which is well known to be the ideal scenario for both industries. Since internal cooperation is still a work in process, many consumer goods companies have outsourced work to vendors to address their need for additional information, while retailers are not addressing this need. Most consumer goods companies have been depending on syndicated scanner data from Nielsen and Information Resources Inc. (IRI) to supplement their data needs to better understand changing consumer demand patterns for their products by geography, retail channel, key account, category, product group, product, SKU, and UPC. The latency of syndicated scanner data has been significantly reduced from 4–6 weeks to 1–2 weeks (or less), as a result of improved Nielsen or IRI syndicated scanner data services.

Syndicated scanner (POS) data from brick-and-mortar stores is the data most frequently purchased from Nielsen or IRI. This data covers a large portion of brick-and-mortar sales for 12 different channels. The data is available to any consumer goods and other manufacturers on both a subscription and ad hoc basis. Although somewhat costly, it's easy to work with coverage of anywhere between 60% and 70% of a company's product portfolio; in most cases, there is 100% coverage of a consumer goods company's key products (20% of their product portfolio), representing 80% or more of their annual volume and revenue. The following six channels would be of interest to most consumer goods companies.

1. Grocery/Food
2. Mass Merchandisers (Walmart, Target, and others)
3. Drug
4. Dollar Stores
5. Warehouse Club
6. Military

There are three more channels covered by Nielsen/IRI which are relevant to many but not all consumer goods companies, depending on their product assortment.

- Gas and Convenience
- Pet
- Liquor

Nielsen and IRI provide very similar information for these channels, offer account-level detail for most key retailers, and include them in their multichannel markets. They essentially collect electronic POS data from stores through checkout scanners across key retailers. In addition, they work very closely with their consumer goods customers to make sure that the syndicated scanner data is standardized, normalized, and aligns with each consumer goods customer's internal corporate product hierarchies.

In emerging markets where POS information is unavailable, field auditors collect sales data through in-store inventory and price checks. Their stringent quality control systems validate the data before it's made available to consumer goods companies. Understanding e-commerce sales has also become increasingly important for retailers and consumer goods companies, thus e-commerce measurement data has become a priority for Nielsen, which now offers a global e-commerce measurement service to help retailers and their consumer goods companies access online sales performance to better understand how their online sales contribute to total sales.

Amazon also provides companies with access to the sales history for their products. Up until the recent COVID-19 crisis, roughly 2–10% of a consumer goods company's products were being sold through Amazon. Most companies forecast demand for products sold on Amazon, but pay little attention given the size of those sales. The e-commerce giant accounts for about half of online sales in the United States, but since the COVID-19 crisis has experienced a significant ramp up in delivery of essential items like food, cleaning supplies, and medicine during the stay-at-home orders to prevent the spread of the coronavirus. According to several financial sources, Amazon sold, shipped, and streamed more food products and video content during the first three months of 2020 (an average increase in revenue of roughly 26% or $75.5 billion) as it became an essential provider for consumers staying at home. So, Amazon is no longer ignored by many consumer goods companies, particularly those companies who sell essential products.

The COVID-19 pandemic has transformed how people shop and how retailers sell. In response, retailers and consumer goods companies are looking to build new analytics capabilities to support the need to change in order to be more effective. Business executives are looking to data, analytics, and technology for answers on how to predict and plan for the surge and, ultimately, the decline in consumer demand. It is significantly easier to shut down facilities than it is to quickly boost production and capacity. The biggest unknown is whether there will be a delayed economic recovery or a prolonged contraction. Regardless of the outcome, retailers and their consumer products suppliers will need to think ahead and be prepared to act quickly.

THE IMPACT OF THE COVID-19 CRISIS ON DEMAND PLANNING

Companies are experiencing unprecedented complexity as they look for growth and market opportunities. Their product portfolios are growing with new product introductions, new approaches for existing products, and new sales channels. The emerging endless aisles of the Internet and mobile shopping channels are expanding product offerings, adding unparalleled supply chain complexity, and making it difficult to manage inventory effectively. Sales and trade promotion spending, designed to grow sales revenue, continues at a staggering pace.

The goal is to grow demand, but it comes at a high cost: the cost of demand complexity. This complexity makes it hard to forecast demand accurately when faced with expanding new items, new channels, new consumer engagement preferences, and global disruptions. Companies are quickly realizing that traditional demand forecasting techniques in this ever-changing complex environment have reached their limitations and are no longer capable of hitting their sales targets. To address these new challenges, companies are striving to become more analytics driven. They are embracing analytics capabilities, which requires emphasis on new data streams as an opportunity to measure the effectiveness of marketing campaigns, sales promotions, product assortment, and merchandising.

The goal is to improve decisions regarding product distribution, and operations across all channels of their business. As direct customer relationships are influenced by mobile devices and in-store IoT, these new data streams are introducing new sources of insights. However, it's taking time to transition from a limited analytics role to a more expansive role. Companies are quickly realizing that their enterprise effort requires a completely different culture that includes different skills, processes, and technology. Although many companies have already started to collect data across all their distribution channels to gain more customer/consumer information, the race to apply analytics to optimize sales and inventory across all channels has taken much more effort than anticipated.

Predicting demand and managing inventory across every channel is hard work. Shorter product life cycles, expanding assortments, frequent price changes, and sales promotions compound the challenges companies are experiencing due to the disruptions created by digital commerce and the current COVID-19 crisis. It's enough to make you wish you had an "easy button" to figure out today's savvy shoppers, and navigate through the four pandemic stages and demand shifts. Figure 1.3 illustrates the four pandemic stages: preliminary,

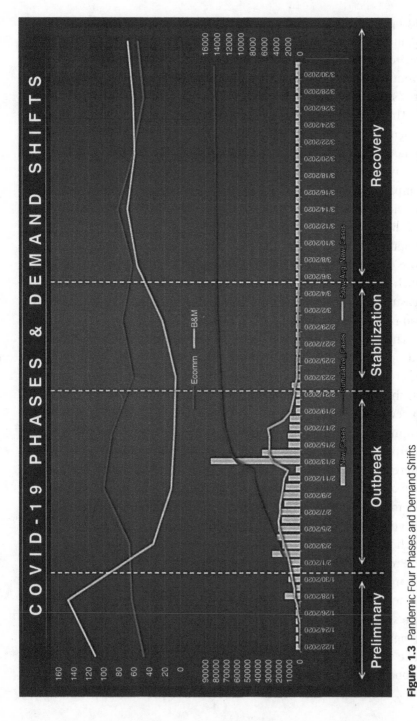

Figure 1.3 Pandemic Four Phases and Demand Shifts

Source: Brittany Bullard, Jessica Curtis, and Adam Hillman, "Retail Forecasting Through a Pandemic," *SAS Voices Blogs*, May 4, 2020. Graphic created by Jessica Curtis and Adam Hillman, SAS Institute Inc.

outbreak, stabilization, and recovery. With the right demand forecasting and planning process, analytics, and technology, you can simplify your demand planning process and create an integrated planning framework that supports multiple forecasting methods with one synchronized view of demand for every type of customer/consumer ship-to combination.

The COVID-19 crisis is transforming how consumers shop, forcing retailers to change how they sell. In response, retailers and consumer goods companies are being forced to build new capabilities and change how they engage with consumers. As a result, the relationship between retailers and consumer goods companies is being strained, with each fighting to stay ahead of the ever-changing digital economy and the COVID-19 crisis. For consumer goods companies, there are additional pressures from niche and private label brands, which are squeezing margins as a result of selling more goods through higher-cost channels. Meanwhile, retailers are trying to increase their online and mobile capabilities while dealing with pressure from discounters and e-commerce giants like Amazon and Alibaba, as well as price-driven consumers.

Because of the disruption caused by the COVID-19 global pandemic, everything has changed. As an unforeseen disruption, COVID-19 is augmenting many trends that have been disrupting the industry for more than a decade. The move to mobile and online shopping is now accelerating at warp speed, with US grocery's penetration into e-commerce doubling and, in some cases, tripling by the end of the initial outbreak stage of the pandemic. As consumers stayed home self-isolating to stop the spread of the coronavirus, they used mobile apps and websites to purchase essential products, and then over time, they added a mix of products that looked very different from what they had previously purchased in brick-and-mortar stores, with a focus on pantry items and products for at-home occasions. Those who did venture into stores found the experience transformed by new rules on physical distancing, hygiene, and the use of masks. In fact, a recent consumer-sentiment survey[3] found that more than 75% of Americans had tried new brands from different retail formats, or otherwise changed how they shop as a result of the COVID-19 crisis. Consumer packaged goods companies bore the brunt of that shift, with their profits falling, while retailers still managed to make some gains.[4]

The pandemic has created more urgency for retailers and consumer goods companies to partner to leverage new technology, data streams, and consumer insights regarding shoppers across all trade channels. With the sudden shift to new forms of buying, the need to coordinate and collaborate has never been greater. As a result, three shifts have surfaced regarding changes in how retailers and consumer goods companies work together—changing consumer preferences, accelerating omnichannel demands, and the need for increased speed and responsiveness, according to McKinsey analytics.[5]

- **Changing consumer preferences.** With the unprecedented size and scope of the lockdowns, consumers have naturally developed a craving for products and services centered on at-home occasions.

- **Accelerating omnichannel demands.** As consumers move more seamlessly between online retailers and brick-and-mortar stores they expect the brands that serve them to do the same. The need for retailers and consumer goods companies to deliver omnichannel excellence has become more critical as the pandemic gives rise to a hybrid model that combines digital commerce with products and services delivered by a neighborhood store.

- **Increased speed and responsiveness.** The continued outbreaks, stabilization, and recovery stages of the pandemic are likely to remain difficult to predict until everyone is vaccinated. Rising infection rates can quickly result in renewed restrictions, which means retailers and consumer goods suppliers will need to adopt a more fluid and dynamic approach to getting goods into the hands of consumers. This will require more accurate demand forecasts that can model the four phases of the shifts in demand as a result of the changing pandemic restrictions.

The question is whether consumer preferences will revert to prepandemic norms once the restrictions are lifted. It is likely that consumers will continue spending large amounts of time at home due to the risk of infection, and as restrictions are lifted, they will revert back to some previous norm. Based on research, it is believed that it could take anywhere from three to ten years for brick-and-mortar channels to fully recover. Within many retail channels, the longer-term shift away from physical stores and higher-priced retail brands has accelerated due to the pandemic. It is estimated that the grocery and convenience channels are likely to lose up to seven points of market share to discounters, hypermarkets, and online sales. This is becoming the new norm. For consumer goods companies, it's time to shift from crisis mode to a more fundamental realignment of their product portfolio and path-to-market strategy to respond to these new consumer purchasing dynamics.

The longer-term effects of failing to predict and anticipate changing consumer demand patterns will result in lost sales, wasted inventory, unproductive marketing investment and promotional spend, inability to effectively plan inventory for key products, and reduced revenue and profit margins. Those companies who embrace predictive and anticipatory analytics and adopt new technology to boost their forecasting and planning capabilities will unlock short- and long-term business benefits. Those same companies will see uplifts in margins as a result of fewer markdowns, and see improved consumer value, accelerated inventory turns, and significant increases in revenue as a result of fewer out-of-stocks.

Selling in the age of the consumer will require foresight, not reaction, to changing consumer demand patterns. Retailers and consumer goods companies will need to establish a pipeline of predictive leading indicators that will allow them to anticipate and predict changes in consumer demand with enough time at the right level of granularity to take corrective actions. In order to maintain their competitive edge, retailers and consumer goods companies must outpace their peers by selecting and implementing new technologies that drive actionable insights critical to adapting to the new digital economy and unforeseen disruptions. Finally, they must drive process and organizational change by hiring data scientists and retraining their people to rely on data and analytically derived consumption-based models to create a more efficient end-to-end supply chain—from consumer to the supplier.

CLOSING THOUGHTS

As digital technologies become more widespread, retailer and consumer goods companies' supply chains will need to evolve, which will require a renewed focus on predicting changing consumer demand patterns.

Transformation will not simply be about new technical capabilities or deployment and use of digital technologies; it will require more transparency. In other words, digital transformation requires extensive changes to the way people in the organization interact and collaborate across processes and corresponding business models. Leadership and workforce talent/skill sets, their attitudes, and ways of working will need to adapt to the new normal. Delivering real benefits for the future will require focus on integration of technologies that are better aligned with the business needs, followed by effective management of those new digital technologies. Those changes will help manage a digitally transformed, consumer analytics–driven organization for the future. Overall, collaboration, new organizational changes, and cultural change must be driven by a champion who reports to an executive sponsor from the C-level suite.

Companies are rapidly transitioning from the hierarchical organizational structure to one that is far more collaborative. Not just because they need to work together to do things faster and reduce delays between organizational silos, but also because now they can share information to create a common view of what needs to be done, end-to-end, within the supply chain. Cross-pollination of understanding among various divisions maximizes the overall business value. Fundamentally, a collaborative culture results in a single source of the truth. Such a culture facilitates connectivity among the various islands of information from downstream consumer strategies and tactics to upstream supply planning, manufacturing, and distribution.

Business executives are looking to data, analytics, and technology for answers on how to predict and plan for the surge, and ultimately, the decline in consumer demand. It is significantly easier to shut down facilities than it is to quickly boost production and capacity. The biggest unknown is whether there will be a delayed economic recovery or a prolonged contraction. Regardless of the outcome, retailers and their consumer goods suppliers will need to think ahead and be prepared to act quickly. Retailers and consumer goods companies are the backbone of the consumer goods supply chain and a lifeline to their customers. Their ability to operate efficiently is determined by the weakest link in the end-to-end supply chain. That link has now been exposed as the result of the digital economy and the coronavirus pandemic—the inability to effectively predict shifting consumer demand patterns.

To make matters worse, the current crisis has changed the makeup of the average grocery basket, making it difficult to predict rapidly shifting consumer demand patterns. As a result, the current supply chain is struggling to keep up. Restoring balance will require changes in the way demand forecasting and planning are conducted by both retailers and consumer goods companies. Navigating the current climate will require new intelligence, resilience, and more dependence on advanced analytics and machine learning.

NOTES

1. Charles Chase, *Next Generation Demand Management: People, Process, Analytics and Technology*, Wiley, 2016: 1–252.
2. Dun & Bradstreet, "Predictive vs. Anticipatory: Understanding the Best Analytics Approach to Address Your Business Goals," 2016: 1–5.
3. Brandon Brown, Lindsay Hirsch, René Schmutzler, Jasper van Wamelen, and Matteo Zanin, "What Consumer-Goods Sales Leaders Must Do to Emerge Stronger from the Pandemic," McKinsey & Company, August 2020: 1–10.
4. Ibid.
5. Ibid.

CHAPTER **2**

A Wake-up Call
for Demand
Management

emand management concepts are now over 30 years old. The first use of the term *demand management* surfaced in the commercial sector in the late 1980s and early 1990s. Previously, the focus was on a more siloed approach to demand forecasting and planning that was manual, using very simple statistical techniques like moving averaging and simple exponential smoothing, and then Excel, and a whole lot of "gut feeling" judgment. Sound familiar? In the mid-1990s, demand planning and supply planning were lumped together, giving birth to supply chain management concepts—demand planning and integrated supply chain planning. Essentially, nothing has changed over the last 30 years other than more focus on planning supply (shipments), using inventory buffer stock to manage variation in the supply plan, and focusing on collaboration. There is very little, if any, focus on advanced analytics and downstream data.

As a result of the current disruptions, supply chain professionals are quickly realizing that their supply chain planning solutions have not driven down costs and have not reduced inventories or speed to market. Companies globally across all industry verticals have actually moved backwards over the course of the last 30 years when it comes to growth, operating margin, and inventory turns. In some cases, they have improved days payable, but this has pushed costs and working capital responsibility backwards in the supply chain, moving the costs to the suppliers. To make matters worse, Excel still remains the most widely used demand forecasting and planning technology in the face of significant improvements in data collection, storage, processing, analytics, and scalability. Not to mention the availability of cloud-ready, web-enabled technology with open-source capabilities that allow the integration of SAS, R, Python, and other advanced analytics, such as machine learning algorithms, to operate in the same ecosystem.

Subsequently, simple moving averaging has now become the preferred statistical model of choice for forecasting demand, digressing from more sophisticated methods like Winters' Three Parameter exponential smoothing based on recent studies. Furthermore, despite all the advancements in analytics and technology, there has been minimal investment in the analytic skills of demand planners. To make matters worse, downstream data with all its improvements in data collection, minimal latency in delivery, and increased coverage across channels is still being used in pockets across sales and marketing, rather than the entire supply chain for demand forecasting and planning.

DEMAND UNCERTAINTY IS DRIVING CHANGE

During normal times companies face numerous uncertainties of varying consequences. Executives deal with challenges by relying on conventional processes and frameworks to solve those challenges. These processes are designed to reduce uncertainty and are normally supported by data-driven decisions. In a crisis, however, uncertainty can reach extreme levels, and the conventional way of working becomes encumbered. As a result, traditional demand planning processes have become inadequate, and executives are quickly finding themselves facing extreme pressure to deliver their products and services to meet shifting consumer demand patterns.

The uncertainty of consumer demand occurs during times when a business or an entire industry is unable to accurately predict demand for its products or services. This can cause several problems for companies, making it difficult to effectively manage customer orders and inventory stocking levels. Uncertainty is measured in magnitude and duration, with both measures determining the uncertainty accompanied by the disruptions, whether they are due to the digital economy or the COVID-19 crisis. The economic damage created by this perfect storm of disruptions is unprecedented in modern history. It is not surprising that companies are looking for new management processes and frameworks for demand planning to sustain their supply chains under such conditions.[1]

The magnitude of the uncertainty that organizations face in this crisis is defined by the frequency and extent of changes in information, which requires continuous learning and flexible responses as the situation evolves. Unfortunately, the duration of the crisis has exceeded the early predictions of many analysts. Now demand planners are having to operate in crisis mode for an extended period. Corporate executives will need to begin assembling the initial elements of this new operating model so that they can direct their organizations under extreme conditions of uncertainty.

CHALLENGES CREATED BY DEMAND UNCERTAINTY

Uncertainty makes it difficult to determine the right quantity of supplies and goods to order for each sales cycle. This also creates back orders on the shelf, high inventories for the wrong products, higher than normal safety stock, waste, and discarded products. Not to mention reduction in revenue and profit margins. Each scenario leads to an increase in unexpected costs. When demand unexpectedly increases, companies with an insufficient supply of goods to sell will experience lower customer service levels (unfilled orders), resulting in dissatisfied consumers who may purchase from a competitor who has a supply of that particular desired product. Some consumers may never return to the original branded product, resulting in loss of business for the company. The costs associated with losing a consumer to a competitor are greater in many cases than the costs of carrying excess inventory. Problems caused by demand uncertainty are not only limited to having the right product availability. When consumer demand patterns fluctuate, it becomes difficult to achieve appropriate staffing levels, especially for retailers. Other areas of expenditure, such as equipment purchases or facility development, are also affected.

ONGOING "BULLWHIP" EFFECT

Demand uncertainty at the retail customer level tends to get magnified from the consumer (downstream) back (upstream) through the entire supply chain to the consumer goods raw materials suppliers. This supply chain phenomenon initially starts when retailers and wholesalers notice that the retail stores they serve have cut back or increased their orders. This in turn creates a chain reaction of cutting or increasing supply from the consumer goods companies, which then over- or underestimate (hedge) their demand plans to compensate for the changes in sales orders. As a result, the flow of orders is amplified upstream throughout the entire supply chain, creating as much as a six-month or greater backlog within the supply chain that began with retailers ordering an additional supply of only three to four weeks. This is known as the "bullwhip effect" because it graphically resembles the action of a bullwhip when the "handle" is moved slightly while the "tail" swings in wider and wider fluctuations. (See Figure 2.1.)

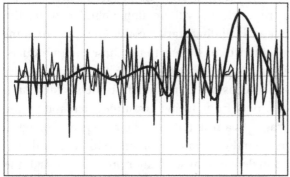

Figure 2.1 The Bullwhip Effect

The bullwhip effect is a distribution channel disruption in which demand forecasts yield supply chain inefficiencies. It refers to increasing swings in finished goods inventory and safety stock (buffer stock) in response to shifts in consumer demand as one moves further upstream in the supply chain. The concept first appeared in Jay Forrester's book *Industrial Dynamics,* and thus it is also known as the Forrester effect.[2]

This situation is augmented even further because consumer goods companies' demand management organizations lack visibility and accessibility to downstream information and data. In fact, most demand planners are embedded upstream in operations planning too far removed from the downstream customer and consumer to accurately forecast future demand. To further exacerbate this dilemma, demand planners are not even forecasting demand, but rather supply or what is referred to as shipments, which is the supply signal. They are backing into a constrained supply plan that they call a demand plan that is based on manufacturing capacity constraints. The closest a demand planner gets to see downstream data is through sales orders from retailers and wholesalers, which is the replenishment signal already inflated by overreaction and hedging. The entire supply chain management process looks backward—looking from supply to consumer, rather than from consumer to supply. How can you possibly react to consumer demand if everything you see and do is about supply, including the historical data being used to predict future demand, or what they are really predicting, supply? Furthermore, the demand planners are restricted by their supply blinders to see the entire consumer landscape, including market conditions and programming that is used to incentivize consumers to purchase their products.

When a supply chain is plagued with a bullwhip effect that distorts its demand information as it is transmitted up the supply chain, it impedes demand planners from seeing consumer demand at the distribution channel stage. As a result, demand planners are forced to rely on the sales orders from their retail customers to forecast and plan demand. Big variations in demand cause a major problem through the supply chain, creating many inefficiencies that lead to increased costs and, in many cases, lost sales revenue and profit. The common symptoms of such variations could be excessive inventory, poor product forecasts, insufficient or excessive capacities, poor customer service due to unavailable products or long backlogs, uncertain production planning due to excessive revisions, and high cost corrections related to the need for expedited shipments and overtime. The order swings that are exaggerated by the retailers and wholesalers, relative to their actual sales, in turn create additional exaggerations of customer orders back to the consumer goods manufacturers and raw material suppliers.

Minimizing the bullwhip effect begins with better predictions of the consumer demand signal (POS/syndicated scanner data—Nielsen, Information Resources Inc. [IRI], and others) not customer demand replenishment (sales orders), which will enable more accurate demand forecasting and planning. This requires a complete re-engineering of the demand management process including people, analytics, and technology.

WHEN WILL WE LEARN FROM OUR PAST MISTAKES?

Many companies continue to rely on the traditional practice of using historical shipment data and simple statistical time series methods deployed by their ERP (Enterprise Resource Planning) systems, along with Excel spreadsheets to develop a constrained demand (supply) plan. It is a labor-intensive, consensus-driven planning process requiring hundreds of manual overrides before it reaches supply planning for final execution by manufacturing and distribution. This traditional approach to demand forecasting is unable to capture many of today's complex market dynamics and is plagued with bias, human error, waste, and inefficiencies. As a result, the demand planning process is unable to capture market dynamics, including price changes and promotions, as well as changing demand patterns and external factors that are caused by COVID-19.

Legacy ERP systems that create transactional history–based forecasts were not designed for the new digital economy. They can only model patterns associated with trends and seasonality. They don't account for the effects of sales promotions, automatically correct for outliers, or include other related external factors that influence demand. In fact, most companies are not forecasting demand, but shipments, which is the supply signal. Some are forecasting sales orders, which is the replenishment signal. The true demand signal for retailers and consumer goods companies is POS/syndicated scanner data.

Furthermore, companies have been focused primarily on the symptom rather than the root cause—using buffer stock to offset poor demand forecasting and planning with a focus on supply planning. In fact, demand planners are backing into a constrained supply plan instead of a demand plan, as they are too far removed from the consumer reporting upstream into supply chain management. As a result, they can't take advantage of downstream information and data, which reflect true consumer demand, to detect shifting consumer demand patterns. This requires working more closely with sales and marketing to integrate marketing, programming, and spending, which influences demand. The result is that consumer goods companies' supply chains lack demand visibility from customer to the consumer. This leads to manual intervention and increases in buffer stock to respond to fluctuations in sales orders and supply.

Companies are essentially backing into a constrained supply plan based on supply chain capacity and are not recognizing the true consumer demand patterns until weeks after they have occurred. This is because their demand planners are really supply planners who are embedded upstream in operations planning, too far removed from the downstream consumer. They have virtually no view of the true consumer demand signal. If they were truly forecasting and planning demand they would need to be located downstream (e.g. in Sales or Marketing) closer to the consumer, with access to POS/syndicated scanner data, as well as access to sales and marketing programming strategies that influence demand. Access to daily POS data and weekly syndicated scanner data would enable them to see the shifting consumer demand patterns due to COVID-19 within the first 1 to 2 weeks, if not days.

Companies have forgotten that without demand there is no need for supply. COVID-19 has surely brought this dilemma to our attention in reverse. Demand planners have no real view into demand, and as such, are not able to react to shifting consumer demand pattens. Think about it.

The result is that retail and consumer goods companies supply chains lack true consumer demand visibility. They are forecasting the supply signal (shipments), or at best the replenishment signal (sales orders), not true demand:—POS/syndicated scanner data. This leads to manual intervention and increases in buffer stock to respond to fluctuations in supply and replenishment, not to mention the impact related to the bullwhip effect.

WHY ARE COMPANIES STILL CLEANSING HISTORICAL DEMAND?

Demand planners spend roughly 80% of their time managing information and cleansing demand (shipment) history. It is a mystery to me why anyone would manually cleanse the actual demand history given all the advancements in data collection, storage, processing, and predicative analytics. In my experience, whenever a company separated historical baseline volume from the promoted volume, and then manually added them back together using judgment (also known as layering), 1 + 1 tended to equal 5, instead of 2. The process of cleansing historical data is a manually intensive and unproductive process.[3]

The actual history is what happened—unless it was entered into your data repository incorrectly. In fact, in all my years of doing demand forecasting, the only time historical demand data were changed (corrected) was if the data were entered into the data repository incorrectly, or if the historical data needed to be restated due to distribution center consolidation. Many companies continue to manually cleanse their historical demand data as a prerequisite for forecasting and planning of their products. I would only restate the data if it were entered incorrectly into the data warehouse, or if the organization was being realigned. There are only a handful of reasons to realign historical demand data (sales orders/shipments):

- Data entry error;
- Warehouse consolidation and realignment;
- Geographic consolidation or realignment; and/or
- Acquisitions and realignment of products.

The true reason for cleansing historical demand is that traditional demand forecasting and planning solutions are unable to predict sales promotions or correct the data automatically for shortages or outliers. To address this shortcoming, companies embedded a cleansing process of adjusting the demand history for shortages, outliers, and sales promotional (incremental) spikes by separating the demand history into baseline and promoted volumes. The cleansing process has become an accepted activity when a company is using a statistical forecasting solution to model and predict future demand. In theory, manually adjusting (cleansing) demand history by removing promotional spikes and outliers improves the forecast results. It is believed that cleansing the actual history will produce a true historical baseline. On the contrary, it makes the forecast less accurate. This is primarily a result of the statistical methods being deployed in their legacy systems—mainly exponential smoothing methods—that are not capable of measuring and predicting sales promotions or do not automatically correct for shortages and outliers.

The definition of *baseline history* of a product is its normal historical demand without promotions, external incentives, or any other abnormal situation that may be caused by outliers. An *outlier* is a too-high or too-low sales number in a product's history that may occur under special or abnormal conditions, such as a disruption or event. Promotional volume is the incremental volume a company sold due to sales promotions and in-store merchandising. Based on these definitions, how would anyone know by how much to raise or lower the data to create the baseline volume? Furthermore, are they removing the correct amount of the sales promotion, or are they removing seasonality as well?

Outliers provide much-needed insights into the actual relationships that influence the data being modeled. They are particularly useful when modeling consumer behavior, where abnormalities between individual responses are a common occurrence. Unfortunately, many people who lack statistical training discard such abnormalities and/or average them out, thinking they are improving the structural integrity of the data being modeled, when in fact they are discarding valuable information that can be utilized to uncover insights otherwise missed because of elimination.

In many cases, sales promotions are executed around annual seasonal holidays (see Figure 2.2). Another reason why traditional demand forecasting and planning systems tend to auto-select non-seasonal models is that the seasonality has been removed along with the sales promotion volume during the cleansing process. In fact, they would have been able to use more sophisticated exponential smoothing methods, such as Holt-Winters, which is one of the best statistical methods for measuring seasonality and predicting the future of highly seasonal products.

Many companies feel data cleansing and transformation are required to facilitate the demand forecasting process. This manual process is both time-consuming and impractical, requiring various rules that use estimates and experimental tests to assess the results of the cleansed data. The cleansing process is usually completed

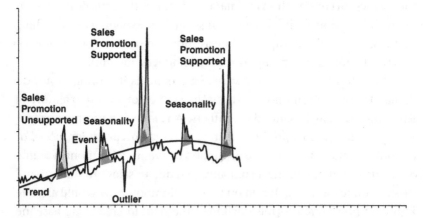

Figure 2.2 Before Data Cleansing

for all historical data during the pre-modeling process. The rules developed must be applied in real time, as historical demand data are generated over time. Beyond cleansing, a transformation process is often applied to normalize the input data for units of measure or changes in product sourcing locations in the future. In addition, for new products that are merely product line extensions, a transformation process is used to fabricate historical data that will provide the necessary inputs for the statistical forecasting engine. There are now three new processes supported by data, analytics, and technology that allow more precision in predicting new product launches. These new processes can now be implemented using new technology capabilities called *product chaining, life cycle management*, and *structured judgment using machine learning*, which require little manual input or rule-based transformations. Data cleansing supposedly removes inaccuracies or noise from the input to the forecasting system. In fact, this so-called normalization tends to create a smoothed baseline that replicates a moving average (see Figure 2.3).

Operations supply planning prefers a moving average forecast for easier planning and scheduling for manufacturing and replenishment purposes. Events such as sales promotions or anomalies are described as unforecastable and are normally turned over to the commercial team (Sales and Marketing) to be handled separately

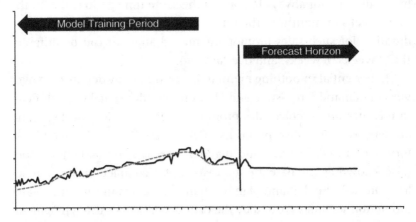

Figure 2.3 After Data Cleansing

using judgment. Removing and separating these events during the forecasting cleansing process is believed to ensure accurate prediction of the impact of future occurrences. These events are used to assess the lift of a sales promotion that occurred in the past, which helps to plan for future promotions. Although more sophisticated forecasting solutions can automatically detect outliers and correct for their impact on the future forecast, companies still manually remove (cleanse) them out from the historical data based on rules and past experience. In my experience, any manual adjustments to the historical data or to the future forecast tend to make the forecast less accurate due to personal bias, whether intended or unintended.

Exponential smoothing methods can only measure trend, seasonality, and level (moving average). As a result, the related sales promotional data need to be stripped away (cleansed) from the demand history, which itself should be adjusted for shortages and outliers. After cleansing the demand history, the baseline volume tends to replicate a predictable smoothed trend with little if any seasonality, which is essentially simulating a moving average ideal for nonseasonal exponential smoothing methods. Smoothed trend and seasonal baseline historical data can be easily forecast with a high degree of accuracy using exponential smoothing methods. The sales promotion volume lifts are then layered back using judgment. It's much more difficult to forecast the sales promotional lifts that occur on a regular basis but may not always happen in the same time periods (i.e. in the same weeks or months in the future) as they did in the past. Also, the duration for such sales promotions may change, or can be different (i.e. 4 weeks, 6 weeks, and overlapping).

Exponential smoothing methods are traditionally deployed in over 90% of demand forecasting and planning solutions, making it difficult to measure and predict sales promotions or adjust for shortages and outliers, as well as disruptions like COVID-19. Once the demand history is cleansed, the demand planner forecasts the baseline history (also known as the baseline forecast). Upon completion of the baseline forecast, the demand planner manually layers in the future sales promotion volumes created by the commercial teams using judgment, as well as other events to the baseline forecast, thus creating the final demand forecast.

Today, new demand forecasting and planning solutions can holistically model trend, seasonality, sales promotions, price, and other related factors that influence demand using predicative analytics and/or machine learning. In addition, these same models can automatically correct for shortages and outliers, including disruptions, without cleansing the actual demand history. Methods such as ARIMA, ARIMAX, dynamic regression, and machine learning models can be deployed up and down a company's business hierarchy in combination to holistically model trend, seasonality, sales promotion lifts, price, in-store merchandising, economic factors, and more. Intervention variables (dummy variables) can be used to automatically adjust the demand history for shortages and outliers. There is no longer the need to cleanse the demand history for shortages, outliers, and sales promotional spikes.

In fact, these same predictive methods can measure the impact of sales promotions—by calculating the lift volumes and predicting the future lifts in different time intervals based on marketing event calendars. In addition, the commercial teams can spend more time running what-if scenarios with precision, rather than judgmentally layering back the sales promotional volumes to the baseline volume. Figure 2.4 illustrates how a holistic model captures the trend and seasonality along with sales promotions while correcting for shortages and outliers without cleansing the data.[4]

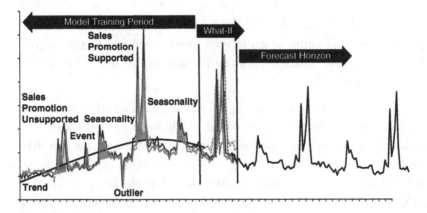

Figure 2.4 Holistic Model Using an ARIMAX Model

CONSUMER GOODS COMPANY CASE STUDY

Recently, while conducting a proof-of-value (POV) with a large consumer goods company, we found that the results of the company's normal demand forecasting process of separating demand history into baseline and promoted volumes was less accurate than using all the data holistically (not cleansing the data). The results were astounding, showing a 5–10% improvement in forecast accuracy by modeling the total uncleansed demand history. What we noticed is that the auto select in their legacy ERP system demand planning module was choosing only nonseasonal exponential smoothing methods (or moving averaging) for the cleansed baseline, rather than seasonal exponential smoothing models. This was unusual, as their business was highly seasonal. So, we decided to send the raw historical shipments data into their ERP solution. As a result, the auto select started selecting Holt-Winters (additive and/or multiplicative) exponential smoothing models 80% of the time. The result, on average, was a 5–10% improvement in forecast accuracy.

The original objectives of the POV were to investigate the potential benefits of using advanced statistical forecasting models. There were three core objectives and activities:

1. Attempt to optimize existing legacy ERP demand forecasting and planning models to improve the accuracy of the current shipment baseline forecasts at item/warehouse level.

2. Use new statistical forecasting technology to determine any benefits using advanced statistical modeling.

3. Show the value of using syndicated scanner data (using consumption-based forecasting and planning) to determine further improvements.

The results of the POC using uncleansed data, or what is referred to as a holistic model, are reflected in Figure 2.5. In the first step uncleansed data was loaded into a new automated large-scale hierarchical solution, but only turned on moving averaging and exponential smoothing models. Without any data cleansing, the forecast accuracy improved by 10–15%. Also, there was no human judgment needed to adjust the final forecasts. We found that roughly 80% of the products

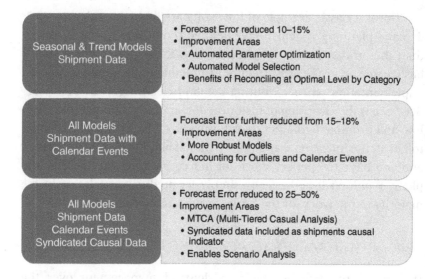

Figure 2.5 Proof-of-Value Results Using Uncleansed Data: Holistic Modeling

were selected using seasonal exponential smoothing (Holts-Winters' exponential smoothing—additive and/or multiplicative), rather than moving averaging and/or nonseasonal exponential smoothing.

In step two, we introduced ARIMA models (seasonal and nonseasonal) with event variables (intervention variables—what is referred to as dummy variables—or binary variables) to capture the lifts of the sales promotions, and to correct for outliers. The results were an improvement of another 15–18%, bringing the forecast accuracy to 83% on average across all the products targeted for the POC, with no data cleansing or judgmental overrides. Their target for the project was 85% for year one.

Finally, we incorporated downstream data (Nielsen syndicated scanner data) into the process, implementing consumption-based forecasting models using a two-step process of nesting two models together up/down their business hierarchy. First, modeling and forecasting the Nielsen syndicated scanner data, and then using the history and shaped future forecast of the downstream data as a leading indicator in a shipment model to predict supply (shipments). In this case, we improved the accuracy of the forecast another 25 to 50 basis points. The result was a forecast in the 87–91% accuracy range on average across all the products selected for the POV.

This is a classic example of how software limitations (legacy ERP/demand planning systems) have defined the business process, rather than the process defining the technology. Even more tragic is that it has created an entire ecosystem of ERP/demand planning vendor and implementation partners touting demand cleansing as a "best practice." So, is the cleansing of historical demand, separating it into baseline and promoted volumes, worth the effort? Layer this dilemma on top of all the intentional and unintentional bias judgmental overrides, and you have the perfect storm for inaccurate forecasts and demand plans. Wouldn't it be better to simply let predictive analytics do the majority of the work, or the heavy lifting? You decide.

PRIMARY OBSTACLES TO ACHIEVING PLANNING GOALS

Despite all the enhancements in demand management over the past decade, companies are still faced with challenges impeding the advancement of demand planning. Many organizations are struggling with how to analyze and make practical use of the mass of data being collected and stored. Others are perplexed as how to synchronize and share external information with internal data across their technology architectures. Nevertheless, they are all looking for cloud-ready enterprise-wide technology solutions that provide actionable insights to improve their IBP (Integrated Business Planning) process to make better informed decisions that improve corporate performance.

Before companies can address all the demand management challenges of people, process, analytics, and technology, they need to address the many existing bad practices and truly embrace the benefits of analytics-based planning. The reality is that the obstacles impeding companies from achieving their goals translate into mistakes and perceptions that hinder the progress of demand management. Those mistakes are still being made today, even after three decades of improvements in data collection, storage, processing, analytics, and technology. In many cases, the conceptual design is sound, but in practice those designs are flawed due to corporate culture and other related political bias.

In fact, no matter what size the company or its location, demand forecasting meetings tend to focus on what happened, rather than why it happened and how it can be corrected in the future, with little or no attention to analytics, and blaming the results on the statistical forecast rather than on the missed assumptions that were used to justify the manual intervention applied to override the statistical forecast. Although the atmosphere in those rooms could be defined by despair, disillusionment, and most of all skepticism, it was far from hopeless. It seemed like déjà vu, taking me back to when I worked for a large consumer goods company back in the early 1990s—no analytics, no technology other than Excel, and 100% "gut feeling" judgment injected into the process by multiple departments including sales, marketing, finance, and operations planning. All in an attempt to create a one-number consensus forecast (technically, a consensus supply plan). The story goes on with no real attention to accountability and little to no attention to the lower product mix, as the focus was always a top-down forecast (plan). The supply chain leaders didn't just say they wanted to improve their demand management process; they said that they had no choice because they were sitting on anywhere from $100 million to over $600 million in finished goods inventory, WHIP, and raw materials. Over $75 million to $400 million was in finished goods inventory alone depending on the industry—the epitome of being supply centric in their approach to demand management. I suppose that using buffer inventory to protect against demand volatility doesn't work after all.

In the face of all the challenges, demand forecasting and planning is still the key focus area for most companies, even more so since the COVID-19 crisis. For most, demand forecasting and planning is the biggest challenge that they will face in their supply chain journey. Companies want to improve demand forecasting and planning but have focused mainly on the process with little or no attention to improving data quality, people skills, analytics, and technology. As a result, their skepticism has become prevalent among their supply chain leaders, as many have conceded that they can never be successful in improving demand forecast accuracy. As indicated in survey after survey, demand forecasting and planning is important to supply chain leaders, but also represents the area with the largest gap in user satisfaction.

Based on my personal experiences visiting companies, I have found that demand management is the most misunderstood supply chain planning process with little, if any, knowledge of how to apply analytics to downstream data (POS/syndicated scanner data). Also, well-intentioned consultants have given bad advice—in particular, that a one-number forecast process is the key to success. The one-number forecast only encourages well-intended personal bias, and is used to set sales targets, financial plans, and other factors that are not directly related to an accurate demand response. What drives excellence in demand management is the ability to incorporate sophisticated data-driven analytics into the process, using large-scale enabling technology solutions to create the most accurate, unconstrained consumer demand response. Once that unconstrained demand response is adjusted for sales, marketing, finance, and/or operational constraints, it becomes a sales plan, marketing plan, financial plan, and supply plan.

WHY DO COMPANIES CONTINUE TO DISMISS THE VALUE OF DEMAND MANAGEMENT?

Today, we live in a polarized world that divides family members, friends, and business colleagues. It affects everything we do, from the way we communicate with one another to how we handle business challenges. I have seen longtime business colleagues have passionate discussions defending their supply chain position regarding what adds more value—demand or supply. As a result, we now work in what I refer to as the *"polarized supply chain,"* where you are either a believer in supply or demand. Sound familiar? We get caught up in what we are comfortable with, or what we believe is the "holy grail" to fixing the inefficiencies in the supply chain. The pendulum seems to swing back and forth from decade to decade, focusing on supply or demand "processes and technologies" with little emphasis on people (skills and changing behaviors), and virtually no attention to predictive analytics.

Based on my personal experiences and observations, I can truly say that we are at a pivotal point in the three-decade-old supply chain journey. Are we going to continue to address the symptoms, or finally take action to fix the root cause of our supply chain challenges?

Everyone seems to be high on supply these days as they continue to smoke inventory crack. They justify their addiction with the fact that forecasts will always be wrong. Well, I have news for our supply-driven friends. *Why is it that* when we under-forecast, companies experience significant backorders, and when we over-forecast, companies sit on millions of dollars of finished goods inventories? What's more, why are our supply-centric colleagues suddenly abandoning their traditional use of buffer inventory (safety stock) to protect against demand volatility? By the way, I agree completely that a 1–3% increase in forecast accuracy may have very little impact, if any, on safety stock or possibly finished goods inventories, particularly if your forecast accuracy is already above 85% on average across the entire product hierarchy. At that point, each additional 1% of accuracy (or reduction in error) requires exponential investment in time and resources with minimal effect on buffer inventories. Of course, that is, if your forecast accuracy at the lower mix levels (i.e. product/SKU or SKU/demand point) is above 70%.

It has been found that over 90% of companies still focus on measuring forecast accuracy at the highest aggregate level of their product hierarchy, with little if any attention to the lower level mix accuracy. Or, what is referred to as the point of execution. In fact, the average forecast accuracy across all industries is between 65% and 70% on average at the aggregate level, and between 35% and 45% at the lower mix levels. How do we know? These numbers have been validated not through self-reporting analyst surveys, but from working directly with over 100 companies during the past 18 years. So, there is a lot of room for improvement regarding demand forecasting accuracy, much more than 1–3%.

A classic case of poor demand forecasting is when a company ships into a channel, or to a retailer, more products than the retailer can sell, while simultaneously incurring backorders. So, you might wonder how could that happen? It's all about the product mix. Not only did the manufacturer ship in more products than the retailer sold, but they shipped in the wrong mix of products. So now the retailer is sitting on excess inventory that is not selling. What does the manufacturer do? The manufacturer discounts the products in inventory at the retailer by running sales promotions and other related consumer incentives in an attempt to reduce the inventory by pulling it through the channel and retailers' stores. This has a negative impact on profit margins and market share.

In addition, the forecasting methods being deployed, which are mainly moving averaging and nonseasonal exponential smoothing, are only accurate for one to three periods into the future. As a result, the upper/lower forecast ranges (confidence limits) that are a key input to safety stock calculations tend to be cone shaped (they get larger exponentially as you forecast beyond one to three periods). This is why the impact in many cases increases safety stock volumes, rather than lowering them. This is not the case when using more advanced statistical methods like ARIMA, ARIMAX, dynamic regression, and machine learning (predictive analytics), as they are more accurate further into the future, so the upper/lower forecast ranges tend to be tighter (more consistent to the forecast, and not cone shaped) as you go further out into the future. These models actually help lower safety stocks not only through more accurate forecasts, but by reducing the upper/lower ranges of the forecast, which is a key input to safety stock calculations. Which demand forecast in Figure 2.6 would you choose to drive your safety stock calculations?

The increase in the use of Excel by demand planners over the past decade and the broader use of moving averaging due to data cleansing are the result of companies' investment in ERP solutions, which were not designed for the digital economy, or for handling abnormal disruptions. In fact, the one area of the supply chain that has received the least attention and investment in people, analytics, and technology over the past decade is demand forecasting and planning. You may have noticed I left out process. Process alone cannot improve your forecast accuracy. It requires investment in people skills and behavior, horizontal processes, predictive analytics, and scalable technology, putting equal emphasis on all four areas.

Using proof-of-values (POVs use a subset of the customer's data in the software vendor's technology to prove the value—that is, whether it improved forecast accuracy) conducted with multiple companies over the last 10 years, SAS Institute Inc. has shown improvements in forecast accuracy of anywhere between 10% to 30% on average up/down companies' product hierarchies by just deploying "holistic" models driven by predictive analytics, rather than by sales targets, financial plans, and/or judgmental overrides. In fact, this has also been proven using historical demand data (uncleansed—that is, not

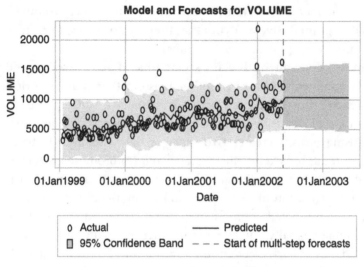

Nonseasonal ESM

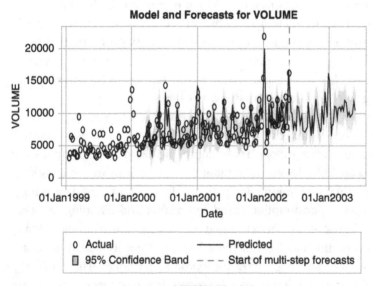

ARIMX Model

Figure 2.6 Comparing Upper/Lower Forecast Ranges for Different Forecasting Methods

segmenting demand history into baseline and promoted volumes) combined with predictive analytics that there is no reason to cleanse demand history (shipments or sales orders).

Cleansing demand history by segmenting it into baseline and promoted volumes, and for any other reason other than historical realignment or true data entry errors is actually a bad practice. In fact, this type of cleansing actually makes the forecast less accurate. The cleansing process creates two separate data streams: (1) baseline, which tends to be a moving average; and (2) promoted, which is supposed to reflect promotional spikes and outlier corrections but is actually a combination of seasonality and promotional volume. Furthermore, the promoted volumes are given to sales and marketing to adjust manually. Finally, the demand planner manually tries to piece these two data sets back together; the result is that 1 +1 now equals 5.

In 95% of the POVs conducted, there were improvements in demand forecast accuracy in the range of 10–25%, significantly lowering buffer inventories (safety stock) and finished goods inventory. In each case, it was found that applying multi-echelon inventory optimization, auto leveling, and other advanced analytics for supply replenishment along with improved forecast accuracy creates a synergy effect of another 15–30% reduction in finished goods inventories, thus reducing costs and freeing up working capital.

Another reason why improved forecast accuracy doesn't have a strong impact on inventory safety stock is that no one is forecasting demand, but rather supply. Those companies who are moving toward becoming analytics driven and ultimately digital driven are engaging sales and marketing, and linking downstream data to upstream data using a process called "consumption-based forecasting and planning, or what can be referred to as "Driver–Based forecasting and planning." Many have seen as much as 25% or more improvement in forecast accuracy for shipments on average across their product portfolios. They have also statistically proven that there is a direct correlation between downstream data and upstream data. So, why do we continue to say that improved demand forecast accuracy has no direct impact on supply?

We need to stop relying solely on either demand or supply as a quick fix to our supply chain challenges. Companies need to take a holistic approach to solving the root cause, which focuses on people skills and behavior, horizontal processes, predictive analysts, and scalable technology that is driven by structured and unstructured data addressing both supply and demand. I call it the *"holistic supply chain."* Successfully implementing an agile analytics-driven supply chain will require a holistic view of demand and supply. We can no longer make a product and hope consumers will buy it. Now we can't only make enough of it, but we can't see what the consumers really want and need. The reason is that we are blindly trying to look from the supplier forward, rather from the consumer back to the supplier.

Companies need to focus across the entire supply chain, starting with downstream consumer demand to create a more accurate demand response to fulfilling that demand with the most efficient supply response. It includes a new definition of Supply Chain Management (SCM), which includes the commercial side (sales and marketing) of the business, which is responsible for demand generation. Finally, in order to achieve this new approach to supply and demand, companies need to invest in new skills; implement horizontal processes with shared performance metrics; rely on predictive analytics to make better decisions; and implement scalable technology to gain the most insights from "big" data. You cannot get it right by just focusing on demand or supply alone; however, we need to start with demand, working with sales and marketing to support demand generation with the intentions of creating the most accurate demand response. Then we can work horizontally across the supply chain to meet that demand response with the most efficient supply response.

SIX STEPS TO PREDICTING SHIFTING CONSUMER DEMAND PATTERNS

Retailers and their consumer goods suppliers are the backbone of the consumer goods supply chain and a lifeline to their customers. Their ability to operate efficiently is determined by the weakest link in the end-to-end supply chain. The current crisis has changed the makeup of the average grocery basket, making it difficult to predict rapidly changing consumer demand patterns. As a result, the current supply chain is struggling to keep up. Restoring balance will require changes in the way demand forecasting and planning are conducted by both retailers and consumer goods companies.

Navigating the current climate will require new intelligence, resilience, and more dependence on advanced analytics and machine learning than ever. Here are six actions that can improve retailers' and consumer goods suppliers' ability to predict changing consumer demand patterns.[5]

1. **Use Downstream Data That Reflects True Consumer Demand.** First and foremost, analyze and forecast the POS data collected through store scanners. Use it to determine the shift in consumer demand patterns for your products in order to more accurately forecast the mix within the average market basket. It is even more important to focus on forecasting the lower product mix, as it will indicate which items have the highest demand velocity as well as those products with the lowest demand. Most consumer goods companies receive POS data directly from their retail customers on a daily and/or weekly basis—POS data is the truest consumer demand signal.

   Several consumer goods companies have been analyzing and forecasting POS data for products sold to their top 20 global grocery retail customers, are recognizing significant shifts in consumer demand patterns almost immediately and are acting accordingly. They have also detected the increase in demand for their products on Amazon.com as consumers shifted from brick-and-mortar stores to online purchases during this same period. Using POS demand history and revised future forecasts as a leading indicator in their shipment models, consumer goods companies can more accurately predict supply replenishment to those same retail customers. This new consumption-based forecasting and planning approach has allowed consumer goods companies to significantly improve not only shipment forecasts but also to detect turning points in demand patterns much faster than traditional shipment models.

2. **Adopt and Implement Advanced Analytics and ML Algorithms in Your Demand Forecasting and Planning Process.** Implementing advanced analytics and machine learning algorithms can help spot abnormalities quickly and adjust immediately. Several consumer goods companies that have recently implemented advanced analytics and machine learning

technology were able to predict the shifts in consumer demand patterns quickly, while their legacy systems were failing to predict those changes.

Retailer Example: Recently, we had a discussion with a large French retailer's data scientist about how the company was coping with the COVID-19 crisis, and how their new demand forecasting solution (designed to forecast warehouse shipments) was handling the shift in demand patterns. The data scientist explained that the new forecasting capabilities were performing very well, while their legacy solution was crashing. This comparison illustrates that even when the shifts in demand patterns were significant, the auto-tuning of advanced hierarchical analytics models quickly adapted.

3. **Implement a Short-Term Demand-Sensing Process.** Implement a short-term (1–8 weeks) forecast that utilizes advanced analytics and machine learning to predict weekly and daily demand based on sales orders and shipments in combination with POS data. Using POS data as a leading indicator in the models (along with sales promotions and events) allows a company to calculate not only the promotion lifts but the shifts (anomalies) in short-term demand patterns. Where available, companies also include trade inventory as another leading indicator.

4. **Incorporate Social Media Information.** Consider incorporating social media into your demand forecasting and planning process by capturing consumer sentiment. Text mining and sentiment analysis allow retailers and consumer goods companies to monitor social channels for consumers' comments on product availability, what's trending, and their store purchases. Once you've gathered a large enough sample of consumer conversations, you can apply sentiment analysis to determine which products are moving rapidly off store shelves and which are completely out of stock, as well as additional changes in purchase patterns and store availability.

Working closely with the marketing and/or consumer insights team, the demand planners can utilize this information to identify in real time the key stores, categories, and products that are affected.

For example, paper goods are moving faster in the northeast regional store clusters in the NYC metro area versus the mid-Atlantic stores. So, the planner should focus demand planning efforts on the northeastern NYC metro area store clusters, categories, and products. This information can be easily integrated into the demand planning process by simply working closely with the marketing and/or consumer insights team. Sharing analytics findings and information across departments is vital to accurately predict shifts in consumer demand patterns. This is a core reason for embedding demand analysts and planners in the sales/marketing organization.

5. **Focus on the Granular View and Regional Geo Areas.** Patterns in consumer demand are varying across countries and product categories more so than usual. Many retailers are experiencing huge spikes across local geographies in excess of 800% for over-the-counter cold and flu medicines, while food items are in excess of 25–50%.

According to a March 16, 2020, McKinsey & Company briefing, the change in consumer demand shifted dramatically in the periods before the Italy lockdown.[6] Sales for cleaning and safety products like sanitizing alcohol, tissues, bleach, hand soap, and toilet paper increased between 23% and 347%, while raw ingredients and long shelf-life products like flour, rice, pasta, pasta sauce, frozen food, and water had lower increases: from 20% to 82%.

Meanwhile, discretionary products like sweets, baking mix, cosmetics, perfume, and salty snacks decreased anywhere from 4% to 52%.

According to the McKinsey briefing, in some geographies, consumers were buying fruit over beer, but after a few days they were returning to beer and snacks as they found themselves at home for extended periods of time. Subsequently, certain store formats like convenience stores were seeing huge declines in sales, while others like e-commerce were experiencing up to 700% increase in consumer demand and were unable to fulfill customer orders.

Collaboration and full transparency between retailers and their consumer goods suppliers are crucial to identify and act upon demand signals and changes in consumer demand patterns. Constant communication will enable retailers and consumer goods suppliers to act fast and appropriately to mitigate root cause threats that contribute to under-predicting demand for essential items.

6. **How Do You Handle the Abnormal Historical Data After Everything Goes Back to Normal?** Another consideration on the minds of many companies is the mid-term: when the COVID-19 crisis begins to subside, and demand returns to normal, how do we adjust the demand history? As the dust settles and we again see normal demand patterns emerge, there will be a need to address the abnormal demand patterns in the historical data.

The biggest challenge for demand analysts will be to cleanse those abnormal demand patterns out of the demand history to reflect normal patterns. Many will fall back to the practice of manually removing the abnormal historical demand without realizing they are erasing key information, as well as possibly over- or under-projecting what the normal demand would have been if the crisis had never occurred. This presents a valuable opportunity to learn from a tragic situation.

The best approach is to view those historical abnormalities as outliers and agree not to manually cleanse the data. This is another opportunity to capture those outliers and adjust the historical demand using advanced analytics. By simply adding outlier variables (also known as dummy variables or intervention variables) to existing models, the demand analyst will be able to capture the abnormal demand patterns whether positive or negative, as well as automatically optimize the historical demand to reflect normal demand patterns. More importantly, they will capture those patterns to be used in future crises. There will be no need to manually replace all or part of the abnormal demand historical data or input missing values for those historical data points. In other words, let's view this unprecedented crisis as a learning event. Using more advanced modeling techniques, we can capture the shape of the event and remove it from the history so it can be reused in the future if something similar happens. We hope it never will, but it's a best practice to capture the impact, so that you can easily add it back into the future to better predict the outcome sooner, rather than later.

The approaches outlined in this chapter offer the rationale to consider a new framework for thinking rigorously and systematically about how to forecast changing consumer demand patterns during a time of uncertainty. These recommended actions should become part of your ongoing demand planning discipline. This will enable retail and consumer goods companies to judge which analytic tools and technology can—and can't—help them make real-time decisions at various levels of uncertainty. This approach provides a playbook to tackle the most challenging decisions that demand analysts and planners face right now, offering a more complete and sophisticated understanding of the implications of capturing and predicting changing demand patterns.

CLOSING THOUGHTS

Many traditional demand forecasting and planning approaches rely heavily on internal historical data—exactly what should not be done. It's time to move away from one-model-fits-all forecasting into a series of more advanced predictive models that collect insights from consumer, market, and internal data. Market impacts are best modeled with data as close to the point of consumer purchase as possible. Consumer goods companies can use these consumption-based models as an input to create a better consumer-driven shipment forecast. While this isn't new to retailers, it certainly might be a new way of thinking for consumer goods companies. POS and syndicated data are often cleaner and more responsive to changing market dynamics than internal shipment or sales order data that is pledged with bullwhip effects, and non-value add demand cleansing activities.

Companies often use syndicated scanner data to understand consumer and market opportunities in examining the effect of sales promotions and in-store merchandising while also gauging trends in distribution. Strategies around these areas are easily integrated into predictive forecast models providing opportunities for tactical what-if scenario planning. Companies should now determine how their business moves with macroeconomic indicators, especially leading indicators. Look at past business results to model this relationship over time. What are those three or four reliable critical metrics that can serve as a two- or three-month lead? Regardless of whether we enter a sustained recession or the global economy rebounds, this is great information for companies trying to understand the impact of long-term demand and supply.

This unprecedented pandemic is a wake-up call to all industries, including retailers and consumer goods companies. It's no longer just about collaborating across internal departments. It's about humans partnering with machines in an autonomous supply chain with full transparency. There is a mandate to leverage the collaboration between humans and machines to fight an invisible enemy that threatens our way of life and our economy like none other. Together, we can detect abnormalities faster, identify immediate shifts in consumer demand patterns, and make decisions in real time. There's no time for hesitation or mulling over options.

NOTES

1. Charles Chase, "Neutralizing the Bullwhip Effect to Manage Extreme Demand Volatility," *Journal of Business Forecasting* 39(4), Winter 2020–2021: 30–33. https://ibf.org/knowledge/jbf-articles/neutralizing-the-bullwhip-effect-to-manage-extreme-demand-volatility-1311

2. Jay W. Forrester, *Industrial Dynamics*, MIT Press, October 1963: 1–480.

3. Charles Chase, "Cleanse Your Historical Shipment Data. Why?," *Journal of Business Forecasting* 34(3), 2015 Summer: 29–33. https://ibf.org/knowledge/jbf-articles/cleanse-your-historical-shipment-data-why-1101

4. Charles Chase, *Next Generation Demand Management: People, Process, Analytics, and Technology*, Wiley, 2016: 1–252.

5. Charles Chase, "6 Steps to Predicting Demand Patterns While Navigating the Coronavirus Crisis," *Consumer Goods Technology*, March 26, 2020. https://consumergoods.com/6-steps-predicting-shifting-demand-patterns-while-navigating-coronavirus-crisis

6. Bill Aull, Dymfke Kuijpers, Alex Sawaya, and Rickard Vallöf, "What Food Retailers Should Do During the Coronavirus Crisis," McKinsey & Company, March 20, 2020. https://www.mckinsey.com/industries/retail/our-insights/what-food-retailers-should-do-during-the-coronavirus-crisis

CHAPTER 3

Why Data and Analytics Are Important

The digital economy is providing companies with unlimited possibilities to create value across the entire organization. Data and analytics have become the primary driver of business organizations with the potential for real-time analytics-driven decision making. It is a significant part of every decision that companies consider before taking actions. However, for many organizations the ability to "think data" and "act analytically" is still a challenge. The transition to a data-driven organization requires data and analytics leaders, such as chief analytics officers (CAOs), CEOs, and CIOs to elevate data and develop analytics strategies, which requires a vision to advance new business problem solving across the entire company. An analytics strategy and vision significantly impacts the work of data and analytics teams and the organization's competencies to solve challenges caused by unexpected disruptions. It requires a corporate cultural shift in philosophy. As data and analytics mature within organizations, the positive returns on their investments will become more evident. Nevertheless, data and analytics leaders must adopt new disciplines and technologies to solve the challenges of data collection, processing, and storage before they can drive business value across the entire organization. As is well known, customer experiences are all connected by data and enabled by analytics.

Advancements in analytics have ignited renewed interest in the consumer products industry, as analytics capabilities are now delivering greater value across major areas of their companies, including marketing, sales, merchandising, supply chain, and others. Advanced analytics is helping consumer goods companies become more consumer and customer focused across all aspects of their business. They are considering next generation AI/machine learning capabilities as the key to unlocking a deeper understanding of their consumers. They are counting on using more data and applying advanced analytics to successfully launch new products, optimize distribution channels and ultimately shape future demand. As consumer goods companies continue to work diligently to achieve this vision, they are quickly realizing that the journey from raw data to actionable insights is a long one riddled with many obstacles. Advanced analytics is not just a tool for better customer and consumer insights—it is also a competitive advantage. As analytics technologies become more widely adopted, the pressure to do more with data increases as companies become more analytics-diagnostic relative to maturity.

ANALYTICS MATURITY

Analytics maturity starts with standard reporting (also known as descriptive analytics), then evolves through statistical analysis and predictive analytics to AI/machine learning capabilities. At highly advanced levels, analytics are used to transform the business by driving new product launches, understanding markets, and creating new business models; however, there is more to analytics adoption and maturity than simply a progression to more sophisticated analytics and technologies. Successful realization of the most advanced applications requires a corporate culture and technology infrastructure that are prepared to implement and make key business decisions based on the results. For example, leveraging more comprehensive data about consumers and developing a hyper view of a target brand for optimizing marketing investment to drive consumption requires investing in new statistical skills and in-house capabilities such as cloud-based analytics solutions. Consumer product companies seeking to move along the maturity curve must find a way to maintain current competencies and integrate them with forward-thinking capabilities. (See Figure 3.1.)

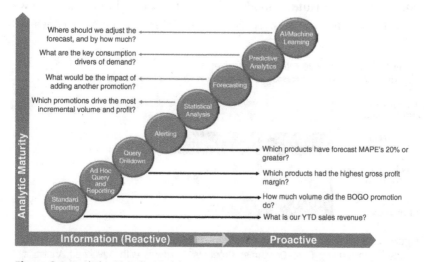

Figure 3.1 Analytics Maturity Model

Standard reporting remains extremely popular and represents the dominant maturity level across many organizations. The exception is marketing, which represents the largest area that taps into more advanced analytics (e.g. statistical analysis, forecasting, and predictive analytics) by using advanced predictive models for predictions to drive more precision in marketing spend, thus improving return on investment (ROI). They also lead the way as the largest group using analytics to transform the business. The supply chain tends to lag behind marketing in the use of more advanced analytics. Ironically, according to a recent custom research report by Consumer Goods Technology (CGT) and IBM, consumer products companies are near unanimous (91.4%) in predicting that the most impact and benefit from advanced analytics will come from forecasting and planning (see Figure 3.2), which includes both consumer as well as supply chain forecasting and planning. This is an area that has already benefited from analytics to date, so it's reasonable to assume that greater advancements will drive greater impact.[1]

The personalized consumer engagement is a dominant theme in the consumer products industry, and the goal of many analytics-driven programs is to gain better insights about consumers. So, it is not surprising that uncovering a broader understanding of consumer insights is an absolute business imperative. One underlying assumption for many consumer goods companies is the ability to factor new data streams into the analysis, such as social media, customer loyalty

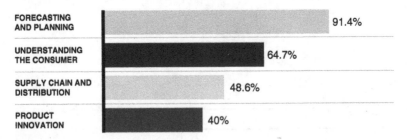

FORECASTING LEADS ANALYTICS BENEFITS
Which functions and processes will be the most affected by advanced analytics

FORECASTING AND PLANNING	91.4%
UNDERSTANDING THE CONSUMER	64.7%
SUPPLY CHAIN AND DISTRIBUTION	48.6%
PRODUCT INNOVATION	40%

Figure 3.2 Functions and Processes Most Impacted by Advanced Analytics
Source: "Transforming Core Consumer Products Functions with Advanced Analytics," A CGT Custom Research Report Partnered with IBM, pp. 1–10.

data, e-commerce, and weather data to achieve not just nuance, but reduce guesswork and latency to take decisive actions. Furthermore, most consumer goods companies are starting to feel less reliance on IT for data access as software vendors have automatically integrated data directly into most business applications. Also, as data scientists are embedded in the business, it will further reduce the dependency on IT. It appears that analytics and insights from these new data sources are being integrated into other processes and systems for many organizations, particularly in the front office.

COLLECTING AND STORING CONSUMER DATA

Consumer goods companies have always desired to collect and store data to help them better understand consumers' buying and consumption patterns. For several decades, the primary sources of data collected by consumer goods companies include point of sale (POS), 66.7%; syndicated scanner, 75.8%; marketing and panel data, 60.6% and 48.5%, respectively; and those trends continue. Many companies purchase data snapshots from each of these sources, packaging data for specific business uses (see Figure 3.3). Two-thirds of consumer goods companies still purchase retail data, despite a decade-long industry-wide effort to demonstrate the value of sharing POS data, which helps

WHAT DATA CONSUMER PRODUCTS COMPANIES ARE PURCHASING... AND WHY
What types of data are you purchasing for internal use (select all that apply)?

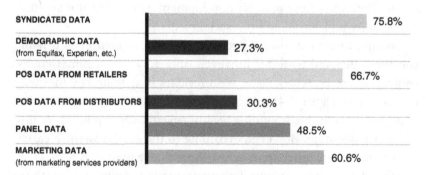

Figure 3.3 Types of Data Being Purchased for Internal Use
Source: "Transforming Core Consumer Products Functions with Advanced Analytics," A CGT Custom Research Report Partnered with IBM, pp. 1–10.

companies to understand consumer demand, driving replenishment and reducing out-of-stocks. This happens, however, only when this data is given rather than sold. Remarkably, consumer goods companies with revenues under $1 billion are most likely buying POS and distributor data. The trend is for large retailers to continue sharing more data and information, particularly from e-commerce, with their large consumer goods supplier partners, even as the gap between leaders and others is growing.[2]

The good news is that options for obtaining data directly from consumers are expanding rapidly. Consumer goods companies are adding new sources such as social media, e-commerce, and digital couponing, among others. According to the CGT custom research report, however, they continue to invest in traditional measures such as surveys, loyalty programs, and panels. Usage of these vehicles could potentially decrease as newer sources become more prevalent and as companies increase their capabilities to best leverage them. Nevertheless, social media adoption is gaining traction with consumer goods companies. They have been investing in various ways to collect and store social media data, and many are counting on it to produce qualitative data needed to gain nearly real-time consumer insights. Social media use, however, is still in its early stages and not yet fully implemented across most companies. Nevertheless, consumer goods companies agree that social media has the potential to foster development of new products based on consumer feedback. Another strong value proposition lies in being able to cultivate key brand drivers (influencers) with a broader reach. They rank new product development as offering the greatest opportunity to drive value from social media.

Weather data has always been a significant influencer in driving consumer demand patterns; however, only 50% of consumer goods companies are currently using weather data in making key business decisions (see Figure 3.4). Historically, those using weather data have done so reactively, incorporating weather events into supply chain and inventory planning. However, according to the CGT custom research report, this lagged other approaches. More than a quarter (26.5%) use weather data proactively for sales and promotion planning. More than one in five (20.6%) use weather data on an ad hoc basis, such as for special projects or immediate weather events.[3] Given improvements

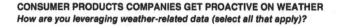

CONSUMER PRODUCTS COMPANIES GET PROACTIVE ON WEATHER
How are you leveraging weather-related data (select all that apply)?

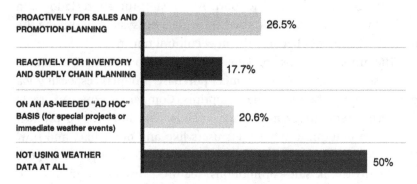

Figure 3.4 Leveraging Weather Data

in the accuracy of weather forecasting models, many companies are beginning to see the biggest benefit in forecasting and planning where demand is known to be affected by specific weather events globally. As a result, many consumer goods companies have been buying weather information from companies who provide weekly weather indices and future predictions by region, category, and product, such as Planalytics (www.Planalytics.com).

Consumer goods companies have a strong potential in moving up the analytics maturity curve, particularly in forecasting and planning as they continue to push forward. They are making headway in circumventing the slow progress regarding retail data sharing by exploring new data streams such as social media. Social media holds promise for new product development as companies learn how to integrate it into the organization. Consumer goods companies realize that by adopting the right data, processes, analytics, and technologies, they can drive considerable gains in consumer advocacy and ultimately, a better ROI.

Why Is the Data Ecosystem Important?

The data ecosystem relates to the data management and technological infrastructure that needs to be in place to enable analytics across the entire organization. This includes implementing technology architectures, governance, and procedures to manage the company's full data needs. It has been proven that those companies that have a strong data-driven decision making corporate culture correlate with executive sponsorship and support. As a result, the appreciation and understanding of the importance of the data ecosystem in driving the benefits of analytics become the new cultural norm.

The primary purpose of data ecosystems is to capture data to produce useful insights. As consumers purchase products, especially via digital formats, they leave data imprints. Companies now can create data ecosystems that capture and analyze data imprints so product teams can determine what their users like and don't like, and how they respond to different marketing programs. Product teams can use insights to tweak sales promotions, features, displays, and more to improve consumer demand. Data ecosystems were originally designed to be relatively centralized and static. The birth of the Web and cloud services has changed the data ecosystem framework. Now data is captured and distributed across organizations with IT professionals having less central control. Hence, the term data ecosystem, indicating these are data environments designed to evolve. There is no one data ecosystem solution framework.

Every business can create its own data ecosystem, sometimes referred to as a technology stack. It starts with a collection of hardware and software to capture, store, process, analyze, and act upon data insights. The best data ecosystems are built around an analytics solution platform that is open source with specific point-design capabilities—such as demand forecasting and planning—which tie the whole ecosystem together. Analytics platforms help teams integrate multiple data sources, provide AI/machine learning tools to automate the process of capturing, harmonizing, and normalizing data, and then conducting analysis and tracking users' performance metrics.

Why Data and Analytics?

The reality is that data and analytics are complicated. However, the results can significantly improve an organization's productivity and performance. The results could be increased revenue, improved profit margins, reduction in inventory costs, or an entirely new business framework. Any successful initiative requires a cultural and mindset shift where data and analytics change from supportive and secondary to fundamental for digital transformation. Data and analytics become central to how organizations do business every day, and thus are the basis for all decisions.

Those companies who make data a part of everything ask the right questions:

- How will the insights uncovered from this data as a result of the analytics change the value proposition for our customers?
- How will it improve our ability to predict shifting consumer demand patterns?
- How will we be able to improve the consumer experience?
- How will this help us deliver value and profitability?
- How will the results drive new business processes, innovation, and consumer response as a result of these new insights?[4]

The ability to answer these questions based on data and analytics will not only add value but will expand data and analytics competencies by encouraging data literacy across the organization. Organizations need to become smarter at understanding what results can be improved and how that investment drives positive outcomes across the company. It might be an investment in access to new data, or the implementation of artificial intelligence, or the ability to easily visualize data, or other activities. A clear understanding that considers data quality, data governance, and data literacy is vital to the success of a company's data and analytics investment.

The challenge at many companies is that demand planners, as well as many businesspeople, don't understand the importance of how data and analytics supports their work. They feel that business knowledge, experience, and intuition play a more practical role. On the other hand, demand analysts and data scientists lack a clear understanding of the business acumen required to successfully model and analyze the business effectively. Data and analytics are increasingly valuable assets to organizations, which requires all employees to embrace, understand, and utilize the relevant analytics information that affects their areas of expertise, particularly during disruptions. In the digital economy, data is as important as the classic business drivers of "people, process, analytics, and technology," making it equally important to become part of the corporate culture.

BUILDING TRUST IN THE DATA

In order to gain more value from predictive analytics and emerging technologies like cloud computing, data collected for the analytics must be trusted. On the other hand, once insights emerge from the application of analytics, individuals throughout the organization must feel comfortable that care was taken to assure the quality and uniformity of the data. Otherwise, the consumers of the insights will not trust the results or use them to make more informed business decisions and take actions. According to recent research, those companies who have advanced their analytics practices to incorporate AI/machine learning foster data quality, safeguard data assets, and develop data literacy cultures that encourage innovation. While most companies have increased access to data, only a few have the right data to make informed decisions. Notably, those companies who report high levels of trust in their data for analytics are more likely to show leadership to ensure that data is of high quality and leads to useful insights.

Leading organizations that have placed priority on building trust in the data that is collected and stored tend to trust the analytic insights it generates, which reinforces a culture that trusts and embraces data-driven decision making. As a result, there tends to be a strong correlation between those companies who use advanced analytics and those whose organizational activity fosters data quality, safeguards data assets, and builds a data-driven culture. They implement measures for governing proper use and security, and follow those practices, achieving results. This means demand analysts (data scientists) trust the data they access from a centralized data hub instead of copying data to work on their own in a siloed environment. This leads to more consistent data, and more accurate results.

Unfortunately, these best practice benefits are still not widespread. Many organizations are still in the process of developing their analytics capabilities to make informed business decisions. According to recent research studies, only 10% of companies are working with predictive analytics and less than 10% are integrating AI/machine learning into their decision-making or supply chain workflows. Most organizations rely on business intelligence (BI) tools and dashboards to support decision-making activities.

AI/MACHINE LEARNING CREATES TRUST CHALLENGES

AI/machine learning (ML) has the potential to solve difficult problems and motivates those who see it ushering in a new era that is comparable to the first machine age driven by the Industrial Revolution. At the same time, the implication that humans are giving machines autonomy—and even some degree of personality, as in the case of automated digital assistants who have names and speak to people—creates a level of anxiety for many. While some of those concerns belong in the dominion of science fiction, using ML does carry real potential risks that organizations need to manage. Mainly because the technology can enable autonomous decision making and actions by machines, questions about its reliability were found in a recent MIT SMR Connections research report (2020) that are more urgent than for other new technologies. The six risks about AI/machine learning that are of high concern:

- Deliver inadequate return on investment (ROI).
- Produce bad information.
- Be used unethically.
- Support biased, potentially illegal decisions.
- Produce results that humans cannot explain.
- Be too unpredictable to manage adequately.[5]

The two risks causing less concern were that AI may disrupt workflows or productivity and that AI may deliver bad customer experiences. An important component of building trust in ML is managing the associated risks, particularly through oversight that seeks to understand and verify how models function, mitigate bias, and anticipate unintended consequences. Organizations that have implemented ML are much more likely to already have a group tasked with setting policies and managing. An important development among some companies that have implement ML is they are establishing management review boards. The biggest item that a lot of companies are doing, especially those that are highly regulated, is to put together boards that review the operationalization of AI/machine learning. These boards often have data scientists as well as business leaders, representatives from the legal department, and other relevant domain experts.

PURSUIT OF EXPLAINABILITY

One of the biggest challenges for many who consider new analytics-driven technology is adequate explainability, or the ability to identify the key factors that a model used in producing its results, which in many cases will be used to make recommendations in a decision-support system or actions in an automated process. It has been found that most action taken based on explainability of ML results is being taken by those with the broadest AI/machine learning implementations. Explainability is important for sales/marketing to determine the appropriate mix of sales promotions, advertising, and in-store merchandising (display, feature, feature and display, temporary price reductions [TPRs], and others) to drive not only incremental volume, but also profitable revenue growth. Although AI/machine learning emerging software applications and tools are getting better at describing correlations that occur within the algorithms and the key variables that matter for the decision, the model must be able to account for the outcome. Explainability also plays a key role in building trust in ML, by providing visibility into how a model works and why it is making a particular recommendation to business stakeholders.

Many business leaders feel that ML models are not mature enough to be used in critical domains because of the black box problem. They believe that there is a need to start using them for problems with low risk to test and learn before taking on more critical problems that require explainability and interpretability of the modes. They also believe these are unsolved problems that need to be addressed before utilizing ML across the broader spectrum of business activities. Managing the risk of bias in ML applications due to inadequate data sets can skew a model and distort the predictions. The question of managing bias becomes particularly urgent with predictive models that make recommendations affecting people, where the potential consequences of doing the wrong thing are greater. Efforts to mitigate bias start with understanding the purpose of any project and then evaluating whether there is appropriate data to build an unbiased model.

Engage with Domain Experts and Business Specialists

Understanding what data is needed may be easier when analytics practitioners work closely with domain experts within their organizations.

Teaming data scientists with domain experts and business specialists who understand data sources and how they can be automated should be a best practice for all companies. The team members would complement one another with different expertise and perspectives, uncovering different patterns and identifying different opportunity pathways that may have been missed without the collaboration. This is particularly true when teaming data scientists with marketing and demand planners to develop driver-based consumption models and forecasts. A marketing expert would expect certain consumer shopping patterns and check with the analytic results as compared to assumptions, and know what questions to ask that were not part of the initial analytics investigation. On the other hand, a demand planner would be able to spot and examine anomalies arising due to field sales activities and know what adjustments to the model would help provide insights as to why those activities should be included or discarded.

Data governance ensures that the right data gets utilized so that results are trusted and actionable. Ensuring that the data is high quality will allow data scientists (demand analysts) to start with good building blocks for their models. There needs to be a common truth in the data, including the underlying data, how it's been processed, and how it's analyzed, which will ultimately create more accurate, scalable analytics. However, companies may find that the challenge may be more complex due to legacy systems architecture and fragmented data sources and data repositories. Many corporate leaders agree that data is an important asset; however, those who back up that view with committed organizational resources will gain competitive advantage from deploying predict analytics and AI/machine learning. As a result, many companies now employ a chief data officer (CDO) or chief analytics officer (CAO).

Why Is Downstream Data Important?

Downstream data has been electronically available on a weekly basis since the late 1980s. But most companies have been slow to adopt downstream data for forecasting and planning purposes.

Downstream consumption data is stored within the commercial side of the value chain. Examples include retailer POS data, syndicated scanner data from Nielsen, Information Resources Inc. (IRI), and Intercontinental Marketing Services (IMS). Prior to electronically available downstream data, manufacturers received this type of data in hard copy format as paper decks (after a 4- to 6-week lag). Once received, the data points were entered manually into mainframes via a dumb terminal (a display monitor that has no processing capabilities; it is simply an output device that accepts data from the CPU). In fact, downstream consumption data has been available to consumer goods companies for many decades. Nevertheless, the quality, coverage, and latency of downstream data has improved significantly, particularly over the past 30 years, with the introduction of universal product barcodes (UPC) and retail store scanners.

In fact, companies receive daily and weekly retailer POS data down to the SKU/UPC level through electronic data interchange transfers (an electronic communication method that provides standards for exchanging data via any electronic means). These frequent data points can be supplemented with syndicated scanner data across multiple channels (retail grocery, mass merchandiser, drug, wholesale club, liquor, and others) with minimal latency (1- to 2-week lag) by demographic market area, channel, key account (retail chain), brand, product group, product, and SKU/UPC. Downstream data are the closest source of consumer demand above any other data, including sales orders and shipments. Unfortunately, most companies primarily use downstream data in pockets to improve sales reporting, uncover consumer insights, measure their market mix performance, conduct price sensitivity analysis, and gauge sell through rates. Very few manufacturers, including consumer goods companies, however, have designed and implemented an end-to-end value supply chain network to fully utilize downstream data.

It is apparent that companies' supply chains have been slow to adopt downstream data, although POS data from retailers has been available for decades. Initially, the decision to use downstream data was a matter of data availability, storage, and processing. Today, this is primarily a question of change management due to corporate culture, particularly from a demand forecasting and planning perspective. So, what are the barriers? In large part, the adoption rate is slow because supply chain organizations have not approached the use of these new forms of downstream data from a holistic standpoint. Instead of mapping new processes based on a strong data and analytics strategy, supply chain organizations have tried to force-fit this data into existing processes using Excel, with no real analytics and a lot of manual manipulation. This is happening even though channel data are now available for anywhere from 50% to 70% of the retail channels, and the delivery time has improved significantly with data latency of 1–2 weeks. Given all these improvements, however, many companies still feel downstream data cannot be used for demand forecasting and planning.

Meanwhile, confronted with demand challenges due to the digital economy and COVID-19, companies have been looking for new ways to predict future demand. Under these changing conditions, the traditional demand planning technology has been ineffective at predicting shifting consumer demand patterns. The main reason for the unsuccessful performance of traditional technology is directly related to the fact that most companies are not forecasting demand, but rather supply—that is, shipments—which is proven to be much more volatile as a result of the digital economy, not to mention disruptions like COVID-19. Customer orders, sales invoices, and shipments are not true demand. They are the reflection of retailer and manufacturer replenishment policies—as seen in the bullwhip effect. To make matters more difficult, traditional demand forecasting processes and enabling technology were not designed to accommodate POS/syndicated scanner data, let alone the more sophisticated analytical methods (predictive and AI/machine learning) required to sense shifting consumer demand patterns and to shape future demand to create a more accurate demand response.

To reduce volatility and gain insights into current shifting consumer demand patterns, companies are turning to POS/syndicated scanner data, but are finding that using those data sources for demand forecasting and planning is complex. Perhaps it is because they are not familiar with downstream data, as most demand planners report into operations planning too far upstream removed from the customer/consumer, rather than downstream in sales and marketing. Another reason is that most companies do not collect downstream data on an ongoing basis over multiple years. They normally collect it on a rolling 104-week basis. This trend is no longer a barrier as companies are creating demand signal repositories (DSRs) to capture downstream data by week for more than 104 weeks, which allows them to compare down-stream consumer demand to upstream shipments and/or sales orders.

Others will admit that what retailers sold last week, or even yes-terday, is not necessarily a good predictor for what they will order next week or tomorrow. This is a myth, as companies have been keeping inventories low with more frequent replenishment because retailers are no longer allowing manufacturers to load up their warehouses at the end of every quarter with their products. As a result, there is a direct correlation with weekly POS/syndicated scanner data at the product level, and in many cases at the SKU/UPC levels (see Figures 3.5 and 3.6). As you can see, there is a strong correlation between weekly shipments and syndicated scanner data. Most consumer goods companies now

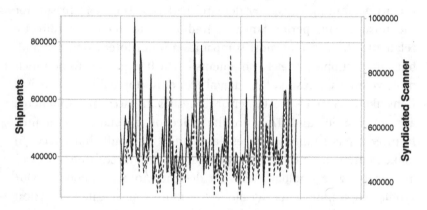

Figure 3.5 Shipments (Supply) Versus Syndicated Scanner Data (Demand)

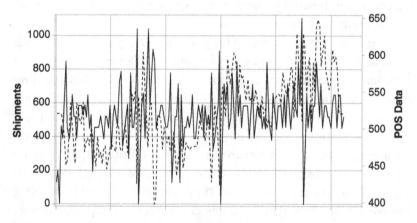

Figure 3.6 Shipments (Supply) Versus POS Data (Demand)

capture their shipment data daily/weekly by channel and key account, down to the SKU warehouse distribution point.

Another barrier has been scalability. Many companies feel that adding downstream channel data to demand forecasting involves a magnitude of effort and complexity that is well beyond what most demand planners can handle to source, cleanse, and evaluate. However, new processing technology (e.g. parallel processing, grid processing, in-memory processing, and cloud computing) leveraging advanced analytics in a business hierarchy along with exception filtering has enabled several visionary companies to overcome these difficulties. The promise of downstream data can be realized with the right technology on a large scale using advanced analytics, as well as AI/machine learning.

The real barriers are internal corporate culture, lack of analytical skills, and the desire to take that first step. The best way to incentivize sales and marketing to participate in your Sales & Operations Planning (S&OP) and Integrated Business Planning (IBP) processes is to integrate downstream data into the demand forecasting and planning process. Without it there is no real reason for sales and marketing to participate. Downstream data are the sales and marketing organizations' "holy grail" to consumer demand. Furthermore, if demand planners were using POS/syndicated scanner data, they would have seen the shifting consumer demand patterns due to COVID-19 within the first or second week of the crisis.

Demand Management Data Challenges

Most demand forecasting and planning initiatives are abandoned or considered failures due in part to data quality challenges. The right data input has several important dimensions that need to be considered for success of any process. Harnessing the right data always appears to be straightforward and relatively simple; however, bad data, or use of the wrong data, often is the real reason behind process failure.

Almost all demand forecasting and planning systems use some form of statistical forecasting methods that require historical data. In most cases, companies choose to use shipment data, or sales orders data, to predict future product demand, as both are readily available and best understood by demand planners who are responsible for the demand planning process. According to recent research close to 70–80% of companies still use either shipments or customer orders data for demand forecasting and planning, which are their supply and replenishment signals, not their true demand signal. Unfortunately, product shipments data, as well as sales orders, contain several undesirable components, including incomplete or partial order fills, delivery delays, and retail channel load effects due to promotions, supply policies that do not always reflect true demand, and sales/marketing strategies designed to generate incremental consumer demand (e.g. sales promotions, in-store merchandising—displays, features, feature/display, temporary price reductions (TPRs) on shelf, and others). Consequently, shipments data represents how operations planning responded to customer demand (sales orders—replenishment), not consumer demand itself (POS/syndicated scanner data—consumer purchases selling through retailer cash registers).

Demand forecasting and planning systems must build plans off a forecast and use shipments data as a measure of effectiveness in meeting those plans. Sales orders from retailers less any customer returns are the next best data representing customer (retailer) demand, but not necessarily the best demand data input for the statistical forecasting process. The closest data to consumer demand is POS and/or syndicated scanner data. Although many companies collect and store POS/syndicated scanner data, less than 40% of companies use POS data for demand forecasting and less than 10% use syndicated scanner data, according to recent surveys. Everyone agrees that POS/syndicated scanner data is the closest data to true consumer demand, yet both these data streams are among the most underutilized for demand forecasting and planning. To make matters worse, roughly 70–80% of companies are using historical shipments "adjusted" for trend and seasonality cleansed of promotions and outliers, separating the data into historical baseline volume and promoted volume creating two separate data streams, which is a bad practice.

HOW MUCH DATA SHOULD BE USED?

An accurate statistically generated forecast has several elements (patterns) including trend, seasonality, holidays, sales promotions, marketing events, and other related causal/explanatory factors. There must be enough demand history in order to statistically model those patterns associated with these elements to produce an accurate forecast for future periods. In most cases, this means a minimum of three years of historical data, and ideally three or more would be best to capture seasonality. Most demand forecasting and planning systems use monthly summaries of product demand (transactional shipments data) separated either by the manufacturing source or the distribution point. In other words, the data must reflect the business hierarchy with the same periodicity (historical time interval) including geography, market, channel, brand, product group, product, SKU, UPC, distribution centers (DCs), and customer ship-to points. Although less data can be utilized—one to two years—the results may not completely reflect the true nature of demand, particularly regarding seasonality, holidays, and promotional effects.

In 2020, demand planners are still spending anywhere from 50% to 80% of their time cleansing, managing, and disseminating data and information across the organization, rather than using the data and information to improve forecast accuracy and uncover insights. They are merely managers of data and information. As data continues to grow in volume, velocity, and variability, and there is more pressure to drive revenue growth, demand planners will be asked to not only improve forecast accuracy but find new insights that are actionable to proactively drive revenue and profit. As such, companies need to invest in data quality, new analytics skills, predictive analytics, and technology. Demand planners will need to transition from managers of data and information to demand analysts (data scientists) with a focus on predictive analytics driving revenue growth and profitability. It has been established that improved forecast accuracy can add as much as 3–7% to revenue and profitability.

Demand-Signal Repositories

There are many challenges to implementing a consumption-based forecasting and planning process. Many of the data sources are new for most companies to manage, so ownership, expertise, and governance are important—not to mention change management requirements to not only gain adoption, but also governance to make it sustainable.

Many executives say that their organizations are still in the basic stages of data integration due to data quality and internal lack of skills about how to maximize analytic benefits. In today's business environment, there are significant financial implications to ineffectively managing all the data streaming from multiple sources. These challenges can take the form of higher costs and lower revenue due to conditions such as ineffective demand planning, non-optimized inventory, strained product launches, and higher out-of-stocks on shelf.

Companies across a myriad of industries understand the importance of transforming into a data-driven company. The challenge is to gather, cleanse, and access the vast amount of downstream demand data, and normalize and harmonize it with upstream transactional information. Downstream data can be difficult to master and govern without a cohesive approach across the organization. Nevertheless, companies are investing in demand signal repositories as an integrated information hub that provides the foundation for breakaway analytics and optimization across the enterprise. Utilizing data to its fullest potential includes such sources as retailer POS; syndicated scanner sources (Nielsen, Information Resources [IRI], and others); loyalty programs; consumer panels; mobile, online, and social media; as well as ERP systems, finance, and internal systems— all of which are available to drive powerful analytics. Downstream consumption data are now more widespread, with many retailers sharing POS data with consumer goods companies daily. As a result, they expect enhanced knowledge from their consumer products suppliers. The demand-signal repository is a central data mart that houses all this information.

The successful implementation of a demand signal repository, supercharged by consumption-based analytics, is dependent upon managing POS/syndicated scanner data effectively, and complementing it with specific internal data, such as the company's product hierarchy. This exercise makes the POS/syndicated scanner data a more robust source of information to analyze with more dimensions that can be "sliced and diced" to gain more actionable insights. This type of data comes from internal corporate systems, local repositories, IoT, and spreadsheets. Furthermore, it is usually manually maintained and thus not subject to good data governance.

What Are Demand Signal Repositories?

A demand signal repository (DSR) is a data repository designed to integrate consumer demand data and leverage that data by consumer goods companies, automotive manufacturers, electronics manufacturers, pharmaceuticals, and others to service retailers and end user consumers efficiently. The focus has been on synchronizing POS/ syndicated scanner data with internal shipment and replenishment data, which allows companies to provide business users with a more complete view of their retail performance. The DSR itself is a data repository that stores the information in a format that allows for easy retrieval so that users can quickly query the database to identify what's selling, where, when, and how. Identifying marketing opportunities, "demand performance," and out-of-stock (OOS), along with control tower tracking and monitoring, are the key requirements for demand forecasting and planning. Leveraging demand signal analytics (DSA) data for demand forecasting and planning using predictive analytics is where the real benefits of such applications can help to identify and measure past, current, and future impacts on consumer demand. With the right architecture, DSRs will continue to grow with the business needs. They will be leveraged across multiple business groups, including demand management, channel marketing, supply chain management, inventory management, promotion, and event management.

Demand signal repositories are defined as centralized data repositories that store and harmonize attributes, and organize large volumes of demand data such as POS data, wholesaler data (electronic data interchange [EDI]), inventory movement, promotional data, and customer loyalty data for use by decision support technologies (channel marketing analysis, shopper insight analysis, demand forecasting and planning, inventory replenishment, and more). Demand signal visualization (DSV) dashboards provide companies with faster decisions and scenario modeling for outcomes and accurate decisions. Furthermore, demand signal analytics (DSA) combines DSV with predictive analytics, allowing companies in real time to conduct root-cause visualization and exploration. DSR, DSV, and DSA are at the heart of being analytics driven. To reap the maximum benefit from a true consumption-based planning process takes commitment and a well-conceived plan, which requires a best-in-class demand signal repository at the core.

Benefits of a Demand Signal Repository

The augmentation of DSR data into the demand planning process improves visibility and control. POS/syndicated scanner data can be a tremendous asset when used properly. By integrating POS/syndicated scanner data with company-specific attributes, consumer goods companies can leverage that data by collaborating more effectively across the organization and with their retailer (customer) networks. POS data can then drive commercial and operational improvements, such as:

- Improving demand forecast accuracy, and enhancing demand-sensing and shaping activities;
- Sensing shifting consumer demand patterns faster and more effectively;
- Improving evaluation of new product information via integration of sentiment analysis;
- Increasing trade promotion effectiveness;
- Reducing out-of-stocks; and
- Lowering inventory and safety stock levels.

WHAT ARE USERS LOOKING TO GAIN?

Users are looking for easy-to-use visualization tools with predictive analytics capabilities to uncover market opportunities with the ability to more efficiently synchronize demand and supply to take advantage of the information stored in their DSRs. If they can't, then they have a point solution that is proprietary, and not a true DSR. An open architecture should have an intuitive point-and-click user interface with strong visualization capabilities that lets users easily access reports to help them understand their sales, manage category and brand information, and more. Users should be able to easily drag, drop, and drill into information. They should be able to pull data from multiple data sources, share reports securely, and create alerts. In addition, users that have specific job requirements, such as price elasticity or analyzing promotional ROI that aren't handled in their DSR, require an exploratory capability that uses predictive analytics that leverages POS/syndicated scanner data and shipments (supply) and replenishment data.

Alerts combined with predictive exploratory capabilities, using visualization, will allow users to pinpoint areas of the business that require immediate attention. The goal of a DSR is to provide faster access to more information, improve retailer relationships, maximize ROI, streamline internal efficiencies, improve performance at all stages of the supply chain, and support multiple departments and teams. Most DSRs fall short of their promise, however, by not providing control towers (dashboards) and descriptive reporting to monitor and track their business year after year, with virtually no predictive analytics to uncover insights into the data that are actionable. Spreadsheets are no longer adequate to take advantage of the information in a DSR, not to mention not scalable enough.

Why Is It Important?

If you want to be more proactive than simply basing replenishment on shipments data, you need access to downstream data, analysis, and insights to make decisions that put you ahead of the demand curve. There is more to it than just forecasting trends and seasonality. Demand sensing is about identifying and measuring market signals, and then using those signals to shape future demand.

Using consumer data effectively requires making an investment in a demand signal repository to harmonize and cleanse POS/syndicated scanner data so that it is usable for data analytics. Consumption-based analytics using downstream data, as well as inventory, shipments, and replenishment data, are current examples of using "structured" data. While the term "downstream data" is most often connected to consumption and inventory data, "unstructured data"—such as loyalty data, social sentiment, consumer perception attitudinal data—is starting to be used for targeting consumers, shaping demand, and improving new product launch effectiveness. Using text analytics, we can now transform unstructured data into structured data that can be combined with the breadth of our data in predictive and machine learning models, and then visualized using control towers and dashboards to create value by enabling faster, more effective business decisions.

What Is Consumption-Based Analytics?

Consumption-based analytics uses the combination of visual analytics and predictive analytics to access the data in DSRs to uncover actionable insights with minimal latency. You can think of DSA as being composed of three layers. The foundational layer is a demand signal repository (DSR), an integrated database of essential data that companies need to provide insight into sales, marketing, inventory, price, demand performance, and operations. The DSR harmonizes, normalizes, and integrates the raw demand and supply data from any source (POS, wholesalers, mobile, online, social media, weather, EDI, inventory, syndicated scanner data, promotional/marketing information, customer loyalty data, and more). It works with any data type or source format from multiple retailers, distributors, and their respective disparate systems to make that data available for retrieval, query, reporting, alerts, and analysis.

In summary, the second layer uses visual analytics to transform the DSR data into DSV to allow for exploration, analysis, and insights that suggest areas of focus, improvement, and action. While typical marketing research only provides answers to predefined questions, DSV provides insight into questions companies didn't initially know to ask. The third layer combines DSR and DSV, creating DSA. The addition of predictive and anticipatory analytics complements the descriptive analytics of DSV, and quantifies the direction, size, scope, and variability of supply chain replenishment. Figure 3.7 illustrates a typical interactive visualization combined with predictive analytics, which allows the demand planner to review both demand and replenishment.

Chapter 4 discusses in depth how using consumption-based forecasting companies can predict shifting consumer demand patterns and their impact on supply by linking POS/syndicated scanner data to shipments using predictive analytics. Effectively adjusting to changing market conditions using consumer demand requires aligned strategies

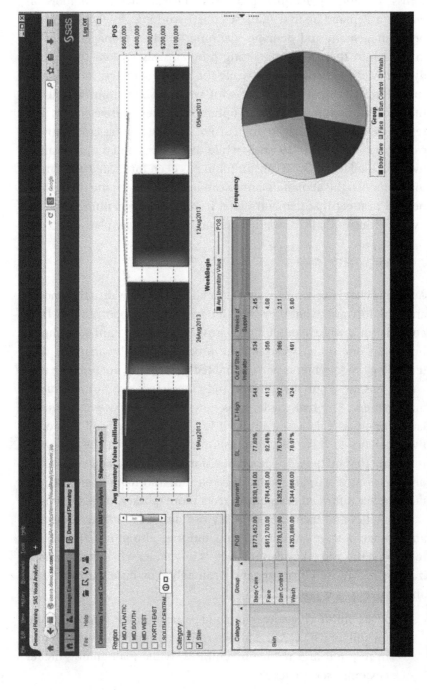

Figure 3.7 Consumption-Based Analytics Combining Descriptive and Predictive Analytics

across a brand's personnel, processes, measurement, and tools, as well as a demand analyst (data scientist) working closely with product management and demand planning. Product managers provide insights into their sales/marketing programs, as well as the overall dynamics of the marketplace, while the demand analyst models consumption, providing marketing with what-if simulation capabilities that test marketing strategies to optimize marketing investment. The results help brands navigate the current volatile market environment caused by the COVID-19 crisis while driving sustained optimization over the long term. Once consumption has been forecasted and linked to shipments, the demand planner can begin to determine the actions needed to meet that demand signal from a supply planning perspective, creating a final constrained demand plan (supply plan).

CLOSING THOUGHTS

As supply chain executives stand at the edge of the new digital economy and look forward, what they see is a new world of opportunities. Data and analytics will shape our lives in ways that are hard to comprehend; but one thing is certain, the processes, people, analytics, and technology requirements will undoubtedly transform not only the way we do business, but will disrupt and completely transform demand management. The real challenge is not that companies are acquiring large amounts of data as a result of IoT, but how they utilize predictive analytics to drive digital transformation. It's what they do with their data that matters. The hopeful vision for data and analytics is that organizations will be able to harness relevant information and use it to make better informed decisions to react more quickly to disruptions.

Analytics and technologies today not only support the collection and storage of large amounts of data, but they also provide the ability to understand and take advantage of its full value, which helps organizations run more efficiently and profitably. For instance, with data and analytics, it is possible to:

- Sense shifting consumer demand patterns, shape future demand for millions of SKUs, and determine optimal prices that maximize profit and reduce inventories, while maintaining higher customer service levels.

- Mine downstream consumer demand data for insights that drive new sales and marketing strategies for consumer retention, campaign optimization, and next best offers.
- Generate retail coupons at the point of sale (POS), based on the consumers' current and past purchases in real time to ensure a higher redemption rate.
- Send tailored recommendations to mobile devices at just the right time, while consumers are in the right location to take advantage of offers.
- Analyze data from online, mobile, and social media to detect new market trends and changes in consumer preferences.
- Determine root causes of failures, issues, and defects by investigating user sessions, network logs, and machine sensors.

Several recent technology advancements are enabling companies to make the most of data and analytics, such as cheap, abundant storage and server processing capacity, faster processors, and affordable large-memory capabilities in the cloud. New storage and processing technologies are designed specifically for large data volumes, including structured and unstructured data. Parallel processing, clustering, MPP (Massive Parallel Processing), virtualization, large grid environments, high connectivity, and high throughputs are making it possible to process data faster. Cloud computing and other flexible resource allocation arrangements are becoming more desirable and cost-effective. Data technologies not only support the ability to collect large amounts of data, but they also provide the ability to understand it and take advantage of its value. The goal of all companies with access to large data collections should be to harness the most relevant data and use it for optimized decision making. The transformation from DSR to DSV and ultimately DSA will require leadership, a strategic vision, a road map of priorities, and the ability to execute against the organization's strategy. Achieving best-in-class status across every measure could merely mean adding unnecessary cost and complexity. What's important is to invest in people, process, analytics, and technology improvements that are valued by customers. Leaders make conscious trade-offs, with an understanding that it may be appropriate to have benchmarks that are at par with industry averages, while at the same time having other measures that reflect best-in-class outcomes.

Now that many companies have created DSRs, the move to the next level will require the migration to DSV, and then ultimately to DSA. Until those companies implement DSV and DSA, they will not have the capabilities to take full advantage of all the data collected, normalized, harmonized, and loaded into their DSRs. In order to take full advantage of their DSRs, companies will need to add a second layer of DSV combined with a third layer of DSA. With DSA, companies can get a nearly real-time picture of retail store level sales and inventory replenishment trends while identifying potential challenges and market opportunities. The entire organization can take advantage of the predictive intelligence of DSA by easily visualizing (using DSV) large data repositories of facts and measures at the lowest granularity across account hierarchies, category/item hierarchies, and geographical hierarchies. In addition, DSA can deliver targeted alerts to enable exception-based processes and workflow.

It is very important to understand that not all data will be relevant or useful. This challenge is widely acknowledged. Most businesses have made slow progress in extracting value from live streaming data by migrating to DSRs. Others attempted to apply traditional data management practices to the data, only to learn that the old rules no longer apply. Investing in DSRs with DSV and DSA capabilities with a set of prepackaged reports, dashboards, and easy-to-use exploration capabilities designed to support demand management, brand management, category management, and product performance along with score carding capabilities, can accelerate time to value.

NOTES

1. *Transforming Core Consumer Products Functions with Advanced Analytics*, A CGT Custom Research Report Partnered with IBM: 1–10. https://consumergoods.com/transforming-core-consumer-products-functions-advanced-analytics

2. Ibid.

3. Ibid.

4. *Design a Data and Analytics Strategy: Advance Your Organization's Strategy by Communicating the Business Value of Data and Analytics*, ebook, Gartner, Inc., 2019: pp. 1–16. https://www.bastagroup.nl/wp-content/uploads/2019/05/Data-analytics-strategy-ebook.pdf

5. *Data, Analytics, & AI: How Trust Delivers Value*, MIT SMR Connections, Custom Research Report, on behalf of SAS, 2019: 1–23. https://www.sas.com/en/whitepapers/mit-data-analytics-ai-110173.html

CHAPTER **4**

Consumption-Based Forecasting and Planning

The ability to predict future demand requires more than the ability to respond to customer needs. The digital economy and current disruptions mandate that companies sense and respond to shifting consumer demand patterns, which necessitates investing in more responsive demand planning technologies. Companies must contend with shifting consumer demand, private-label, and smaller "lateral" direct-to-consumer digital competitors (start-ups). In order to effectively compete, companies need to invest in predictive analytics that will allow them to anticipate markdowns, sales promotions, inventory allocation, fulfillment, and assortment so they can be prepared not only for customer requirements, but also to provide consumers with a great purchasing experience.

The current disruption related to COVID-19 has been a wake-up call for retailers and consumer goods companies, causing havoc with their categories, brands, and products and making it harder to predict supply requirements due to the acceleration of these new market trends. The new, changing shopping preferences continue to differentiate how consumers prefer to shop and pick up their purchases. According to recent research, more than half of brand management professionals are struggling under the weight of increased consumer demand for home delivery, online purchasing, and in-store pickup preferences. Many feel these new expanded behaviors are unlikely to subside, even as COVID-19 eventually disappears. So, thinking about waiting out these new shifting demand patterns is not a practical long-term strategy. This has given rise to the need for consumption-based forecasting and planning; however, it will require a complete redesign of a company's demand planning process, including new people skills, integrated horizontal processes with shared performance metrics, the use of predictive analytics, and open-source cloud-ready solutions. It's no longer a matter of if, but when companies realize they can no longer effectively run their business from the supplier to the consumer. They need to run their business from consumer to supplier. This is a radical change that will require change management supported by the C-level management suite. Those companies that realize this situation as a "burning platform" and make the appropriate changes will reap the benefits.

The ability to anticipate and predict shifts in consumer demand patterns allows companies to influence demand effectively and efficiently, while more accurately planning supply. Consumption-based analytics enables brands to get ahead of shifts in demand, markdowns, promotions, allocation, and fulfillment, allowing brand teams to identify those factors influencing demand. The future of demand forecasting and planning requires more than the ability to respond to consumer demand; it must have a direct link to supply. The new digital economy dictates that companies sense and respond to demand by investing in more responsive analytics and planning processes that can anticipate shifts in consumer demand and plan inventory replenishment accordingly to create a positive consumer engagement.

Effectively adjusting to changing market conditions and demand requires alignment of strategies across the organization, including horizontal processes, shared performance metrics, and technology. Unfortunately, vertical processes leave organizations unprepared for shifts in consumer demand and leave their business environment exposed to risks. Their applications and technology aren't aligned in a way that enables them to predict, identify, and act on changes to the market environment. Companies' applications and technology are not ready for the challenges, as few retailers and consumer goods companies are able to anticipate and predict consumers' changing preferences as a result of these new disruptions. If they are correct in their assessments, and correctly and appropriately align their supply chains, they will have a competitive advantage over poorly equipped competitors.

A CHANGE OF MINDSET IS REQUIRED

We have all heard the phrase, "forecasts are always wrong." This folklore, which has been passed down by business executives from generation to generation, is misleading. It is the underlying rationale used by executives to support the belief that their business is too unique and unpredictable to be forecasted, when in fact it's more predictable than they realize. Business executives should not accept forecast inaccuracies as a way of doing business. This belief causes companies to "leave too much money on the table." Nothing is perfect in life including sales and marketing plans, financial plans, or supply plans. They too will never be 100% accurate. Striving to improve their accuracy inevitably drives companies to improve the execution of their plans. When plans are well executed, companies are top performers in their industries.[1]

The challenge for those who seek to improve their demand planning process must demonstrate the return on investment in concrete terms that directly relate to business performance. This requires a change in mindset. The burden is on the business managers to make a compelling analytics-based case for change. Creating the case for change and investment starts with determining what needs to improve: process, people, analytics, and technology. Many organizations believe that improved forecast accuracy alone is the goal of demand planning initiatives. They spend considerable time and effort on trying to get the numbers right. In doing so, they fail to consider what data scientists know—that every statistically derived forecast has an upper and lower confidence range. In the realm of data scientists, forecasts are wrong only if actual demand falls outside the confidence range. So, if your forecasts fall within the confidence range 9 out of 10 prediction periods, then your forecast accuracy is 90%. (See Figure 4.1.)

A better and more practical approach captures the impact of demand planning based on the well-being of the business. It involves a holistic understanding of:

- Why an accurate statistical forecast that reflects consumer demand is needed
- Why a demand plan is needed
- How the demand plan affects the way other business functions perform
- How the demand plan drives decision making that has an impact on business performance

When demand plans are well thought out and credible to the rest of the organization, execution across the business improves. This is

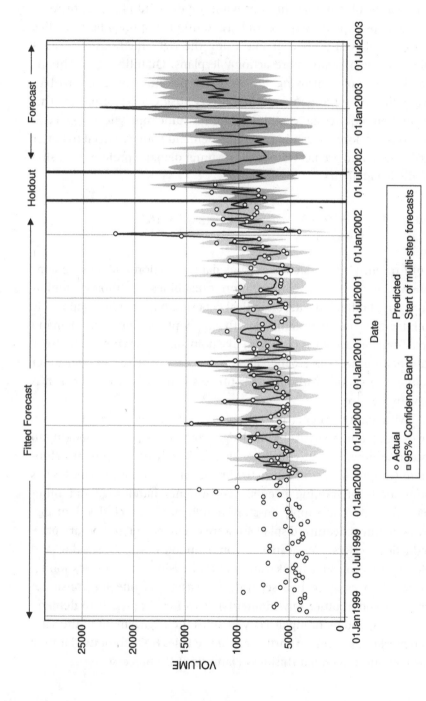

Figure 4.1 Forecasts That Fall in the 90% Upper/Lower Confidence Range

where a lot of value lies in improving the demand planning process. It also helps explain why technology solutions require a best practice process and well-trained people using the right methods and capabilities to help create more actionable plans. Quantifying the financial benefits of improving the demand planning process involves evaluating how the demand plan affects business performance. This evaluation requires data gathering and consumer analytics–driven calculations. Before we can improve the demand plan, we need to better understand and predict changing consumer demand preferences using predictive analytics.

WHY CONSUMPTION-BASED FORECASTING AND PLANNING?

Until recently many factors such as data collection and storage constraints, poor data synchronization capabilities, technology limitations, and limited internal analytical expertise have made it impossible to integrate consumer demand with supply plans. Consumer demand data from key accounts (retailers) like point-of-sale (POS) and Nielsen/ Information Resources Inc. allows for easy linkage of consumer demand to supply. Although this process is not new in concept, it is new in practice.

With improvements in technology, data collection and storage, processing, and analytical knowledge, companies are now looking to integrate downstream consumer demand with their upstream shipment (supply) plans to capture the impact of marketing activities (sales promotions, marketing events, in-store merchandising, and other related factors) on supply. In-store merchandising includes floor displays, features, feature/display, in-store circulars, and temporary price reductions (TRPs). We can use consumption-based forecasting and planning to consider marketing and replenishment strategies jointly rather than creating two separate forecasts (i.e. one for consumer demand and another for shipments). This new approach to demand forecasting and planning directly justifies the engagement of the sales and marketing teams to participate in the Sales & Operations Planning (S&OP) and Integrated Business Planning (IBP) processes.

In those industries where downstream data are available, consumption-based forecasting and planning is used to model the push/pull effects of the supply chain by linking a series of predictive analytics models together based on marketing investment strategies and replenishment policies. The theoretical design applies in-depth causal analysis, as well as machine learning to measure the effects of sales and marketing activity on consumer demand at retail (pull), and then links it, via consumer demand, to supply (push). This is known as a two-tiered model. In the case of companies with more sophisticated distribution networks, a three-tiered (or more) model could incorporate wholesalers (i.e. consumer to retailer to wholesaler to manufacturer) and/or distributors.

WHAT IS CONSUMPTION-BASED FORECASTING AND PLANNING?

The consumption-based forecasting and planning process is designed to identify and model the factors that influence consumer demand. Then, using the demand model parameters, it executes various what-if scenarios to shape and predict future consumer demand. Finally, it links consumer demand to supply (sales orders or shipments) as a leading indicator in a shipment model, rather than using "gut feeling" judgment. Once the causal factors that influence consumer demand are determined, and those drivers of consumption are sensed and used to shaped future demand, a second model is developed using consumer demand as the primary leading indicator to link consumer demand to supply. The supply model can also include such factors as trade promotions, wholesale gross price, cash discounts (or off-invoice allowances), co-op advertising, trade inventory, trend, seasonality, and more.

In many cases, consumer demand is pulled forward one or more periods to account for the buying (replenishment) patterns of the retailers. For example, mass merchandisers, such as Walmart, buy in bulk prior to high periods of consumer demand, usually one or more periods (weeks) prior to the sales promotion. Other retailers, such as Publix, carry large varieties of products and hold small inventories.

This shortens their purchase cycle and requires them to purchase products more frequently with virtually no lag on consumer demand when introduced into the supply model. With that, if consumer demand (D) of Product A is:

$$\text{Demand}(D) = \beta0 \text{ Constant} + \beta1 \text{ Trend} + \beta2 \text{ Seasonality}$$
$$+ \beta3 \text{ Price} + \beta4 \text{ Advertising} + \beta5 \text{ Sales Promotion}$$
$$+ \beta6 \%\text{ACV Feature} + \beta7 \text{ Store Distribution}$$
$$+ \beta8 \text{ Competitive Price} + \beta n$$

Note: Distribution is percentage of stores in where products will be sold.

Then Product A's supply (S) would be:

$$\text{Supply}(S) = \beta0 \text{ Constant} + \beta1 \text{ D } (\text{lag1} + n) + \beta2 \text{ Trend}$$
$$+ \beta3 \text{ Seasonality} + \beta4 \text{ Gross Dealer Price}$$
$$+ \beta5 \text{ Factory Rebates} + \beta6 \text{ Trade Discounts}$$
$$+ \beta7 \text{ Co} - \text{op Advertising} + \beta8 \text{ Trade Promotions} + \beta n$$

In consumption-based forecasting models, some of the explanatory variables (key performance indicators, or KPIs) are held static while others are changed to simulate the impact of alternative marketing strategies on consumer demand, using what-if scenario analysis. The impact of the selected scenario is linked to supply. The goal here is to simulate the impact of changes in those key performance indicators such as price, advertising, in-store merchandising, and sales promotions; determine their outcomes (predict future consumer demand); and choose the optimal strategy that produces the highest volume and ROI. The key assumption is that "if all things hold true" based on the model's parameter estimates when any of the explanatory variables is changed, it will have "X" impact on future consumer demand, resulting in "Y" change in supply. The most difficult explanatory variables to simulate are those we have no control over such as weather, economy, local events, and competitor activity. However, those data streams can be forecast using time series methods, and in many cases, forward projections are available from outside resources, often at no or little cost.

CONSUMPTION-BASED FORECASTING AND PLANNING CASE STUDY

This case study shows the step-by-step process application of consumption-based forecasting and planning at a large consumer goods manufacturer to sense, shape, and predict demand, then link consumer data to shipment data, thus synchronizing demand and supply. A brand manager, demand analyst (data scientist), and demand planner all work together to evaluate the efficiency and productivity of the company's sales and marketing efforts, by sensing the demand signal and measuring the impact of the key business drivers that influence consumer demand; then shape future demand with the goal of driving more profitable volume growth; proactively predict future consumer demand; and finally, link predicted demand to supply to create a supply plan (shipment forecast). The brand manager has the domain knowledge of the market, category, channel, brand, products, SKUs, and marketplace dynamics; the demand analyst has the statistical experience and knowledge to apply the appropriate predictive analytics models; and the demand planner has the demand planning/supply planning expertise. This raises three major questions:

1. What sales and marketing activities are working to influence the demand signal within the retail grocery channel? This process of identifying and measuring the KPIs that influence demand is known as demand sensing.

2. How can they put pressure on those KPIs to drive more volume and profitability using what-if analysis? In other words, what alternative scenarios can be identified to maximize their market investment efficiency? This is known as demand shaping.

3. How does the final shaped demand influence supply replenishment (shipments)?[2]

CONSUMPTION-BASED FORECASTING AND PLANNING SIX-STEP PROCESS

Step 1: Gather all the pertinent data for consumer demand and shipments. In this example, syndicated scanner data (153 weeks) were downloaded from the company's database at the total US market, grocery channel, brand, product group, product, package size, and SKU levels. This example focuses on the product group weekly case volume (consumption), in-store merchandising vehicles (average retail price, displays, features, features/displays combined, temporary price reductions [TPR]), and weighted distribution percentages by product, which were downloaded along with major competitor information. The marketing events calendar (sales/trade promotions calendar) from the sales and marketing plan was downloaded as well. Finally, weekly supply volumes were downloaded along with wholesale price, case volume discounts (off-invoice allowances), trade inventory, and local retailer incentives being offered by the consumer goods manufacturer.

This consumer goods brand is nationally distributed with several size and package configurations. It was decided that it made more sense to use models at the pack size level (middle-out), which was three levels deep into the product hierarchy (see Figure 4.2) to override the lower-level statistical forecasts, rather than at the individual SKU level and customer ship-to-location models. Then, disaggregate the product case volumes down to the individual SKU and customer ship-to-locations, using the bottom-up statistical consumption forecasts to build in the lower-level trends associated with the lower-level SKU/customer mix. This creates a dynamic disaggregation process that is not static, but based on the lower-level trends and seasonality creating a more accurate product mix level forecast.

Once selected, the statistical engine will automatically reconcile the entire product hierarchy back up to the US grocery channel level. Building the statistical models, disaggregation, and reconciliation of the product hierarchy uses first-generation artificial intelligence (AI), also known as an "expert system." It automatically diagnoses all the data, builds a series of competing models at every level of the business hierarchy using different categories of models (exponential smoothing, ARIMA, ARIMAX, dynamic regression, Stacked Neural Networks + Times Series

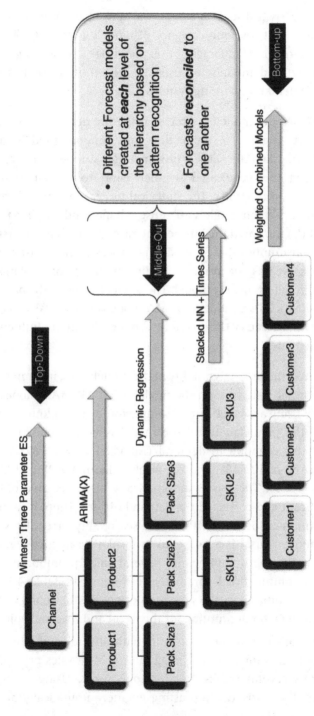

Figure 4.2 Large-scale Hierarchical Forecasting with Automatic Reconciliation

models—we will discuss machine learning in the next chapter), and others. Not just one category of models (simple time series methods—moving averaging, exponential smoothing, and regression trend models) as used in ERP (Enterprise Resource Planning) demand planning systems.

Step 2: Start the modeling process using the demand forecasting auto-select engine to build the consumption models using downstream data to sense consumer demand drivers; in this case, using the syndicated scanner data from their Demand Signal Repository (DSR). The statistical forecasting engine creates consumption-based models to sense, shape, and predict future demand (D) up/down the business hierarchy, which is the first tier in the consumption-based modeling process. The consumption forecast serves as the primary leading indicator or explanatory variable in the supply (S) model. The model chosen at the pack size level is an ARIMAX model (ARIMA model with causal variables) that identifies causal factors that are significant in influencing future demand.

Step 3: Test the predictive ability of the model using in-sample and out-of-sample data to train the models. The ARIMAX model was validated using a 6-week out-of-sample forecast (holdout sample). Overall, the predictability of the model is very good, capturing 78% of the variation in demand (Adjusted R^2 = .7767) with a fitted MAPE of 12.41%, and a 6-week holdout MAPE of 12.94% (see Table 4.1). The model automatically identified two outliers as significant and corrected the demand history. Then, it captured the volumes associated with trend, seasonality, irregular shifts, and multiple causal factors (features/displays, category segment, special holiday promotion, and several sales promotions). See the third column titled parameter "estimates" in Table 4.1. The parameter estimates for the sales promotions are the actual volume lifts captured after accounting for the trend and seasonal volumes.

The statistical model also automatically adjusted the sales promotions lifts for cumulative lag affects. Most sales promotions run across several weeks, not just one week. Using predictive analytics, the statistical forecasting engine automatically applied

Table 4.1 Consumption Model Analytic Results

Component		ARIMA (X) Model			
		(1,0,0) (0,1,0)			
Component	Param-eter	Estimate	Standard Error	t-Value	Approx Pr > |t|
Volume	Con-stant	72.13227	205.1025	0.35	0.7258
Volume	AR1	0.18191	0.09837	1.85	0.0671
ACVFND	Scale	60.75919	7.81686	7.77	0.0001
Category Segment	Scale	0.12568	0.0249	5.05	0.0001
Jan201905Promo	Scale	2459.2	446.81778	5.5	0.0001
Aug201810Off	Scale	903.6	1274.9	2.04	0.0436
Feb101815OFF	Scale	3262.7	1274.4	2.56	0.0118
HolidayPromo	Scale	2624.6	1362	4.74	0.0001
HolidayPromo	Num1	2456.2	1968.5	4.03	0.0001
HolidayPromo	Num2	503.5	1518.2	1.75	0.4561
HolidayPromo	Den1	0.98415	0.17999	5.47	0.0001
July20175Off	Scale	5058.5	910.53912	5.56	0.0001
June2017Cou-pon	Scale	2912.7	905.13238	3.22	0.0017
Outlier-July212018	Scale	–5036.7	1289.5	–3.91	0.002
Outlier-Mar112017	Scale	–1708.6	904.7353	–1.89	0.0616
R² = .8021	Weekly Fitted MAPE 12.41%			MAE = 941-89 (units)	
Adj R² = .7767	Weekly Holdout (6wks) 12.94%				

what is known as a "transfer function" to model the lagged cumulative effects of the sales promotions across several weeks. For example, the holiday sales promotion lift volume after trend and seasonal volumes have been automatically captured (removed), are 2,624.6 cases in week one, 2,456.2 cases in week two, and 503.5 cases in week three, respectively. This reflects the sales promotion volumes across the three-week promotional period indicating that the first two weeks tend to sell over 90% of the promotional volume and the balance (503.5 cases) in the third week. To obtain the baseline volume, all you need to do is subtract all the sales promotion lift volumes from the total case volume along with other promotional vehicle volumes (Feature/Displays, TPRs and others). No data cleansing is needed to separate the demand history into baseline and promoted volumes.

It should be noted that not all promotions are significant, and as such, may not be significant in the model—that is, they may not show up in the model output. Others may be significant in driving volume but are not profitable. Finally, as you go further down into the product hierarchy you may experience more noise in the data, making it difficult to build a robust model that picks up all the causal relationships. On the other hand, as you go higher in the product hierarchy, due to aggregation, you may not pick up all the promotional effects. The aggregation effect is also prevalent when using monthly data, as promotions are normally run weekly rather than monthly. We found that middle-out levels in the product hierarchy tend to work best focusing on brands/product groups/products based on the promotional calendar normally managed by the marketing team. Most promotions target specific groups of products.

The system uses simple statistical methods (exponential smoothing and others) to forecast the lower-level SKU/customer ship-to-location mix using a bottom-up forecast. Then, using the middle-out models (brand/product groups) volumes, the system automatically overrides the lower-level mix based on the bottom-up volume trends and seasonality allocating the middle out volumes down the hierarchy. Finally, the entire hierarchy is then automatically reconciled to assure all levels sum to the top level. This method of allocating middle-out forecast volumes up/down the product hierarchy is dynamic (floats) as each period is updated, and as the system allocates out across future periods (weeks/months). In other words, the lower-level product mix splits are not static. As a result, the lower-level product mix is much more accurate.

All the consumption drivers (independent/exogenous variables) in the model are significant in predicting future consumption (consumer demand). If the demand analyst finds a week(s) in the out-of-sample (holdout) sample test that is outside the 95% confidence range, the brand manager may know what happened and can identify additional inputs that need to be added to the model. This is where domain knowledge, as opposed to "gut feeling" judgment, can help. The demand analyst can then go back into the statistical forecasting engine to tweak the model(s) to improve its accuracy incorporating the additional information and data. This is a holistic modeling approach that is transparent, requiring no data cleansing. A legacy ERP demand planning solution does not have this capability.

Step 4: Refit the model using all the data. After identifying and verifying the consumption model parameter estimates for all the explanatory variables and testing the model's predictive capabilities, the system automatically refits all the models up/down the product hierarchy with the 6-week out-of-sample data using all 153 weeks of data (see Figure 4.3). The final model fit and forecast for all levels of the product hierarchy are now disaggregated down the product hierarchy from the pack size (middle-out) level to the SKU and customer ship-to-location; and then automatically reconciled to the channel (top) level to maintain the integrity of the entire product hierarchy.

Step 5: Run what-if scenarios to shape future demand. Using the consumption-based model parameter estimates, the product manager or marketing planner can shape future consumer demand by conducting several what-if scenarios (simulations) by varying future values of different explanatory variables that are under their control. Upon completion of the simulations, the product planner chooses the optimal scenario that generates the most volume and profitability, which then becomes the consumption future forecast for the next 52 weeks. The optimum scenario can be selected in a matter of minutes using a demand planning workbook with either a Web or Excel user interface (UI). Here is an example of a marketing planner's workbook using a Web-interface. See Figure 4.4.

The marketing planner's workbook is set up by month and week from left to right. At this point, we are three levels deep in the product hierarchy at "pack size" and "key accounts" (customer ship-to-locations). In the right-hand column the marketing planner can view POS actuals for the first two weeks of February 2019 and

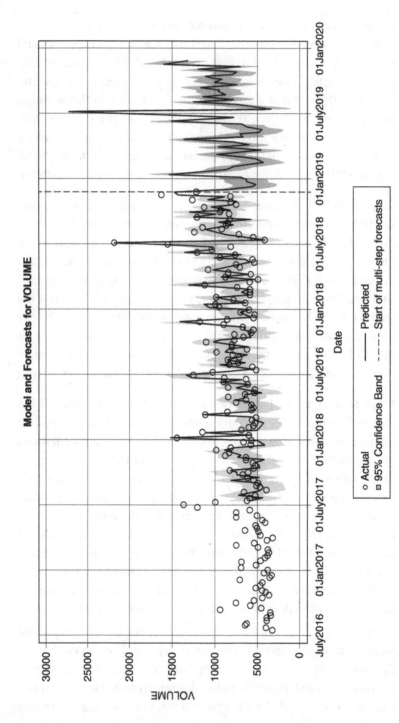

Figure 4.3 Consumer Demand (D) Forecasting Graphical Model Fit and Forecast

Sheet1

Version: PREDICTED (PREDICTED) Product: Pack Size 3 Key Account: KOL003 Units of Measure: USD FAW_INTERNAL_ORGANIZATION: FAW_DEFAULT Frequency: FTD Source: Total (Total) TRADER: EXT

	FEB2019	WEEK07OF2019	WEEK08OF2019	MAR2019	WEEK09OF2019	WEEK10OF2019	WEEK11OF2019	WEEK12OF2019	WEEK13OF2019	APR2019	WEEK14OF2019
Point of Sale / Sell-led Plan	34,520.00	8,350.00	8,561.00	42,995.00	8,441.00	8,799.00	8,771.00	8,672.00	8,330.00	34,169.00	8,343.00
Sales / Sell-out units (Baseline)	32,230.00	8,350.00	6,271.00	46,237.00	6,183.00	8,291.00	8,711.00	8,672.00	8,380.00	34,169.00	8,343.00
Sales / Sell-out units (Promo)	2,290.00	0.00	2,290.00	2,758.00	2,258.00	500.00	0.00	0.00	0.00	0.00	0.00
POS / Sell-out Promo uplifts adjustments	0.00	0.00	0.00	0.00	0.00	0.00	0.00	0.00	0.00	0.00	0.00
Shipments / Sell-in Baseline forecast	45,213.09	17,600.00	6,000.00	39,980.53	6,131.30	8,221.67	8,656.15	8,599.45	8,599.52	41,239.98	10,660.49
Total promotion events	1.00	0.00	1.00	1.00	1.00	0.00	0.00	0.00	0.00	0.00	0.00
Temp price reduction 15%	0.00	0.00	0.00	0.00	0.00	0.00	0.00	0.00	0.00	0.00	0.00
Temp price reduction 10%	0.00	0.00	0.00	0.00	0.00	0.00	0.00	0.00	0.00	0.00	0.00
Temp price reduction 5%	0.00	0.00	0.00	0.00	0.00	0.00	0.00	0.00	0.00	0.00	0.00
Holiday promotions	1.00	0.00	1.00	1.00	1.00	0.00	0.00	0.00	0.00	0.00	0.00
Display no price reduction	0.00	0.00	0.00	0.00	0.00	0.00	0.00	0.00	0.00	0.00	0.00
Coupon	0.00	0.00	0.00	0.00	0.00	0.00	0.00	0.00	0.00	0.00	0.00
Buy one get one	0.00	0.00	0.00	0.00	0.00	0.00	0.00	0.00	0.00	0.00	0.00
Revenue (Total sales)	466,020.00	119,425.00	115,573.50	590,432.50	113,963.50	118,679.50	117,595.50	117,072.00	113,130.00	461,201.50	112,930.50
Revenue (Baseline)	435,105.00	119,475.00	84,658.50	540,199.50	83,479.50	111,929.50	117,388.50	117,072.00	113,130.00	461,201.50	112,930.50
Revenue (Promo)	30,915.00	0.00	30,915.00	37,233.00	30,483.00	6,750.00	0.00	0.00	0.00	0.00	0.00
Cost of goods sold (Total)	271,160.14	69,295.50	67,929.17	333,619.36	66,977.04	64,915.53	68,207.13	67,001.76	65,615.40	267,543.27	63,325.09
Cost of goods sold (Baseline)	252,560.90	69,295.50	48,181.93	315,055.71	48,432.89	64,915.53	68,207.13	67,001.76	65,615.40	267,543.27	65,325.09
Cost of goods sold (Promo)	18,627.24	0.00	16,627.24	18,564.15	18,564.15	0.00	0.00	0.00	0.00	0.00	0.00
Gross Margin %	41.81	42.00	41.22	42.52	41.22	45.38	42.00	42.00	42.00	42.00	42.00

Figure 4.4 Marketing Planner Workbook

the last two weeks of forecasts. Then the month of March and the corresponding five weeks of March, etc. The market planner can scroll from left to right to view additional months and weeks for as many weeks into the future that has been set for this view—in this case, 52 weeks into the future.

This is a Web user interface (UI), not a spreadsheet; however, the marketing planner can click on the menu to go into Excel if they prefer a spreadsheet UI. If the marketing planner wants to change products, key accounts, or units of measure, they can click on those items on the top menu bar and a dropdown menu will appear to change the product level or metrics. Finally, the marketing planner can have a different view from the demand/supply planner(s). The different workbooks can be linked together through a common element, so that when the marketing planner makes a change it will affect the demand/supply planner's workbook. There is also workflow and an approval process, including comments, built into all the workbooks. Each time the demand analyst updates the statistical models after each forecasting cycle all the workbooks are updated with the new updated forecasts, along with any calculations.

The workbook shows the POS total sell-out (left-hand column), which in this case is the syndicated scanner data. The promoted volume is simply the total sales promotional lift volumes summed from the statistical models. It was not broken out by cleansing the data, or human judgment. The promotion volumes reflect the parameter estimates generated by the statistical models. The POS/syndicated scanner baseline volume is simply the statistical promotion lifts minus the total volume. There are several promotions that were found to be significant in the statistical models. Where you see a "1" in that row, the promo is turned on, and a "0" turns off the promo impact. As you can see, the consumer goods company is running the special holiday promotion in the last week of February (Week 8) and the first week of March (Week 9). The holiday sales promotion impact is 2,290 cases and 2,258 cases, respectively. There is also some sales promotion volume in March (Week 10) of 500 cases. This is the residual effect of the two-week sales promotion captured by the statistical model. As you scroll down the left-hand side of the workbook there is revenue broken out into baseline and promoted—again, as a result of the statistical model, not data cleansing. Finally, the last row is gross margin. In this case the goal is to maintain a gross margin of 42% or greater.

The company discovered excess inventory for this pack size group in the grocery channel at several key accounts. The market planner's goal is to assure that all the inventory, including the holiday sales promotion volumes, sell through the channel for all key accounts. The marketing planner runs a what-if simulation by turning on the Temp Price Reduction (TPR) of 10% off for Week 10 of March to determine the impact on volume, revenue, and profit margin. Originally, the TPR 10% sales promotion was run in August 2018, and now the market planner is hoping to run it again in March (Week 10) 2019. That's fine; the impact from August 2018 will be replicated into March (Week 10) 2019. The result is that it increases March (Week 10) volume by 912 cases, increasing revenue from $118,678.50 to $130,990.64, and maintains a gross margin of 44.44%, slightly less than the original gross margin of 45%. (See Figure 4.5.)

In this case, adding the TPR 10% off sales promotion not only increases volume in March (Week 10) by over 900 cases, but it also increases revenue and maintains a gross margin over 42%. This sales promotion not only increases volume and revenue, it is also highly profitable. The market planner submits this scenario to their manager for approval. Then, the impact is sent to the demand planner's workbook electronically for further evaluation along with comments to determine if there is enough inventory to cover the promotion volumes. (See Figure 4.5.)

Once the marketing planner receives the approval from their manager, the demand planner's workbook is automatically updated, so they can determine how to adjust the supply (shipments) plan. (See Figure 4.6.)

As you can see, the demand planner's planning workbook is slightly different from the marketing planner's workbook: they have scrolled down the planning view to the product hierarchy at "pack size" and "key accounts" (customer ship-to-locations) level. The demand planner can scroll from left to right to view additional

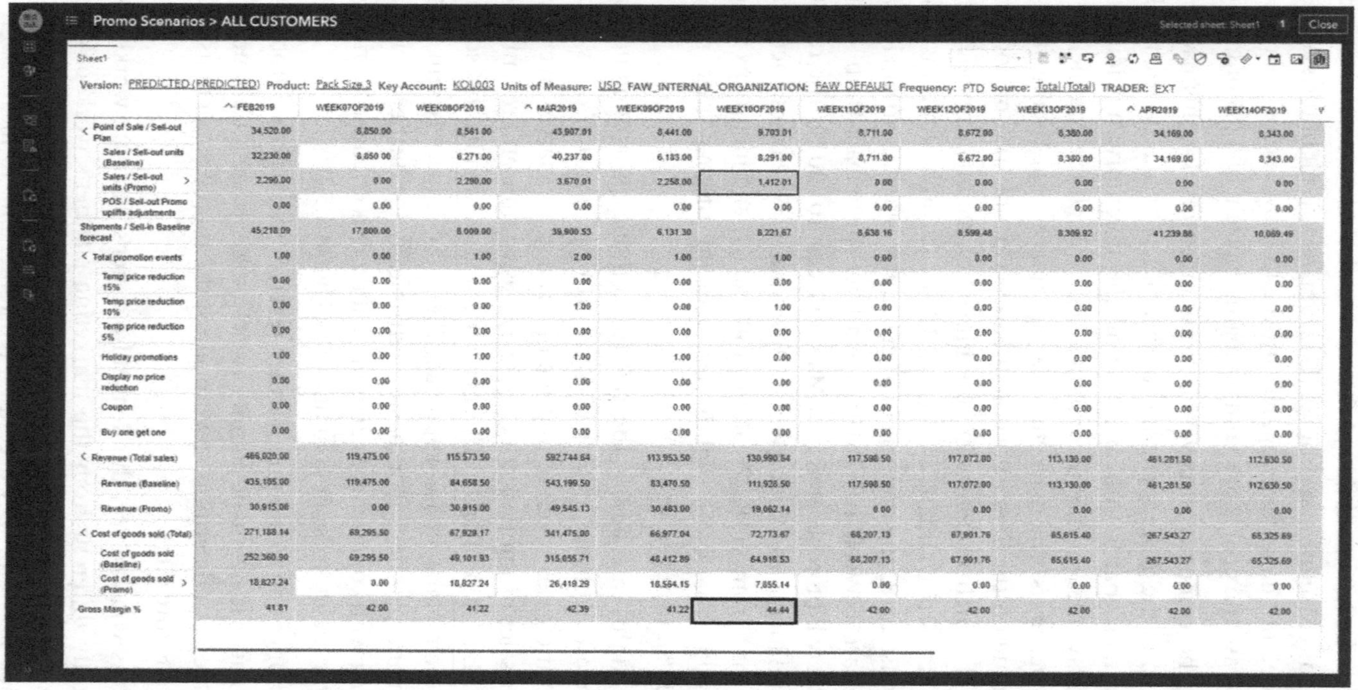

	^ FEB2019	WEEK07OF2019	WEEK08OF2019	^ MAR2019	WEEK09OF2019	WEEK10OF2019	WEEK11OF2019	WEEK12OF2019	WEEK13OF2019	^ APR2019	WEEK14OF2019
< Point of Sale / Sell-out Plan	34,520.00	8,850.00	8,561.00	43,907.01	8,441.00	9,703.01	8,711.00	8,672.00	8,380.00	34,169.00	8,343.00
Sales / Sell-out units (Baseline)	32,230.00	8,850.00	6,271.00	40,237.00	6,183.00	8,291.00	8,711.00	8,672.00	8,380.00	34,169.00	8,343.00
Sales / Sell-out units (Promo) >	2,290.00	0.00	2,290.00	3,670.01	2,258.00	1,412.01	0.00	0.00	0.00	0.00	0.00
POS / Sell-out Promo uplifts adjustments	0.00	0.00	0.00	0.00	0.00	0.00	0.00	0.00	0.00	0.00	0.00
Shipments / Sell-in Baseline forecast	45,218.09	17,800.00	8,009.00	39,900.53	6,131.30	8,221.67	8,638.16	8,599.48	8,309.92	41,239.86	10,089.49
< Total promotion events	1.00	0.00	1.00	2.00	1.00	1.00	0.00	0.00	0.00	0.00	0.00
Temp price reduction 15%	0.00	0.00	0.00	0.00	0.00	0.00	0.00	0.00	0.00	0.00	0.00
Temp price reduction 10%	0.00	0.00	0.00	1.00	0.00	1.00	0.00	0.00	0.00	0.00	0.00
Temp price reduction 5%	0.00	0.00	0.00	0.00	0.00	0.00	0.00	0.00	0.00	0.00	0.00
Holiday promotions	1.00	0.00	1.00	1.00	1.00	0.00	0.00	0.00	0.00	0.00	0.00
Display no price reduction	0.00	0.00	0.00	0.00	0.00	0.00	0.00	0.00	0.00	0.00	0.00
Coupon	0.00	0.00	0.00	0.00	0.00	0.00	0.00	0.00	0.00	0.00	0.00
Buy one get one	0.00	0.00	0.00	0.00	0.00	0.00	0.00	0.00	0.00	0.00	0.00
< Revenue (Total sales)	466,020.00	119,475.00	115,573.50	592,744.64	113,953.50	130,990.64	117,598.50	117,072.00	113,130.00	461,281.50	112,630.50
Revenue (Baseline)	435,105.00	119,475.00	84,658.50	543,199.50	83,470.50	111,928.50	117,598.50	117,072.00	113,130.00	461,281.50	112,630.50
Revenue (Promo)	30,915.00	0.00	30,915.00	49,545.13	30,483.00	19,062.14	0.00	0.00	0.00	0.00	0.00
< Cost of goods sold (Total)	271,188.14	69,295.50	67,929.17	341,475.00	66,977.04	72,773.67	68,207.13	67,901.76	65,615.40	267,543.27	65,325.69
Cost of goods sold (Baseline)	252,360.90	69,295.50	49,101.93	315,055.71	48,412.89	64,918.53	68,207.13	67,901.76	65,615.40	267,543.27	65,325.69
Cost of goods sold (Promo) >	18,827.24	0.00	18,827.24	26,419.29	18,564.15	7,855.14	0.00	0.00	0.00	0.00	0.00
Gross Margin %	41.81	42.00	41.22	42.39	41.22	44.44	42.00	42.00	42.00	42.00	42.00

Figure 4.5 Marketing Planner Promotion Simulation Results

months and weeks for as many weeks into the future that has been set for this view—in this case, 52 weeks into the future. (See Figure 4.6.)

As the demand planner scrolls down the left-hand column, they can review the POS data, which in this case is syndicated scanner data, including total, baseline, and promoted volumes that link the marketing planner's workbook to the demand planner's workbook. March Week 10 reflects the results of the marketing planner's scenario, adding the impact of running the TPR 10% off promotion (1,412.01 units). However, the remainder of the workbook is totally different showing "Shipments/Sell-in Plan" (total, baseline, and promoted shipment volumes). In addition, showing trade inventory receipts, opening and closing inventory, weeks coverage (forward inventory coverage of forecast) and target, last month consensus demand plan (CDP) and annual CDP.

As a result of the marketing planner's added TPR 10% off promotion volume in weeks forward coverage of trade inventory for March (Weeks 9–10) is below one-week coverage. The company target is two-week forward trade inventory coverage. In addition, the gap between target and actual trade inventory for March (Weeks 9–10) is 11,195.20 and 10,642.67, respectively. To shore up inventory to protect customer service levels and mitigate any backorders, the demand planner reaches out to the supply planner to determine if incoming product can be pulled forward to cover the increase in demand. In this case, the supply planner advises the demand planner that 5,000 additional cases can be expedited into March (Weeks 9–10). The demand planner then runs a scenario to determine the best way to allocate the 5,000 additional cases. They add 3,000 cases to March (Week 9), and 2,000 cases to March (Week 10) in the "Shipments/Sell-in Adjustment" row in the workbook to increase the demand plan, thus increasing forward weeks trade inventory. The result is that forward weeks trade inventory increases from below one week to 1.34 forward weeks coverage. (See Figure 4.7.)

Step 6: Link the consumer demand forecast to supply (shipments). The process just described (adding the TPR 10% off promotion to

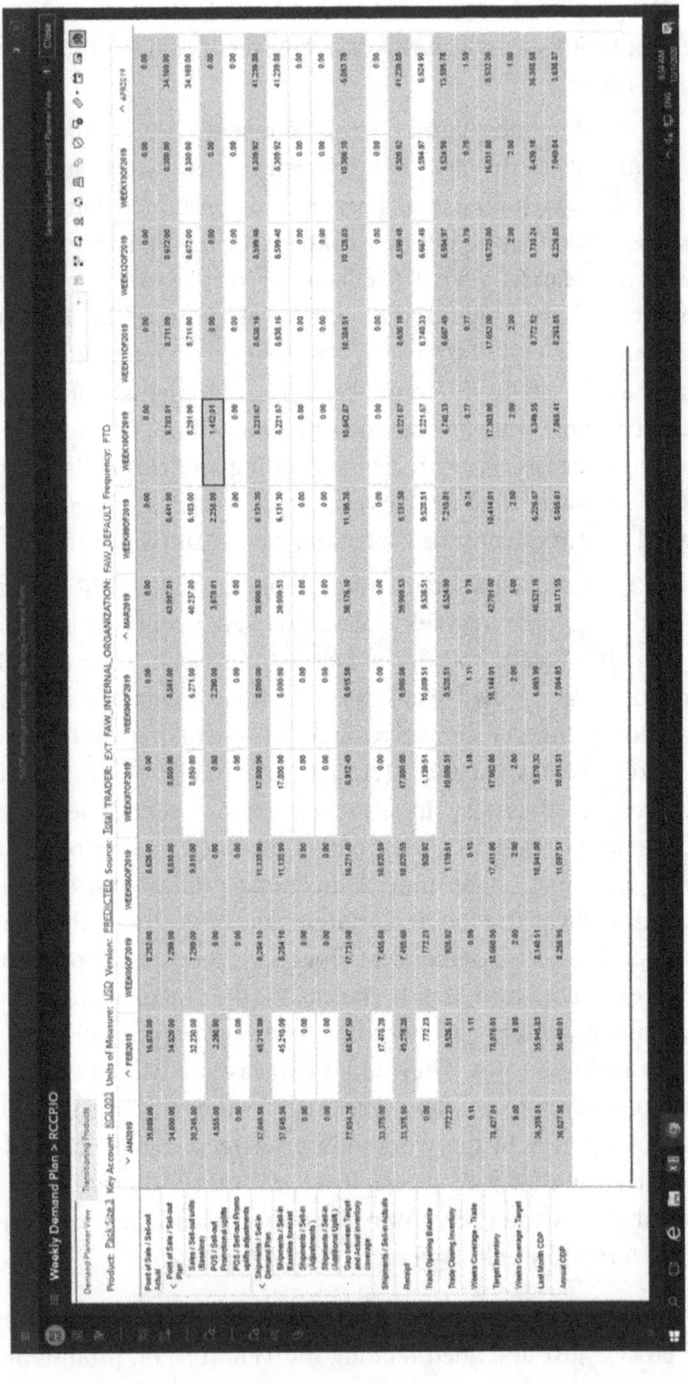

Figure 4.6 Demand/Supply Planner Workbook

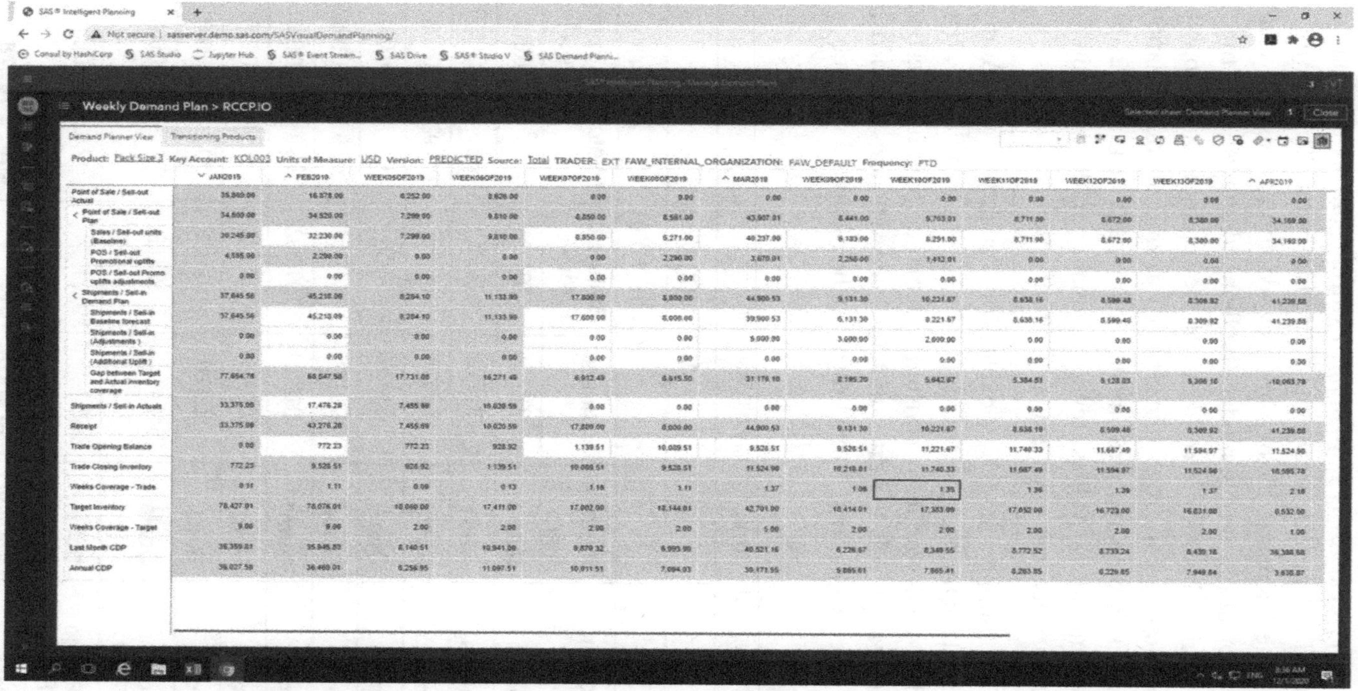

Figure 4.7 Demand Planner Supply Simulation Results

March (Week 10) is now applied (turned on) in the consumer demand (D) model, recalibrated, and forecasted. Then, using the consumer demand history and revised forecast as the leading indicator in the supply model, the demand analyst links the first tier (demand) to the second tier of the supply chain (supply) by incorporating consumer demand (D) as one of the explanatory variables in the supply (S) model. The results in Table 4.2 shows how demand, as well as trend, seasonality, trade promotion and inventory are influencing supply (shipments).

The supply model is explaining roughly 83% (Adjusted R^2 .8321) of the variation in supply. One of the significant variables in the supply model is consumer demand (parameter estimate = .70894), which indicates that for every 10 cases shipped into the grocery channel, 7.0894 cases are being pulled through (sold

Table 4.2 Supply (Shipments) Model Analytic Results

Component	Parameter	ARIMA (X) Model			
		(0,1,1) (1,1,0)			
		Estimate	Standard Error	t-Value	Approx Pr > |t|
Shipments	MA1	−0.23606	0.094	−251	0.0135
Shipments	AR521	−0.45192	0.12835	−352	0.0006
Demand	Scale	0.70894	0.04752	14.92	0.0001
Demand	Den1	0.99365	0.01458	68.17	0.0001
Inventory	Scale	−0.01739	0.0091598	−1.9	0.0602
Inventory	Num1	0.05061	0.0073022	6.93	0.0001
Inventory	Num2	0.03759	0.073072	5.14	0.0001
Inventory	Den1	0.9937	0.01413	70.31	0.0001
Outlier 05Jan2019	Scale	2544.4	.923.08	2.76	0.0068
Trade Promo Feb2019	Scale	2905.1	996.09	2.92	0.0043
R^2 = .8445	Weekly Fitted MAPE 7.61%			MAE = 767.78 (units)	
Adj R^2 = .8321	Weekly Holdout (6wks) 10.01%				

through) the grocery channel by consumer demand at the pack size level. Conversely, roughly 3.0 cases (10 − 7.08 cases = 2.91 cases) are being pushed into the channel by offering trade incentives to retailers, as well as other related factors. This indicates some inventory loading is occurring in the retail grocery channel for these products as the consumer goods company is shipping in more than the retailers are selling through the channel to the consumer. This will eventually lead to higher inventory at the retailer's distribution centers (customer ship-to-locations).

It is interesting to note that the fitted MAPE for the supply forecast is 7.62% and the 6-week out-of-sample MAPE is 10.01%, which is well below the average industry accuracy of 17.0% to 35.0%. Keep in mind the industry average is based on one month (lag1) aggregated (top level) monthly forecasts, while the consumption-based supply (shipments) model accuracy is based on a 1- to 6-weeks ahead weekly forecast accuracy at the pack size level (three levels deep in the product hierarchy). These results are not uncommon using the consumption-based forecasting and planning process.

The supply model identified a February 2019 trade promotion as significant, as well as an outlier (week of January 5, 2019) and trade inventory. Working with the marketing planner, the demand analyst learned that the outlier was another trade vehicle (off-invoice allowance) designed to encourage retailers to backfill product inventory after the Christmas holiday season. Again, it is important to remember that the combination of predictive analytics and domain knowledge (not "gut feeling" judgment) are required to effectively implement consumption-based forecasting and planning.

After identifying and verifying the supply model parameter estimates for all the explanatory variables and testing the model's predictive capabilities, the system automatically refits all the models up/down the product hierarchy with the 6-week out-of-sample data using all 153 weeks of data (see Figure 4.8). The final model fit and forecast for all levels of the product

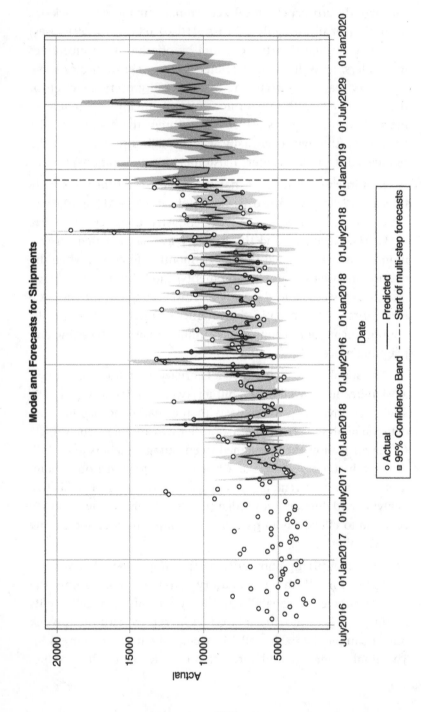

Figure 4.8 Supply (S) Forecasting Graphical Model Fit and Forecast

hierarchy are now disaggregated down the product hierarchy from the pack size (middle-out) level to the SKU and customer ship-to-location; and then automatically reconciled to the channel product (top) level to maintain the integrity of the entire product hierarchy.

UNDERSTANDING THE RELATIONSHIP BETWEEN DEMAND AND SUPPLY

In some situations, you may find little or no statistical significance between consumption (consumer demand) and supply (shipments). There are two potential reasons this could be occurring. First, this could be an indication that your company has been pushing supply into the retail channels, rather than pulling products through the channel. As a result, the relationship between consumer demand and supply is minimal. Also, your company may be focused on utilizing trade vehicles (trade promotions, off-invoice allowances, and others) to influence retailers to purchase your products. This push strategy, although a good short-term fix to lagging sales, cannot be sustained over long periods. In the short term you can build those trade incentives into your supply models in the hope that you don't load up the channels with too much inventory. On the other hand, it is advised that you work closer with sales and marketing, using the supply models to statistically demonstrate that trade spend is pushing too much inventory into the retail channels. In fact, you should consider rebalancing your marketing P&L to focus more on consumption—sales promotions and in-store merchandising—features, displays, feature and displays, TPRs, and others—to drive more consumer demand to pull through (sell through) their products in those retail channels. If so, over time a stronger relationship (correlation) between consumer demand and supply will result, thus lowering channel inventory and increasing profit margin. In fact, less trade incentives will be needed to sell products through those channels, allowing marketing to reallocate the trade spend to the consumer side of the P&L, thus increasing consumer spend to drive more consumer demand, revenue, and profit.

Second, another more common reason is the lag between ship-ments and POS/syndicated scanner data. Depending on the channel and the retailer's replenishment policies, there could be a lag bet-ween supply replenishment and demand from anywhere between 1–4 weeks. For example, grocery retailers reorder products every 3–5 days (weekly), so there is little if any lag between demand and supply, as we have seen in the consumer goods example discussed earlier in the chapter. The main reason is that grocery retailers carry many SKU facings on shelf, requiring more frequent reordering due to warehouse replenishment constraints and thin margins. Not to mention that they carry many perishable products with short shelf life, such as bread, fruit, vegetables, and others. On the other hand, mass merchandisers like Walmart, Target, and others have less SKU facings on shelf and sell more volume, so they tend to reorder every three to four weeks and carry large inventory stocks for nonperish-able products.

Depending on the channel where you are implementing consumption-based forecasting and planning you may have to "pull forward" POS/syndicated scanner data (consumption) in the supply (shipments) model anywhere from one to four weeks in order to successfully model the relationship—that is, find significance. For example, let's take a canned food product in the grocery channel that has a two-year shelf life.

Figure 4.9 is a comparison between syndicated scanner data and actual shipments over the same 153 weeks for a canned food prod-uct at the product group level, one level above product SKU. If you look closely, there appears to be a one-week lag between the actual consumer demand and shipments. In other words, the product is shipped into the grocery channel one week earlier than it is pur-chased by the consumer (sell through). This is a highly seasonal prod-uct with several sales promotions occurring between January and May to entice consumers to purchase the product early in the season (October/December), and then again in mid-season (January). In fact, when a regression model is applied the adjusted R^2 = .60, which means the correlation (relationship) is moderate between demand and supply—that is, not too significant. In fact, when additional explan-atory variables are added to the model, the syndicated scanner data

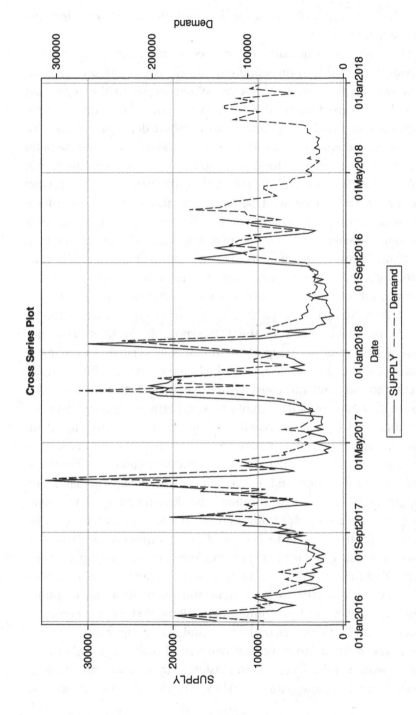

Figure 4.9 Canned Food Product Demand and Supply Comparison

becomes less and less significant, having little impact on shipments due to trade incentives.

In Figure 4.10 demand (syndicated scanner data) was "pulled forward" one week in the shipment model. As you can see, demand now falls in place with shipments. When we rerun the regression model, the revised adjusted R^2 =.87, which means demand is highly correlated to supply (shipments). Now when demand increases or decreases, we will see a similar impact on supply because demand is a leading indicator in the supply model. Demand leads supply, not the reverse. This is a critical relationship that helps not only predict short-term shifting demand patterns, but also mid- and long-term demand, turning (infection) points. The shifting demand patterns are now influencing shipments, reflecting those changes faster than traditional time series models (i.e. moving averaging, exponential smoothing, and others) that normally don't react well to turning points until several periods after the inflection point takes place.

A demand planner reporting upstream into operations planning would not have access to the POS/syndicated scanner data, nor have a solid understanding of the nuances associated with demand and supply. In addition, they don't have the analytics skills to implement and maintain the consumption-based predictive models. As a result, they may think that there's no significant relationship between demand and supply. Subsequently, a data scientist reporting upstream into operations planning would have the analytics skill necessary to build the models, but they would lack the same domain knowledge and thus not understand the relationship between demand and supply. This is another justification why demand analysts and planners need to be embedded downstream in sales and marketing. If so, they would have access to POS/syndicated scanner data, marketing events calendars, and other related marketing tactical information and data. Over time, the demand analysts and planners would learn how to apply the analytics to implement and maintain a consumption-based forecasting and planning process. Plus, they would become a valued analytical resource to the sales and marketing teams.

I was fortunate to have met two VPs of marketing early in my career who had the foresight and vision to delve into consumption-based forecasting and planning. They also agreed to be accountable

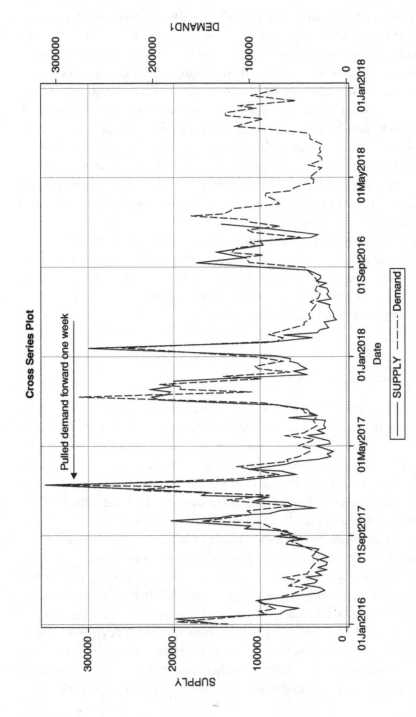

Figure 4.10 Canned Food Product Demand and Supply Comparison-Demand Pulled Forward One Week

113

for forecast accuracy and leading the S&OP (Sales & Operations Planning) process for both demand and supply. At the time, we didn't realize we were 30 years ahead of the consumer goods industry. Those two individuals went on to become CEOs of major international consumer goods companies, and have since retired. It was during those first few years we successfully implemented consumption-based forecasting and planning across the entire company product portfolio. I went on to successfully implement consumption-based forecasting and planning at three more companies. In each case, I either reported into the VP of marketing, or the president/CEO of the company, not supply chain. Still today, only a handful of companies have had the desire and fortitude to successfully implement consumption-based forecasting and planning. Unfortunately, over 90% of companies are in denial and reluctant to invest the time and resources to change the paradigm. They are stuck in a viscous 1980s demand forecasting and planning ecosystem that is supported by outdated ERP technology.

WHY MOVE DEMAND PLANNING DOWNSTREAM CLOSER TO THE CONSUMER?

Most executives consider demand management a futile effort, and a "waste of time." As a result, they rely heavily on lean manufacturing and supply chain planning, utilizing inventory safety (buffer) stock to manage demand volatility caused by poor forecasts, and the bullwhip effect. Essentially, they are focusing on the symptom, rather than the root cause—failing to recognize the true demand signal (POS/ syndicated scanner data), and doubling down on supply. Although this approach initially improves manufacturing efficiencies, companies are quickly realizing that it does require an enormous amount of effort to improve customer service and reduce excess finished goods inventories. In fact, inventory safety stock and finished goods inventories have increased over the past decade in many cases. Making matters worse, the excess inventory is the wrong mix of products due to lack of focus on true consumer demand. They are essentially forecasting from supply to the consumer, rather than the consumer to supply. They have forgotten that demand drives supply, not the reverse.

Consumption-based planning is a combination of horizontal business processes, analytics, and technologies that enable companies to analyze and execute against the precise mix of customer, product, channel, and geographic segments that achieves their customer-facing business objectives. Based on recent observations and research, demand planning on average is driven 60% by process, 30% by analytics, and 10% by enabling technology, depending on the industry, market, and channel dynamics that influence how companies orchestrate a demand response. Although enabling technology represents only 10%, the other 90% cannot be achieved without the enabling technology due to scalability and analytical requirements, not to mention data integration requirements that span across the organization. The need for an improved demand planning process focuses not only on process, analytics, and technology but also on the importance of integrated collaboration internally across the organization, as well as externally with key accounts (customers).

Consumption-based planning utilizes data from market and channel sources to sense, shape, and translate consumer demand into an actionable demand response that is supported by an efficient supply plan, or supply response. A true consumption-based forecast is an unconstrained view or best estimate of the market and of the dynamics influencing consumers to purchase your products through various channels including traditional brick-and-mortar, mobile, online, and other IoT devices.

True demand shaping is the process of using what-if analysis to influence unconstrained consumer demand in the future and matching that demand with an efficient supply (shipments) response. Based on various industry research studies conducted over the past several years, demand shaping, just like demand sensing, includes three key elements:

1. *Ability to increase volume and profit.* This can be achieved by using predictive analytics to proactively influence future unconstrained demand using what-if analysis. Using predictive analytics, companies can measure the impact of changing price, sales promotions, marketing events, advertising, and product mix against demand lift and profitability to make optimal business decisions that affect future demand.

2. *Supply plan/supply supportability analysis.* This refers to how much product can be made based on existing capacity, and where, when, and how fast it can be delivered.

3. *Demand shifting (steering).* This refers to the ability to promote another product as a substitute if the one originally ordered was not available, and/or to move a sales and marketing tactic from one period to another to accommodate supply constraints. This ability is especially useful if demand patterns or supply capacity changes suddenly steer customers from product A to product B, or shift demand to a later time period.

Over the past several years, many companies have begun to invest in demand-sensing and shaping processes along with enabling technology; however, in almost every case, they are doing demand shifting rather than true demand shaping. If anything, they have implemented short-term demand sensing (1–6 weeks into the future). Even in those cases they are sensing sales orders, which is a replenishment signal, not the true consumer demand signal. No one is truly sensing and shaping consumer demand, POS, or syndicated scanner data (Nielsen/ IRI/IMS); neither are they linking unconstrained demand to sales orders and shipments (supply) using consumption-based forecasting and planning, as described early in this chapter.

Demand shaping happens when companies use sales and marketing tactics such as price, promotion, new product launches, sales incentives, and/or marketing programs to influence future consumption, not just to generate incremental unit volume, but also to increase revenue and profit. All too many times, companies believe that they are shaping demand but find that they are just shifting demand (moving demand from one period to another). Shifting demand and selling at a lower margin without improving market share and revenue growth creates waste in the supply chain. The first step in the consumption-based forecasting and planning process is sensing market conditions based on demand signals and then shaping future demand using technologies such as price optimization, trade promotion planning, new product launch plan alignment, and social/digital/mobile convergence (see Figure 4.11). Demand sensing reduces the latency of the demand signal by 70–80%, allowing the company to better understand and

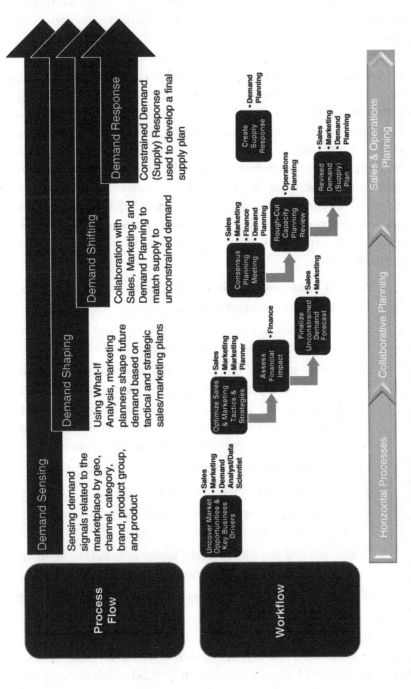

Figure 4.11 Consumption-based Forecasting and Planning Process

view true channel demand. Demand shaping combines the tactics of pricing policies, sales promotions, sales and marketing incentives, and new product launches to influence demand at the point of purchase.

Traditional demand forecasting and planning ERP systems were not designed to sense demand patterns other than trend/cycle, seasonality, and level (unexplained variance). For that reason, it is impossible for traditional demand planning systems to conduct demand-sensing and shaping activities associated with price, sales promotions, channel marketing programs, and other related factors. As the global digital economy has become increasingly volatile, fragmented, and dynamic, and as supply chain lead times have become overextended, companies are quickly coming to the realization that their demand forecasting and planning systems are no longer adequate to predict shifting consumer demand patterns. There are two primary factors that have contributed to this situation:

1. *Limited statistical methods* available in traditional demand forecasting and planning systems:

   a. Can only sense and predict stable demand that is highly seasonal with distinct trend patterns.

   b. Primarily use only one category of statistical models, called time series methods, with a focus on exponential smoothing models, and moving averaging, such as simple exponential smoothing, Holt's two-parameter exponential smoothing, and Winters' three-parameter exponential smoothing.

2. Process *requires domain knowledge* versus judgment to:

   a. Define data availability, granularity, and sourcing.

   b. Assess the dynamics of the market and channel segments to identify factors that influence demand.

   c. Run what-if analyses to shape future demand based on sales and marketing tactics/strategies.

   d. Link demand to supply using data and analytics, versus "gut feeling" judgment.

Research continues to show that there is a strong correlation between demand visibility and supply chain performance. As demand visibility yields higher accuracy in assessing demand, efficiencies continue to accumulate throughout the supply chain. Yet in most companies, there is still a wide gap between the commercial side of the business, with its understanding of the market and plans for demand-sensing and shaping (e.g. sales/marketing tactics and strategies, new product commercialization, life cycle management, and social media), and the supply chain organization, with its ability to support those efforts.

Demand sensing as a core capability isn't new; retailer POS data, syndicated scanner data, customer insights, and focus groups have guided marketing and sales promotional programming for over three decades. The challenge is how to translate these demand insights into actions that can drive an efficient supply response. The ability to sense, shape, and translate consumption into an accurate demand forecast and a corresponding supply plan requires more transparency and collaboration between the organization's commercial and operational functions. The key to demand shaping is cross-functional collaboration between sales and marketing, demand planning (demand analyst/planner) and among the other members of the supply chain (e.g. finance) by coordinating and agreeing on demand-shaping programs (see Figure 4.12).

The core purpose of such programs is to influence consumers to purchase the company's products (increase unit volume) while maintaining profit margins across the company's product portfolio. At first, these activities typically are monitored and managed independently by each functional department, such as sales, strategic marketing, and product management, with little cross-functional integration. For example, a price change occurring simultaneously with a product sales promotion could erode the profitability of the product or create an unexpected out-of-stock situation on the retailers' shelves. Cross-functional collaboration among sales, marketing, demand planning and finance requires companies to pivot to a cross-departmental market orientation that balances the trade-offs of each tactic and focuses on revenue generation and profit (see Figure 4.13), and not focusing entirely on reducing inventory costs. It also requires transition from traditional Sales & Operations Planning (S&OP) to Integrated Business Planning (IBP). This is the main reason why demand analysts and planners should be embedded downstream in the commercial side of the business.

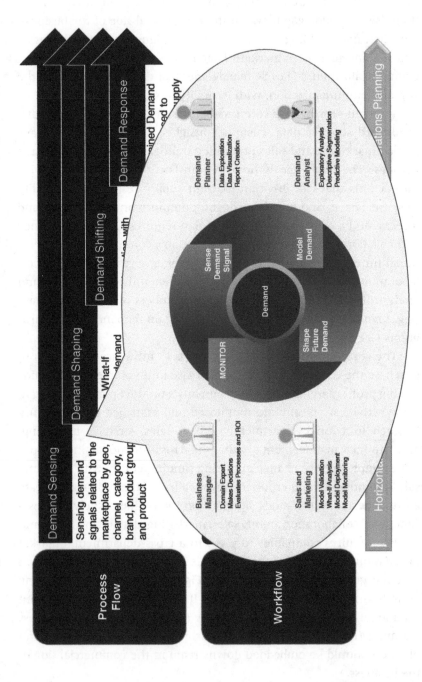

Figure 4.12 Consumption-Based Forecasting and Planning Demand Sensing Workflow

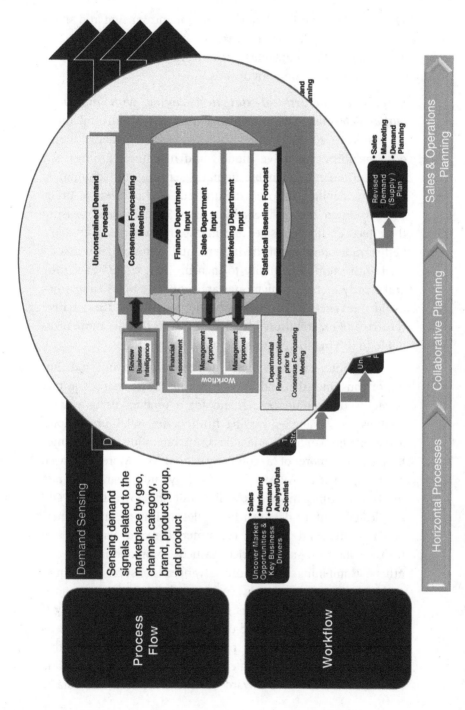

Figure 4.13 Consumption-Based Process Collaborative Planning Workflow

121

To better understand the dynamics of demand sensing and shaping, we need to break down the consumption-based forecasting and planning process into a capability framework made up of five key components. Those key components are:

1. *Large-scale hierarchical statistical engine with automatic outlier detection.* A set of more sophisticated statistical models that span across all analytics categories (time-series methods, including predictive models and machine learning) is a key requirement to enable demand sensing and shaping, as well as scalability, to forecast hundreds of thousands of products up/down the business hierarchy. Such models measure the effects of different sales and marketing events and enable a better understanding of the incremental volume that is associated with them. The ability to measure past events over time and clearly identify which ones are profitable helps companies avoid unexpected planning disruptions that produce negative returns and exploit those identifiable events that are more profitable in driving incremental demand and profit.

   Companies can proactively influence the amount and timing of consumer demand by varying the future marketing mix elements that influence demand for a product using what-if analysis. For example, varying future price, sales promotions, levels of merchandising, and advertising can influence consumers to purchase more of a company's products. More advanced methods, such as ARIMA, ARIMAX, dynamic regression, and machine learning models as well as utilizing downstream POS/syndicated scanner data can help sales and marketing planners better understand shifting consumer demand patterns and uncover insights, such as price elasticity, promotional lifts, and others. Combining these more advanced statistical techniques with decision-support tools, such as what-if analysis, enables sales and marketing planners (supported by a demand analyst) to determine the right trade-offs within the marketing mix by geography, channel, brand, product group, and product that drive incremental unit volume and profit. Demand analysts and planners need to move toward the use of downstream data to help capture consumer insights to build on current trends and seasonality, utilizing marketing programs based on the combination of historical data and domain knowledge, not "gut feeling" judgment. The only way to achieve all the above requires embedding demand analysts and planners downstream in sales and marketing.

2. *Visualization Analytics (VA).* VA capabilities combine the power of descriptive analytics associated with monitoring, tracking, and reporting with the power of predictive analytics to uncover actionable insights with user friendly interfaces. Visual Analytics' control towers/dashboards along with predictive analytics allow sales and marketing personnel to collect, integrate, and apply data from the statistical engine and the field to support business tactics and strategies, such as pricing, sales promotions, and measuring results against strategic and tactical business plans. Demand shaping can be used to reduce demand volatility, thereby reducing the need for supply network agility. For example, corporate leaders in various industries (e.g. retailers, consumer goods companies, and direct-to-consumer companies) are looking to use Web channels to sense demand signals and shape future demand using distributed network architectures (DNA).

3. *Post reconciliation of performance.* It is important to measure demand-sensing and shaping programs after each completed demand forecasting cycle to determine the success or failure of the programs implemented to drive demand. Historically, it took weeks to review and assess the success or failure of a sales promotion after its completion. With new enabling technology along with downstream data collection and synchronization processes, as well as market sensing and shaping capabilities, today it is much easier and faster to monitor, track, and report on the effects of demand-shaping programs. This allows companies to manage the demand-shaping process around real-time demand signals. Adjustments can be made to demand-shaping programs within a daily or weekly period to better manage the outcome.

4. *Executive alignment to support change management.* Establish clear decision criteria, empower senior managers and their staff, and develop an appropriate incentive program that includes rewards for accurate demand forecasts. Decentralize tactical knowledge-based decision making while balancing corporate strategic unit volume and profit objectives. Stress the importance of building a demand forecast based on sales and marketing programs that are profitable, not just volume generators. There will be a paradigm shift, moving from a view of unit volume in isolation of profitability (not considering profit, but only incremental volume for trial purposes) to a more focused view of how unit volume increases can affect profitability.

5. *Continuous business process improvements.* Short- and long-range business strategy and planning, operational tactical planning, and post-event analysis must be coordinated in the organization. Sophisticated analytics shared across the various departments within a company through well-designed decision support networks will provide more consistency and alignment of internal processes and workflow to drive profitability.[3]

Demand shaping focuses on creating an unconstrained demand forecast that reflects the sales and marketing activities that shape demand, rather than using supply to manage demand volatility. Demand shaping is a process that requires predictive analytics supported by enabling technology. The system should be flexible and easy to use, with quick response time, and closed-loop feedback to measure and report the value of those adjustments made to the initial statistical forecast. Without access to the intuitive system, the sales and marketing organizations have legitimate reason to resist participating in the forecasting process, as well as the S&OP process.

The consumption-based planning process relies on data, domain knowledge, and advanced statistical techniques to sense (measure) the key performance indicators (KPIs) that influence the demand signal, then using those KPIs to shape future demand to accurately predict shifting consumer demand patterns and react to changes in the marketplace. The process provides an unconstrained view or best estimate of market demand based on corporate specific historical sales demand

(POS/syndicated scanner data) and translates the demand response into a supply (shipment) plan. The KPIs ("demand drivers") used to predict demand (POS/syndicated scanner data) normally include retail price, sales promotions, advertising, in-store merchandising, competition, weather, and other related market factors. Figure 4.14 outlines the key components of the consumption-based forecasting and planning process.

Consumption-based planning is the set of business processes, people, analytics, and technologies that enable companies to analyze, choose, and execute against the precise mix of geographic segments, key accounts (customers), channel, brand, product group, and products that achieves their customer-facing business objectives. Consumption-based forecasting and planning utilizes data from market and channel sources to sense, shape, and translate demand requirements into an actionable demand response that is supported by an efficient supply response. The core focus areas in the process are:

- **Sensing Demand Signals:** Sense true consumer demand (POS/syndicated scanner data) to understand market shifts in demand for a company's products by measuring the impact of KPIs that influence consumer demand using predictive analytics.
- **Shaping Future Demand:** Using what-if scenario analysis to shape future demand by varying the future values of price, sales promotions, marketing events, and other related factors that influence consumer demand.
- **Demand Shifting:** During the S&OP process, collaborate across sales, marketing, and demand planning to influence short- and mid-term demand, by negotiating where necessary to shift future constrained demand based on supply capacity constraints—thus providing more time for supply planning to build capacity to meet short- and mid-term sales and marketing tactics.
- **Cross-functional Collaboration:** Traditionally, companies have adopted techniques of collaboration to increase dialogue between internal supply chain members in order to create more accurate short- and mid-term plans. Those supply members are

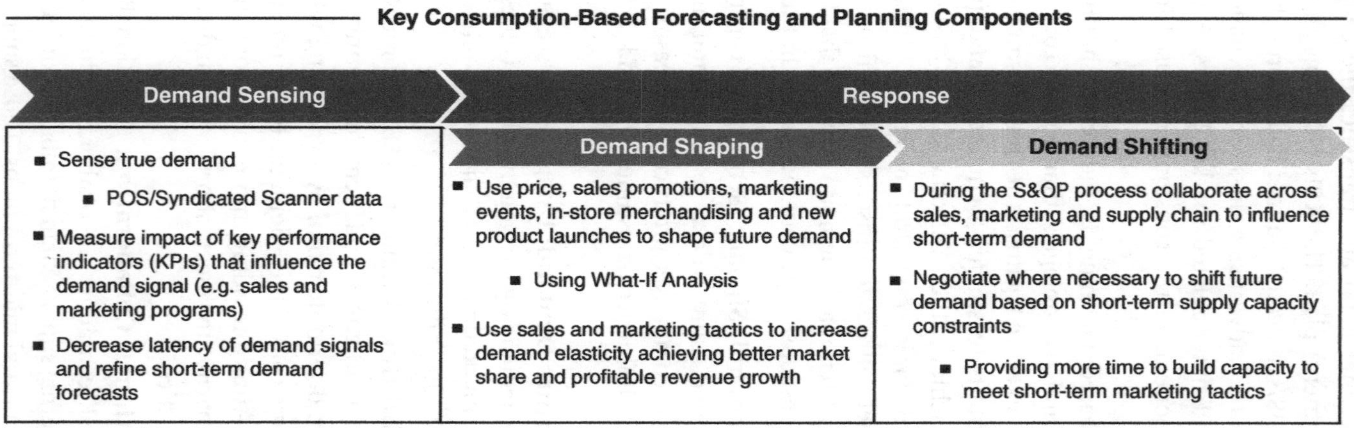

Key Consumption-Based Forecasting and Planning Components

Demand Sensing	Response	
	Demand Shaping	Demand Shifting

Demand Sensing

- Sense true demand
  - POS/Syndicated Scanner data
- Measure impact of key performance indicators (KPIs) that influence the demand signal (e.g. sales and marketing programs)
- Decrease latency of demand signals and refine short-term demand forecasts

Demand Shaping

- Use price, sales promotions, marketing events, in-store merchandising and new product launches to shape future demand
  - Using What-If Analysis
- Use sales and marketing tactics to increase demand elasticity achieving better market share and profitable revenue growth

Demand Shifting

- During the S&OP process collaborate across sales, marketing and supply chain to influence short-term demand
- Negotiate where necessary to shift future demand based on short-term supply capacity constraints
  - Providing more time to build capacity to meet short-term marketing tactics

Figure 4.14 Key Components of the Consumption-Based Planning Process

sales, marketing, finance, and demand planning, but could be others—such as retail customers. More and more companies are attempting to collaborate with their retail channel partners/customers like Walmart, Publix, Walgreens, and others.

■ **Forecast Value Add (FVA):** Implementing FVA with the intent to reduce touch points in the demand forecasting process thus increases forecast accuracy and efficiency (reduced cycle time) by eliminating those touch points that are not adding value. The FVA process measures each touch point in the demand forecasting process before and after someone manually adjusts the forecast. If they are not adding value, then eliminate that touch point, or discount it through weighting or minimizing the bias in the forecast, thus reducing forecast error. This topic will be discussed in more detail in Chapter 6.

There have been several research studies conducted over the past decade by various research organizations indicating that anywhere from 10% to 30% improvement in demand forecast accuracy delivers on average between 3% and 11% improvement in revenue and profit. Improved forecast accuracy, when combined with software that translates the consumer demand forecast into its individual drivers, will decrease inventory and operating cost by as much as 15–30%, increase service levels, and improve cash flow and return on investment (ROI), as well as increase pretax profitability. In the last decade, a host of seasoned and practiced supply chain professionals have presented and published a number of articles and research highlighting the returns for companies that create accurate demand forecasts to drive their digital supply chains with a focus on customer excellence. According to those professionals, implementing consumer-driven supply chain strategies allows companies to:

■ Support periods of shifting consumer demand patterns with less finished goods inventories;

■ Improve demand forecast accuracy for products that are slow moving while keeping pace with consumer demand for those products that are fast moving; and

■ Achieve higher ROI, profits, and overall lower inventory costs and working capital.

The journey to become consumption-driven requires rethinking demand holistically by understanding (1) the source of demand signals, and (2) the integration of demand into corresponding horizontal supply chain processes. Consumption-based forecasting and planning is the use of forecasting technologies along with demand-sensing, shaping, and translation techniques to improve supply chain processes. This journey starts with outside-in thinking and focuses on identifying the demand signals and translating them into the drivers of consumer demand. Consumption-based plans focus on accurately predicting what consumers will buy, not on what companies think consumers want. This is in sharp contrast with the traditional supply-centric processes that determine what companies will manufacture or ship. The input signals are from the consumer to supply, not from supply to the consumer. There are many possible inputs, including seasonal responses, sales promotions, marketing events, pricing, economic factors, competitive pressures, in addition to epidemiological data, stringency indices, Google trends, and social media.

Companies have limited ability to reduce supply chain costs via supply-centric levers due to increasingly high demand volatility as a result of the digital economy and unexpected disruptions like COVID-19. Focusing on the consumer demand drivers will address the root cause and yield significant benefits to both supply and demand. It has been proven that those companies who have implemented consumption-based forecasting and planning have experienced decreasing inventories simultaneously with increasing sales. With improved demand forecasting and planning, those companies that adopted consumption-based forecasting and planning manufactured less of the products that were low selling and kept pace with consumer demand for what was selling. This led to better gross margins, ROI, higher profits, and lower inventory costs, waste, and working capital.

THE INTEGRATED BUSINESS PLANNING CONNECTION

Sales & Operations Planning (S&OP) has been adopted worldwide by many companies to help them synchronize demand and supply. In the early 1980s Oliver Wight first wrote about S&OP, and they continue to find that the quantity, quality, and sustainability of business performance improvements depend on how the process is implemented and deployed across the organization. Those companies who have adopted S&OP as the primary process to manage their business tend to get the most significant and wide-ranging results when implemented correctly across all the participating functions—sales, marketing, and operations planning.

Most companies, however, have not seen sustainable results as their businesses have matured while the digital economy emerged, with its impact on markets and consumer preferences. The primary reasons for experiencing minimal results is related to the lackluster participation of sales and marketing, as the their focus is too supply centric, and the absence of horizontal shared performance metrics. Furthermore, the core component of balancing "supply and demand" lends itself to supply chain planning, which is not related to true consumer demand. It's about supply. The focus needs to be on balancing "demand and supply" with a focus on profitable demand. As mentioned in earlier chapters, "without demand there's no need for supply." Make it and they will come (buy) only works in the movies. As a result, many companies have not experienced the true benefits of their S&OP efforts.

The biggest contributor to S&OP failing, as mentioned, is too much focus on operations planning and reducing inventory costs. Most companies forget that the "S" stands for sales and marketing. Sales and marketing are not measured as much on cost cutting as they are on market share, revenue, and profitability—that is, demand generation. In other words, the performance metrics are vertically aligned, rather than horizontally aligned—not to mention they are conflicting, which creates an antagonistic environment. Furthermore, the S&OP meetings themselves are focused almost exclusively on reducing inventory costs, customer service levels, and production scheduling, all of which are operations planning centric, not customer/consumer focused. The only real common metric that sales and marketing share with operations planning is customer service levels. There is little if any connection between consumer demand and supply (shipments), as well as shared performance metrics. This is how S&OP has failed to deliver on its promise. Furthermore, it is too supply centric with no connection to downstream data and marketing tactics and strategies. There are little, if any, benefits for the commercial teams to participate in the S&OP process. Consumption-based forecasting and planning, linking consumption to shipments, is the combination required to take S&OP to the next level: Integrated Business Planning (IBP).

S&OP's failure to deliver upon its promise led to *integrated business planning (IBP)*, which focuses on balancing demand with supply chain resources. Integrated business planning is broader than S&OP; it is an approach that combines Enterprise Performance Management (EPM) and S&OP. Enterprise performance management is a field of measuring business performance which considers the visibility of operations in a closed-loop model across all facets of the organization. It is explicitly related to financial operations and activities of the chief financial officer. EPM also supports financial planning and analysis, which is synonymous for "enterprise performance management." As such, many analyst firms have officially retired the concept of "Customer Relationship Management (CPM)" and reclassified it as part of "financial planning and analysis." This new approach reflects two significant trends: (1) increased focus on planning across the entire enterprise, and (2) supporting the management of the financial plan. In doing so, the IBP process addresses challenges that financial and operational planning professionals have struggled for years to overcome. The intent is to open opportunities for step-change improvements as to how companies plan, manage, and govern their business.

The purpose is to focus on strengthening the financial integration and reconciliation of all plans, and on increasing the responsiveness of the supply chain. This new approach requires what-if scenario analyses to better predict customer/consumer demand by detecting shifting consumer demand patterns and identify opportunities to increase revenue and profit. This is exactly what the consumption-based forecasting and planning process addresses by integrating POS/syndicated scanner data with shipments using predictive analytics. Then, by using what-if scenario planning, it creates a sales and marketing plan that increases revenue and profit. Finally, this approach links the sales and marketing forecast and plan directly to supply, using data and analytics to generate an efficient supply response. The consumption-based forecasting and planning process captures the key consumer and supply drivers, allowing marketing and demand planners to collaborate across the supply chain from consumer to supply by using predictive analytics and domain knowledge, rather than "gut feeling" judgment, to balance demand and supply to increase revenue and profit.

Educating sales and marketing, creating a well-structured consumption-based forecasting and planning process with clearly defined organizational roles and responsibilities, and increasing access to information are all important to help incentivize the commercial teams to participate in the IBP process. Among these, there are two underlying adages that should be understood:

1. What gets measured gets done; and

2. Performance incentives drive behavior.

Sales team performance metrics often fall into a revenue-generation category. Typical measurements are based against a sales quota (gross or net value) and may also be measured based on a margin or profitability target. As a result, the focus moves to how much revenue can be generated by the sales organization and how profitable that revenue is for the company. At its basic level, the quota is a sales plan, not a forecast. Since compensation is determined by the results compared to a plan, there is a tendency to understate the forecast in order to improve the chances of exceeding the target. Another common measure for the sales team may be based on customer service. This may be an order-fill-rate, such as Delivered In Full, On Time (DIFOT), or some other similar measure, such as perfect order. When customer service measures are used to determine compensation, the tendency is to over forecast demand to make sure adequate inventory is available to maximize order fill rates.

The forecast isn't a number pulled off the top of someone's head, although in many cases that's not too far from the truth. The demand forecast is the sum of many parts working together toward a common goal. The sales and marketing teams can add significant value to the forecasting process; however, the process must harness the intelligence the sales and marketing organizations provide to align consumer demand at strategic and tactical levels with the company's marketing capabilities, resulting in improved revenue and profitability.

At the strategic level, the emphasis is on aligning long-term marketing investment strategies with long-term consumer demand patterns while maximizing marketing investment effectiveness. At the tactical level, the focus is on understanding shifting consumer demand patterns, and proactively influencing demand to meet available supply, using the marketing mix to sense and shape price, sales promotions, marketing events, and other related factors to influence demand generation and profitability.

DEMAND MANAGEMENT CHAMPION

Companies are quickly realizing that an internal "champion" who has executive sponsorship is required to drive the change management required to gain "adoption" of this new radical design called "consumption-based forecasting and planning." It also requires investment in demand analysts (data scientists). Even if you get adoption, you need it to be "sustainable." Many companies gain adoption but cannot sustain it overtime due to lack of commitment to make it part of the corporate culture. Ongoing champion involvement will be required until this new approach to demand planning becomes part of the corporate culture. The champion must have the knowledge and experience to demonstrate that this is a burning platform situation and doing business as usual will only lead to poor performance and results.

These interdependencies are also influenced by the strategic intent of a company's demand planning process. In other words, is the intent to create a more accurate demand response, a financial plan, marketing plan, supply plan, and/or a sales plan (target setting)? These different intentions are all conflicting, and are not really forecasts, but rather plans that are derivatives of the unconstrained demand forecast. Understanding this simple nomenclature is key to solving the corporate culture.

CLOSING THOUGHTS

Consumption-based forecasting and planning is a simple process that links a series of predictive analytics models—in this case two ARIMAX models—through a common element (consumer demand) to model the push/pull effects of the supply chain. It is truly a decision-support system that is designed to integrate statistical analysis with downstream (POS/syndicated scanner) data and upstream shipment/supply data to analyze the business from a "holistic supply chain" perspective. This process provides both brand managers and demand planners with the opportunity to make better and more actionable decisions from multiple data sources.

The objective is to link consumer demand to supply replenishment via a structured approach that relies on data, analytics, and domain knowledge rather than "gut feeling" judgment and a whole lot of manual overrides. The key benefit of consumption-based forecasting and planning is the ability to capture the entire supply chain by focusing on sales and marketing strategies to shape future consumer demand, and then link demand to supply. These relationships are what truly define the marketplace and all marketing elements within the supply chain.

Today, technology exists that enables demand analysts to leverage their data resources and analytics capabilities as a competitive advantage, offering a true, integrated demand management perspective to optimize the entire supply chain from the consumer to supply replenishment. Relying only on constrained supply plans is like taking a picture of inventory replenishment through a narrow angle lens; while you can see the impact within your own supply chain network (upstream) with some precision, the foreground (downstream) is either excluded or out of focus. As significant (or insignificant) the picture may seem, too much is ignored by this view. Consumption-based forecasting and planning provides a wide-angle lens to ensure a complete and clear picture of where a company is and where it wants to go.

There are no longer challenges preventing companies from moving to this new demand management approach. Today, data collection, storage, and processing are no longer a barrier; scalable cloud technology can run millions of data series in a matter of a minutes and hours; and advanced analytics and machine learning are able to automatically run hundreds of iterations using a broad array of methods (including open source) up and down a business hierarchy. Universities now teach advanced analytics as required courses in most undergraduate and graduate business programs. It is simply a matter of investing in people (advanced analytical skills), process (horizontal processes), analytics (predictive analytics), and technology (scalable cloud native technology).

NOTES

1. Charles Chase, Todd Ferguson, and Greg Spira, "Making the Case: The ROI of Demand Management," Oliver Wight Paper series, *Information Guides on Industry Best Practices*, November 24, 2020: 1–16. https://www.oliverwight-americas.com/whitepapers/making-the-case-the-roi-of-demand-management/

2. Charles Chase, "Building A Holistic Supply Chain with Consumption-Based Forecasting & Planning," *Journal of Business Forecasting* 39(3), Fall 2020: 5–11. https://ibf.org/knowledge/jbf-issues?date=&keywords=&quarter=Fall&year=2020

3. Charles Chase, *Next Generation Demand Management: People, Process, Analytics and Technology*, Wiley, 2016: 1–252.

CHAPTER **5**

AI/Machine Learning Is Disrupting Demand Forecasting

A rtificial intelligence (AI) and machine learning (ML) are the new buzzwords being touted as a vital business capability to digital transformation. AI/machine learning algorithms are being embedded into every key business function throughout the enterprise, providing forward-thinking companies with unapparelled insight, control, and performance. Machine learning is providing consumer goods companies with unprecedented analytic firepower to enhance technology by raising the bar in such business functions as demand planning and supply chain execution. The interesting aspect is how leading consumer goods companies are developing these game-changing enhancements to their corporate technology stack.

It would be difficult to find a technology executive who does not completely believe in the power of AI/machine learning. Technology supported by ML is becoming a dynamic tool and will only become more vital in the coming years as it is refined, and use cases become more abundant. Having clear and tangible benefits does not necessarily mean a technology solution has organizational support. Fortunately, that is not the case with AI/machine learning. In fact, according to a recent 2020 Consumer Goods Technology (CGT) targeted research report,[1] 70% of consumer goods company executives are committed to leveraging AI/machine learning for technology business designs, execution, and implementing for field operations.[2]

In that same 2020 CGT targeted research report, however, 60% of the surveyed consumer goods leaders said they are willing to invest the time and resources required to validate new AI/machine initiatives through proof-of-value (POV), and 40% of consumer goods companies indicated that they are unwilling to invest the time to validate new AI/machine learning initiatives.[3] Many consumer goods companies are not early adopters when it comes to new processes and technology, which may leave many playing catch-up in the years to come. In addition, although most consumer goods companies are committed to developing and deploying AI/machine learning now and into the future, many do not have the appropriate data and analytics culture or the capacity to fully leverage these next-generation analytics technology platforms. It will also require change management lead by executive cross-functional leadership to gain adoption and ownership of AI/machine learning initiatives.

136

Developing a successful AI/machine learning executional roadmap requires more than just committing to its development and deployment. It requires identification and understanding of the areas where AI/machine learning technology can make a meaningful contribution to the company and the bottom line. That said, 63% of those companies who responded to the 2020 CGT targeted research report said demand planning was the top area where AI/machine learning would have the most positive impact and benefits.[4] Those same respondents mentioned that uncovering shifts in demand before they occur has always been and will remain a cornerstone of their success. Also, promotion execution was another area of benefit along with revenue growth management and supply chain execution.

Artificial intelligence development and deployment requires a specialized tool set, as well as highly skilled individuals to effectively execute those capabilities on a large scale. Many consumer goods companies have not invested in data scientists, nor do they have the in-house talent, technical architects, subject matter experts, data experts, and model governance experts in place to implement and deploy AI/machine learning. Although AI has the potential to supercharge almost every major business function, many companies lack the internal wherewithal and the cultural desire to successfully deploy AI/machine learning. There are a handful of savvy consumer goods companies who are hard at work developing, field testing, and deploying AI/machine learning technology that will set them apart from the competition; and once this technology has been developed and tested, who will own the change management initiatives needed to ensure success? Embedding meaningful AI into these business functions would significantly increase their capabilities, but many consumer goods companies lack the internal resources to build and deploy these competences.

In the face of all these challenges, machine learning is slowly taking on a role in many big data initiatives today. Large retailers and consumer goods companies are using machine learning combined with predictive analytics to help them enhance consumer engagement and create more accurate demand forecasts as they expand into new sales channels like the omnichannel. With machine learning, supercomputers learn from mining masses of big data without human intervention to provide unprecedented consumer demand insights. Predictive analytics and advanced algorithms, such as neural networks, have emerged as the hottest (and sometimes controversial) topics among senior management teams. Neural network algorithms are self-correcting and powerful but are difficult to replicate and explain using traditional predictive analytics like multiple linear regression models. For years, neural network models have been discarded due to the lack of storage and processing capabilities required to implement them. Now with cloud computing using supercomputers' neural network algorithms, along with ARIMAX, dynamic regression and ensemble models like "neural networks plus time series" are becoming the catalyst for machine learning–based forecasting.

According to a Consumer Goods Technology custom research report, through pattern recognition there will be a shift from active engagement to *automated engagement*.[5] As part of this shift, technology (machine learning) takes over tasks from information gathering to actual execution. Compared to traditional demand forecasting methods, machine learning–based forecasting helps companies understand consumer demand that, in many cases, would be otherwise impossible. Following are several reasons why.

Incomplete versus complete information and data. Traditional demand forecasts are based on time-series forecasting methods (exponential smoothing, ARIMA, and others) that can only use a handful of demand factors (e.g. trend, seasonality, and cycle). On the other hand, machine learning–based forecasting can combine learning algorithms (gradient boosting, random forest, neural networks, and others) with traditional predictive models (exponential smoothing, ARIMA, ARIMAX, dynamic regression, and others) along with big data and cloud native computing to analyze thousands—even millions—of products using unlimited amounts of causal factors simultaneously up and down a company's business hierarchy. Traditional demand forecasting and planning systems are restricted to only the demand history, whereas machine learning–based forecasting can take advantage of limitless data, determine what's significant, and then prioritize available consumer insights (demand sensing) that influence future demand using what-if analysis (demand shaping). Compared to traditional time-series forecasting systems, machine learning–based forecasting solutions identify the underlying consumer demand drivers that influence demand, uncovering insights not possible with traditional time-series methods. In addition, the self-learning algorithms get smarter as they consume new data and adapt the algorithms to uncover shifting consumer demand patterns.

Holistic models using multiple dimensions versus single dimension algorithms. Traditional forecasting systems are characterized by a few single-dimension algorithms, each designed to analyze demand based on certain data-limited constraints. As a result, much manual manipulation goes into cleansing data and separating it into baseline and promoted volumes. This limits which algorithms can be used across the product portfolio.

Machine learning–based forecasting takes a more sophisticated approach. It uses pattern recognition with a single, general-purpose array of algorithms that adapt to all the data. They fit many different types of demand patterns simultaneously across the product portfolio up/down the company's business hierarchy without data cleansing handling multiple data streams (e.g. price, sales promotions, advertising, in-store merchandising, and many others) in the same model—holistically—without cleansing the data into baseline and promoted volumes. For example, traditional forecasting systems have a specific purpose leading to multiple inconsistent forecasts across the product portfolio. With machine learning–based forecasting, the same algorithm is useful for multiple processes including pricing, sales promotions, in-store merchandising, advertising, temperature, store inventory, and others, thus creating one vision of an integrated forecast.

Partial versus complete use of item history. When creating demand forecasts, traditional demand forecasting and planning systems analyze the demand history for a particular product/SKU, category, channel, and demographic market area. Machine learning–based forecasts leverage history for all items, including sales promotions, to forecast demand for every item at every level (node) in the business hierarchy simultaneously.

STRAIGHT TALK ABOUT FORECASTING AND MACHINE LEARNING

There's been a lot of hype about using machine learning for demand forecasting and planning—and rightfully so, given the advancements in data collection, storage, and processing along with technology improvements, such as cloud-native software supported by super-computers. There's no reason why machine learning can't be used as another demand forecasting method among the array of existing predictive and time-series forecasting methods. To be honest, there's no single tool—mathematical equation or algorithm—designated just for demand forecasting. All ERP demand management solutions use "best fit" selection based on how well a model fits to the historical demand using basic time-series methods—moving averages and exponential smoothing—nonseasonal and seasonal. They do not, however, use predictive or machine learning methods as part of the standard selection using their "best fit" capability.

Some stand-alone forecasting software solutions do include ARIMA models, multiple linear regression, and other predictive models using an expert system (rules based) that's built on an automatic large-scale hierarchical forecasting platform. Used at all levels of the business, these packages contain all categories of models, including moving averages, exponential smoothing, dynamic regression, ARIMA, ARIMA(X), unobserved component models, weighted combined models, and only a handful include machine learning ensemble models (combined machine learning plus time-series models). This type of forecasting system requires minimal human intervention as the system does all the heavy lifting from a modeling standpoint, and uses not only model fit, but also in-sample/out-of-sample analysis to determine the appropriate model automatically. Given these capabilities, it could be mistaken for a machine learning–based forecasting solution. It automatically builds the models based on patterns in the data, and it requires minimal human intervention, but must also include learning algorithms (Neural Networks, Random Forest, Gradient Boosting, and others) to be a true AI/machine learning solution.

WHAT IS THE DIFFERENCE BETWEEN EXPERT SYSTEMS AND MACHINE LEARNING?

Expert systems are an integral part of artificial intelligence (AI), also known as symbolic artificial intelligence. This type of AI, that's designed to think like a human, is differentiated from sub-symbolic artificial intelligence, which includes the newly revived research area of neural networks and deep learning. Deep learning is a type of machine learning that trains a computer to perform humanlike tasks, such as recognizing speech, identifying images, or making predictions. Instead of organizing data to run through predefined equations, deep learning sets up basic parameters about the data and trains the computer to learn on its own by recognizing patterns using many layers of processing.

So, it would be fine to say that automatic large-scale hierarchical forecasting systems use first-generation AI using symbolic artificial intelligence; however, expert systems aren't really a part of machine learning, unless you have a decision tree learning the rules of the expert system from the data. In that case, it would indeed be a so-called "meta learning" approach. The most successful form of symbolic AI is expert systems, which use a network set of production rules. Production rules connect symbols in a relationship, like an if-then statement. The expert system processes the rules to make deductions and to determine what additional information it needs and what questions to ask, using human-readable symbols. In other words, they run the same way every time. They are completely deterministic. They are mathematical models in which outcomes are precisely determined through known relationships among conditions and events, without any room for random variation. In such models, a given input will always produce the same output, such as in a known chemical reaction. Given the same data, they give the same answer every time.

There are new cloud-native open-source SaaS (Software as a Service) solutions that allow companies to add their own code—*any code (R, Python, and others)* that can be generated with machine learning algorithms or any other algorithms. Those same machine learning algorithms can also be added to the open model repositories to complement existing forecasting algorithms to enhance forecast accuracy across a company's entire product portfolio. Many feel the next generation of machine learning will also include cognitive computing where the supply chain becomes self-healing. This would improve upon machine learning by going beyond predictions to making decisions to automatically correct for anomalies in the supply chain.

DO MACHINE LEARNING ALGORITHMS OUTPERFORM TRADITIONAL FORECASTING METHODS?

The forecasting industry has been influenced over the past three decades by linear statistical methods such as exponential smoothing, ARIMA, and linear regression models. Over the past five years, however, machine learning models have drawn attention and are establishing themselves as serious contenders to traditional time-series methods for demand forecasting and planning. Machine learning methods have been proposed by both academia and many data scientists as alternatives to traditional predictive analytics for use in forecasting future demand. In fact, recent research by Makridakis, Spiliotis, and Assimakopoulos have documented evidence based on the M4 and M5 competitions that there is much promise for ML algorithms for demand forecasting. They have found that the combination of ML and traditional time-series methods seems to work best versus pure ML models for predicting future demand.

M4 COMPETITION

The M4 competition was the continuation of three previous competitions started more than 45 years ago. The purpose was to learn how to improve forecasting accuracy and use those learnings to advance the theory and practice of forecasting. The key learnings of the M1 Competition proved that simple methods were at least as accurate as statistically sophisticated methods.[6] The most interesting finding of the M2 competition established that the use of additional information and judgment did not improve the accuracy of time-series forecasting.[7] Yet today, over 25 years later, adjusting statistically derived forecasts using judgment based on collaboration across the organization is standard practice for demand planners. Finally, the M3 competition reconfirmed the findings of M1 and introduced a couple of new more accurate algorithms.

The purpose of the M4 competition was to replicate the results of the previous competitions and extend them into three categories: (1) significantly increase the number of series, (2) include ML forecasting methods, and (3) evaluate both point forecasts and prediction intervals. The five major findings of the M4 Competition are:

1. Out of the 17 most accurate methods, 12 were "combinations" of mostly traditional statistical approaches.

2. The major surprise was a "hybrid" approach that utilized both traditional statistical and ML models. Those methods' average MAPEs (Mean Absolute Percentage Errors) were close to 10% more accurate than the combination benchmark used to compare the submitted methods.

3. The second most accurate method was a combination of seven statistical methods and one ML model with the weights for the averaging being calculated by a ML algorithm that was trained to minimize the forecasting error through holdout tests.

4. Out of the 17 most accurate methods, two successfully specified the 95% prediction intervals correctly.

5. The six pure ML methods performed poorly, with none of them being more accurate than the combination benchmark and only one being more accurate than a Naïve2 model.[8]

A naïve model utilizes the last period's actuals as the one-period-ahead forecast without adjusting or attempting to establish any causal factors. It is used mainly for comparison purposes with forecasts generated by more sophisticated methods.

The conclusion from the M4 competition findings is that the accuracy of individual statistical or ML methods was low. However, hybrid approaches and combinations of methods are the best way forward for improving forecast accuracy. The most interesting finding was that pure ML models were the least effective, while the combination of ML algorithms with traditional time-series methods were the most accurate.

M5 COMPETITION

The M5 competition focused on a retail sales forecasting approach and extended the results of the previous four competitions by significantly expanding the number of participating methods, especially those in the category of machine learning, included causal (explanatory) variables in addition to the time-series data, using grouped correlated time series, and focused on series that display intermittency (spare data). The main objective was to produce the most accurate point forecasts for 42,840 data series (time series) that represent the hierarchical unit sales for Walmart—the largest retail company in the world. The products are sold across 10 stores, located in three states (California, Texas, and Wisconsin). The retail hierarchy included disaggregated data by product store unit sales, which can be grouped based on either location (store and state) or product-related information (department and category). The hierarchy included total volume including three states, three categories, seven departments, and eight products.[9] (See Figure 5.1.)

The M5 competition data set included causal/explanatory variables, including calendar-related information and retail prices. In addition to past unit sales of the products and the corresponding timestamps (e.g. date, weekday, week number, month, and year), there was also information available about:

- Special events and holidays (e.g. Super Bowl, Valentine's Day, and Orthodox Easter), organized into four classes, namely Sporting, Cultural, National, and Religious.

- Selling prices, provided on a week-store level (average across seven days). If not available, this means that the product was not sold during the week examined. Although prices are constant on a weekly basis, they may change with time.

- Supplemental Nutrition Assistance Program (SNAP) activities that serve as promotions. A binary variable (0 or 1) was used as indicator for whether stores allow SNAP purchases. A 1 indicated that the SNAP was allowed (turned on).[10]

The M5 competition attempted to address several concerns and suggestions that surfaced from the M4 competition by introducing the following innovative features:

- A large data set of 42,840 series was introduced along with 24 benchmarks. That way, existing and new forecasting methods could be objectively evaluated, and the results of previous studies effectively tested for replicability.

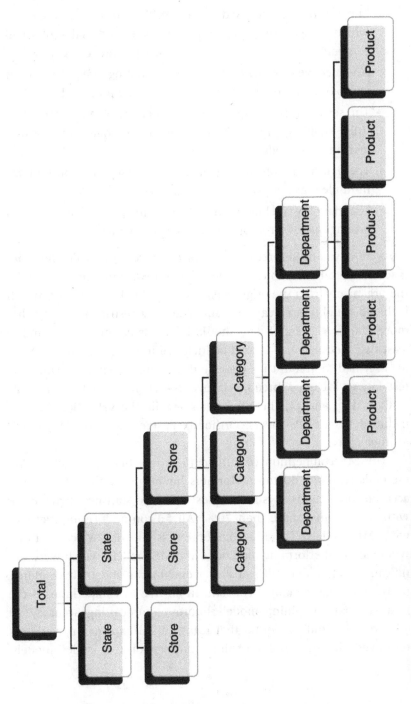

Figure 5.1 M5 Competition Retail Business Hierarchy

- The competition focused on a specific forecasting challenge, which is accurately predicting the daily unit sales of retail companies across various locations and product categories.
- An objective measure was used for evaluating forecast accuracy, approximating the mean of the series being predicted.
- The series of the data set were grouped and highly correlated, thus enabling the utilization of multivariate and "cross-learning" methods.
- The data set involved daily data which requires accounting for multiple seasonal patterns, special days, and holidays.
- The data set included causal/explanatory variables, such as product prices, promotions, and special events.[11]

A 28-days-ahead forecast was utilized based on how decisions are made at typical companies. The test data set was randomly chosen by the organizers from the original data set provided by Walmart, which included roughly six years of data. The only restrictions being that more than five years of data should be available for training and at least two special events should be included in the validation. The test data set had to account for possible deviations in demand. Thus, the test data set included three special events—(1) Memorial Day, (2) part of Ramadan, and (3) the NBA finals—while the validation data set included Pesach (Passover), Orthodox Easter, Cinco De Mayo, and Mother's Day.

The M5 competition continued to prove the superiority of ML methods with the 50 top performers having more than 14% more accurate predictions versus the most accurate statistical benchmark with the top five more than 20%. All 50 top-performing methods were ML models. The M5 competition is the first M competition where all top-performing methods were ML models, which were significantly better than all statistical benchmarks and their combinations. What has remained constant in all five M competitions is the findings that combining models improves forecasting accuracy. In addition, the findings found that using causal/explanatory variables improved the overall forecasting accuracy of time-series models.

For instance, ARIMAX models that included promotions and special events as explanatory variables were found to be 13% more accurate than ARIMA models.[12] Furthermore, deep-learning ML methods showed potential for further improvements in forecast accuracy when predicting retail sales in a business hierarchy format.

As companies find increasing availability of large amounts of historical data within their organizations and have an immediate need to accurately predict shifting demand patterns, they are finding opportunities to introduce AI/machine learning. However, it begins by building trust not simply because data collected for analytics must be trusted, but due to the consistency they experience over time. Leadership and management practices that support a culture of analytics-driven decision making tend to be successful, but this requires continuous support from senior management to facilitate the necessary skills and mindset throughout the organization.

Machine learning and hybrid modeling strategies are beginning to emerge as possible complements to traditional time-series forecasting due to the volume of data being collected and the processing power brought about by the second machine age. Neural networks are becoming more popular. The main reason is that they can estimate most functional relationships and are very well suited for modeling nonlinear relationships. A neural network (NN) model may seem somewhat intimidating because it has many parameters, but successfully applied to forecasting problems, NNs tend to increase forecast accuracy. To get the most benefits you need to understand what types of data work well with NN models depending on the forecasting challenges at hand. Whether the volume of data is medium size, large, or huge, these modeling techniques can help identify complex relationships between variables and increase the predictive power of your demand forecasts.

BASIC KNOWLEDGE REGARDING NEURAL NETWORKS

Many of the advancements in AI have been driven by neural networks. Neural networks (NNs) are the connection of mathematical functions linked together in a format like the neural networks found in the human brain. NNs can extract complex patterns from data and then apply the patterns to unseen data to classify (recognize) the data. This is how the machine learns. In other words, NNs learn through an iterative cycle of training and validation.

Within NNs there are structures that connect nodes to nodes called "weights." Weights are assumptions about how data points are related as they move through the network. In other words, weights reflect the level of influence that one neuron has over another neuron. The weights pass through an "activation function" as they leave the current node, which is a type of mathematical function that transforms the data. They transform linear data into nonlinear representations, which enables the network to analyze complex patterns. The analogy to the human brain implied by a "neural network" comes from the fact that the neurons which make up the human brain are joined in a similar fashion to how nodes in a NN are linked. (See Figure 5.2.)

NNs learn through an iterative series of training and validation. Training data are fed forward through the NN to calculate an output value, then back propagation is used to update the connection weights and reduce the error. Back propagation is short for "backward propagation of errors." It is an algorithm for supervised learning of neural networks using gradient descent. Gradient descent is a first-order

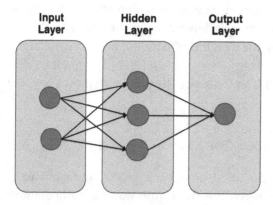

Figure 5.2 Neural Network Architecture

iterative optimization algorithm for finding a local minimum of a differentiable function. The idea is to take repeated steps in the opposite direction of the gradient, or approximate gradient of the function at the current point, because this is the direction of steepest descent. Conversely, stepping in the direction of the gradient will lead to a local maximum of that function, thus the procedure is then known as gradient ascent. Gradient descent is by far the most popular optimization strategy used in machine learning and deep learning at the moment. It is used when training data models, can be combined with every algorithm, and is easy to understand and implement.

Given a neural network and an error function, the backward propagation method calculates the gradient of the error function with respect to the neural network's weights. It is a generalization of the delta rule for perceptrons to multilayer feed-forward neural networks. The "backwards" part of the name stems from the fact that the calculation of the gradient proceeds backwards through the network, with the gradient of the final layer of weights being calculated first and the gradient of the first layer of weights calculated last. Partial computations of the gradient from one layer are reused in the computation of the gradient for the previous layer. This backwards flow of the error information allows for efficient computation of the gradient at each layer versus the naïve approach of calculating the gradient of each layer separately. Back propagation's popularity is experiencing a resurgence given the widespread adoption of deep neural networks for image recognition and speech recognition. It is considered an efficient algorithm, and modern implementations take advantage of specialized GPUs to further improve performance.

WHY COMBINE ML MODELS?

One of the most preferred machine learning techniques is ensemble models. Ensemble models combine multiple machine learning algorithms, and machine learning algorithms with tradition time-series models (for example, NN + Time Series, Multistage, and others) to improve the reliability and accuracy of predictions. The ensemble model process combines the training of multiple machine learning models and their outputs together. The different models are used as a base to create one optimal predictive model. Combining various sets of individual machine learning models can improve the stability of the overall model, which leads to more accurate predictions. Ensemble learning models are frequently more reliable than individual models and, as a result, many placed first in the M5 competition. (See Figure 5.3.)

Evaluating the prediction of an ML ensemble model typically requires more computation than evaluating the prediction of a single model. In a way, ensemble learning may be thought as compensating for poor learning algorithms by performing a lot of extra computation. An ensemble model may be more efficient at improving overall accuracy for the same increase in computing, storage, or communication resources by using that increase on two or more methods than would have been improved by increasing resource use for a single method. Fast algorithms such as decision trees are commonly used in ensemble methods (for example, random forest models), although slower algorithms can benefit from ensemble techniques as well. An ensemble model is a supervised learning algorithm because it can be trained and then used to make predictions (forecasts). ML ensemble models have been shown to have more flexibility in the purposes they can be used. This flexibility can, in theory, enable them to overfit the training data more than a single model would, but in practice, some ensemble models reduce problems related to overfitting.

The goal of any machine learning application is to find a single model that will best predict the outcome. Rather than creating one model and hoping this model is the best or most accurate predictor, an

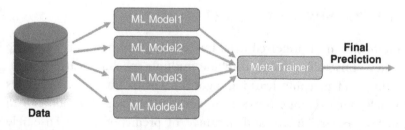

Figure 5.3 ML Ensemble Architecture

ensemble model takes several models into account. Then it averages those models to produce one final prediction.

CHALLENGES USING MACHINE LEARNING MODELS

Unlike traditional statistical methods the models created by machine learning algorithms can be extremely complex. Although there is an ML methodology, it is not always immediately obvious or linear. The exact path through a neural network, for example, is not easy to trace. Thousands (and even millions) of rules or parameters can define the model. As a result, the exact internal processing pathways can be a black box even to the data scientist.

First and foremost, you need to understand the limits of current machine learning technology. Data scientists, analysts, and managers tend to overestimate the present capabilities of machine learning. They expect the algorithms to learn quickly and deliver precise predictions to complex situations. They expect magical things to happen immediately. Because of the hype and media buzz about the coming of general superintelligence, people perceive AI/machine learning as a magic wand that will quickly solve all their challenges.

In fact, commercial use of machine learning, especially deep learning methods, is still relatively new. These methods require vast sets of properly organized and prepared data to provide accurate answers. A business working on a practical machine learning application needs to invest time and resources, while taking substantial risks. A typical neural network model can have millions of parameters, and some can have hundreds of millions. A training set usually consists of tens of thousands of data points. While a neural network can model the training set and provide answers with a high degree of accuracy, it may prove completely useless when given new data. This situation is called overfitting (or overtraining) and is just one of the limits of ML algorithms.

DATA CHALLENGES AND CONSIDERATIONS

The second challenge to consider for ML algorithms is the data used to build the original models as well as the data used once the model is in production. Not only can there be data bias but there are plenty of other challenges that can be introduced by the data. With data, you can have many different challenges including:

- **Data quality:** Do you know where your data has been, who has touched it, and what is the quality of the data you have decided to use? If not, the data you think is correct with the utmost quality in the appropriate format may be designed for descriptive (reporting) analytics versus predicative analytics. Furthermore, it may not be in the appropriate business hierarchy, or have all the appropriate levels to create accurate predictions.

- **Not enough data:** A great ML model can be built on a small amount of data, but that model won't provide very accurate output over the long term. Unless all your future data looks exactly like the small amount of data you used to build it, it won't provide continued accurate predictions. When building ML models, whether they are machine learning models or traditional models, there needs to be as much data as possible—particularly for ML models, which tend to be data hogs.

- **Homogeneous data:** Similar to not having enough data, this challenge comes from a lack of data, but not necessarily the lack of the amount of data; rather, the challenge is in the lack of variability of the data. For example, if you want to forecast consumer demand, you probably want to get as many different explanatory variables (data sets) as available, as well as POS and syndicated scanner data. Don't just use shipment history alone, particularly if the trend and seasonality of the historical shipments has been disrupted by COVID-19. Find a couple of different data sets, such as epidemiological, Google trends, local economic, and other data sets, with many different types of regional data points to find the best model inputs to generate accurate outputs.

- **Valid data:** Make sure you validate all your data to assure it is the correct data for the products you are trying to forecast. For example, if you are trying to forecast demand for a large global consumer goods company with offices in North America, South

America, Europe, and Asia, make sure the data you've pulled together is the correct data.

- **Data compliance issues:** Make sure the available data can be used. Every company sets and maintains policies to govern business processes and data usage. Typically, the owner of these policies is identified by executive leadership, and leadership ratifies them to put them into effect. Simple as this may sound, it is a policy that annoys many data scientists and one that doesn't have an easy answer.

Black Box Effects

ML is often called a "black box" because the processes between the input and output are not transparent. The only things people can observe are how the data is entered and what the results reveal. As NNs become more complex when the number of nodes increases, the model itself becomes less and less transparent. As a result, people have no idea how ML makes the decisions and can't view its internal workings, leading them to lose confidence in the model because they cannot fully control it. Subsequently, the lack of "trust" usually leads to many AI/machine learning failures. The best way to solve this situation is to carefully design the ML model to make it more transparent and let the users analyze why the model makes certain decisions. Use external tools to monitor how the ML model works. Visual analytics dashboards and reports are a good way to show users how the automated ML process works. A lack of model explainability has the potential to thwart adoption of AI/machine learning, which can lead to wasted investment and the risk of falling behind the competition. Without an explainable model, adoption by frontline workers is most likely impossible. Workers need to be able to trust ML judgment not only for the sake of taking the most efficient action but also for delivering to the bottom line: revenue growth and profit.

Interpretation of the ML Model Output

Data scientists may spend a lot of time making sure they have good data, the right data, and as much data that is available. They do everything right and build a very good ML model and process. Then, their boss looks at the output and interprets the results in a way that is so far from accurate that it no longer makes sense. This happens more times than one would think. The ML model output is misinterpreted, used incorrectly, and/or the assumptions that were used to build the model are ignored or misunderstood. A model provides estimates and guidance, but it is up to the demand analyst (data scientist) and/or demand planner to interpret the results and ensure the models are used appropriately. This is true not only for ML models, but for any model used to predict future demand. A good data demand analyst needs to be just as good at interpreting the outputs and reporting on findings to senior management as they are at building the models. Demand analysts need to be just as good at communicating as they are at understanding the data and model building. This requires being able to explain very sophisticated predictive analytics in terms a senior-level executive can understand and act upon.

There are some promising findings regarding the success and adoption of AI/machine learning. According to a McKinney & Company 2020 AI global study those companies seeing significant value from AI/machine learning are continuing to invest in it during the pandemic. Most respondents who are high performers say their organizations have increased investment in AI across each major business function in response to the pandemic, while less than 30% of other respondents say the same. In addition, the findings suggest that companies who are experiencing more EBIT (Earnings Before Interest and Taxes) contribution from AI/machine learning are experiencing improved year-over-year growth overall than are other companies.[13]

Machine learning is another tool in our analytics toolbox. Like any tool, it must be thoughtfully applied for fear that it may become the proverbial hammer looking for a nail. As machine learning capabilities emerged, early adopters often found themselves expending significant time and effort on challenges that could have been easily solved with traditional statistical methods. Therefore, machine learning is best seen as a supplement, not a wholesale replacement, for traditional statistical forecasting methods.

CASE STUDY 1

Using Machine Learning to Enhance
Short-Term Demand Sensing

Consumer goods companies account for some of the biggest industries in the world and provide items that are used regularly by consumers, including food, beverages, and other household products. Since many products provided by consumer goods companies have short shelf lives and are intended to be used quickly, companies need to routinely replenish products on store shelves to meet consumer needs. Effective supply chain management is critical to ensure the timely replenishment of products by properly managing the movement and storage of raw materials and finished goods from the point of origin to the point of consumption.

A key component of supply chain management for retailers and consumer goods companies is forecasting short-term consumer demand accurately to assure that their products are available to consumers when they need them in the near-term. Implementing short-term (1- to 8-week) forecasts is critical to understanding and predicting shifting consumer demand patterns associated with sales promotions, events, weather conditions, natural disasters, and other unexpected shifts (anomalies) in consumer demand. Short-term demand sensing allows retailers and consumer goods companies to predict and adapt to changing consumer demand patterns.

Traditional time-series forecasting techniques that model patterns associated with trend and seasonality are typically used for demand forecasting at retailers and consumer goods companies. These models can only uncover those two historical demand patterns to provide an estimate of demand into the future. In addition to the historical demand data, consumer goods companies have access to other data feeds like POS information, future firm open orders, promotional events, and others that collectively constitute the demand signal. Traditional predictive and ML models can include those additional data feeds as leading indicators to improve the overall accuracy of short-term demand sensing.

A Practical Application of Demand Sensing Using Machine Learning

A large global consumer goods company implemented a patent pending machine learning (ML) approach for short-term demand sensing (1–8 weekly and daily forecasts).[14] They applied this new demand-sensing capability to seven years of order "shipment" history by Product (Prod), Shipping Location (ShipLoc), and Customer Location (CustLoc) using weekly and daily data. (See Figure 5.4.) The shipping locations corresponded to the consumer goods distributions centers (DCs) and retail customer DC locations. The order shipment history corresponded to the number of daily product shipments from ShipLoc to CustLoc. They also included future open orders for both data sets at the lowest (Prod–ShipLoc–CustLoc) level. The order shipment history and future open orders were the main inputs in the advanced analytics models. In addition, POS data and inventory data for one specific consumer goods retail customer was included as causal/explanatory variables.

In addition to the order shipment history, future open orders and POS data provided by the consumer goods marketing team included weekly estimated forecasts using their current forecasting procedures

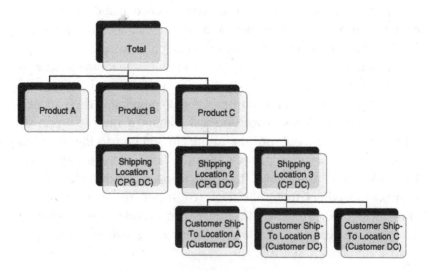

Figure 5.4 Graphical Representation of the Provided Data

and technology. Two such forecast estimates were provided—one was generated using standard procedures using traditional time-series methods (FC-Base) and the other was generated by consumer goods experts who had adjusted FC-Base to further refine the existing forecasts (FC-Base+Expert). Each of these two forecast estimates was provided at the (Prod) and (Prod–ShipLoc) levels. The main goal of this project was to generate better short-term (1–8 weekly and daily) forecast estimates compared to FC-Base and FC-Base+Expert at both (Prod) and (Prod–ShipLoc) levels. It should be noted that the forecasts for comparison were only provided at the weekly level. The consumer goods company did not include daily forecasts for comparison, as they currently do not have the resources to forecast in daily intervals. However, the goal is to determine if daily forecasts can be created for the same product/ship-to-locations utilizing the weekly forecasts.

Several rolling weekly forecasts for different forecast starting dates were generated. Order history data prior to a given forecast start date was used for training and 12 weeks of data after the start date was used as the holdout data for validation. The project team compared performance for the current week (Lag0) and up to 12 weeks into the future (Lag11). For each rolling forecast, they used two methods to generate forecasts:

1. Traditional time-series based forecast (various exponential smoothing, ARIMA, ARIMAX, and other methods).
2. Neural Network + Time-Series (NNTS) ensemble models.

Neural Network + Time-Series (NNTS) models generate forecasts using stacked models that include a neural network model (NN) and a time-series model (TS). This modeling strategy captures the non-linear relationship between the dependent and independent variables as well as time series characteristics in the data, such as seasonality and trend. As the diagram in Figure 5.5. shows, it models the time series in two steps:

1. In the first step, the neural network model is used to generate the forecasts.
2. In the second step, the residuals from the first step are passed to the time-series model to generate residual forecasts.

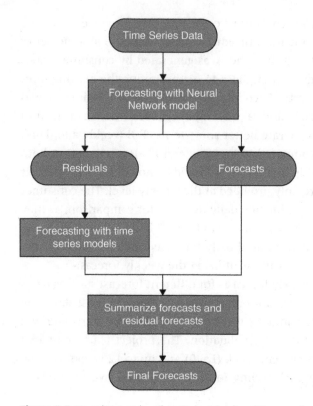

Figure 5.5 Neural Network + Time Series High Level Process Overview

The first and second steps run sequentially. The final forecasts are the sum of the forecasts from the neural network and the residual forecasts from the time-series model.

For the based forecast, traditional time-series methods were used to diagnose the statistical characteristics of each {Prod–ShipLoc–CustLoc} data set identifying the appropriate forecasting models. The diagnosis of the results was used to generate a time-series forecast estimate and a trend estimate for each Prod–ShipLoc–CustLoc combination.

For the NNTS models, the project team trained a neural network for each product separately by using the following inputs:

- ShipLoc
- CustLoc
- Previous four years of order history

- Forecast estimates
- Trend estimates

Next, the project team incorporated future open orders data to further refine the enhanced forecast. For each rolling forecast over the validation period, they compared the enhanced forecast estimate with the future open orders and replaced the forecast estimate with the open order quantity, if the open order quantity exceeded the forecast estimate. For analyzing the impact of using POS data and customer inventory data, the project team created two versions of the NNTS forecast. One forecast used inputs to the neural network listed earlier, and the other one with two additional inputs corresponding to POS and customer trade inventory data.

The data was also segmented using segmentation analysis into two different categories based on seasonality, nonseasonality, and availability causal data. Given that machine learning models require a lot of data, it was felt that the NNTS models would work best applied to products with long seasonal history, and would use the additional causal information (e.g. POS and customer trade inventory) where it was available. It made sense to apply traditional time-series methods to the nonseasonal products, which had much shorter history—in many cases less than one year. The objective was to apply ML models where they work best for products with long history and additional causal data sets, and time-series models across those products with short history and no additional causal data. Focusing specific models across product groups (seasonal and nonseasonal) it would increase the accuracy of the overall forecasts by taking advantage of all available analytic methods.

Converting Weekly Forecasts to Daily Forecasts

Daily forecasts were generated by disaggregating (or breaking down) the enhanced weekly forecasts for each Prod–ShipLoc–CustLoc level in the hierarchy to enhance the daily forecasts. The project team achieved this by estimating the relative daily order proportions to disaggregate the weekly forecast into daily forecasts. They estimated the proportions for each {Week–Prod–ShipLoc–CustLoc} combination and then used the proportions to multiply the weekly forecast estimate and obtain a daily forecast estimate. The weekly disaggregation proportions were estimated using three separate models:

1. **Seasonal model.** This model was used to capture the slow-moving seasonal nature of daily order patterns. For each week, they analyzed the daily order patterns over the last three years and averaged the proportions for each day to estimate the weekly disaggregation proportions for each {Week–Prod–ShipLoc–CustLoc} combination.

2. **Trend model.** This model was used to capture the more recent daily order trends. For each week, they analyzed the daily order patterns over the previous 13 weeks and averaged the proportions for each day to estimate the weekly disaggregation proportions for each {Week–Prod–ShipLoc–CustLoc} combination.

3. **Neural network model.** This model was used to estimate daily order quantities based on the previous two years of daily order history using a neural network. For training, they used the daily order history from two years to estimate the daily order quantities of the subsequent year as a holdout using a neural network model. After training the neural network for 100 iterations, they used the daily order quantities from two years prior to predict daily order quantities for the current year. The estimated daily order quantities for the current year were normalized to get weekly disaggregation proportions for each {Week–Prod–ShipLoc–CustLoc} combination.

The weekly forecasts were disaggregated into daily forecasts using the three methods just described. For each forecast, the project team calculated the mean absolute percentage error (MAPE) for each {Prod–ShipLoc–CustLoc} hierarchy level over the training period and used the forecast with the lowest MAPE as the enhanced daily forecast for a given level in the hierarchy.

Overall Results

The project team generated enhanced weekly and daily forecasts for the products that passed their data validation criteria—that is, order

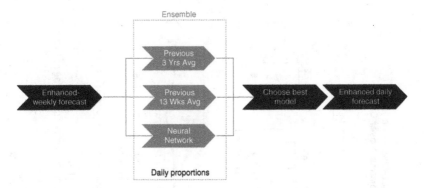

Figure 5.6 Process Methodology for Converting Weekly Forecasts to Daily Forecasts

shipments in the current year and at least one year of order history. The performance of weekly and daily forecasts was evaluated using two metrics:

1. The absolute error between the forecasted order quantity and the actual order quantity.

2. Bias, which considers the ratio between the actual order quantity and the forecasted order quantity. A negative bias is interpreted as an under-forecast of the actual quantity whereas a positive bias is interpreted as an over-forecast of the actual order quantity.

For weekly forecasts, they evaluated the above measures for the enhanced forecast (FC-Enhanced) and the two forecasts provided by the consumer goods company—FC-Base and FC-Base+Expert at both {Prod} and {Prod– ShipLoc} levels. (See Figure 5.6.)

Weekly Forecast Results

This approach demonstrated a significant improvement in forecast accuracy using the FC-Enhanced models compared to both FC-Base and FC-Base+Expert as shown in Figure 5.7, and results summarized in Table 5.1. At the {Prod} level, the project team observed that FC-Base+Expert is better than FC-Base for Lags0–5; however, FC-Enhanced forecast was better than both the forecasts across all 8 lags. At the {Prod–ShipLoc} level, they observed a dip in accuracy for

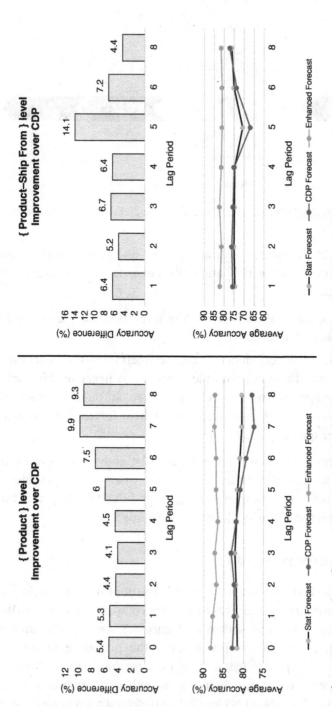

Figure 5.7 Comparison of Forecast Accuracy Using Three Forecasts at (a) {Prod} Level and (b) {Prod–ShipLoc} Level
Source: Roger Baldridge, Kedar Prabhudesai, Varunraj Valsaraj, Dan Woo, and Jinzin Yi, "Using Machine Learning and Demand Sensing to Enhance Short-Term Forecasting," SAS White Paper 2020.

Table 5.1 Summary of Weekly Forecasting Accuracy at {Prod} and {Prod–ShipLoc} Levels from Figure 5.7, Summarized Using Mean ± Standard Deviation

Forecast level	FC-Base	FC-Base+Expert	FC-Enhanced
{Prod}	81.18 ± 0.36 %	81.70 ± 1.48 %	86.71 ± 0.57 %
{Prod - ShipLoc}	73.49 ± 1.80 %	74.46 ± 2.56 %	80.58 ± 0.74 %

Source: Roger Baldridge, Kedar Prabhudesai, Varunraj Valsaraj, Dan Woo, and Jinzin Yi, "Using Machine Learning and Demand Sensing to Enhance Short-Term Forecasting," SAS White Paper 2020.

both the FC-Base and FC-Base+Expert forecast. However, they did not observe such a dip in accuracy using the FC-Enhanced forecast. Note, Lags0 and 7 are missing in the {Prod–ShipLoc} level, because forecasts for those lags were not available in the data utilized by the consumer goods company.

The weekly FC-enhanced forecast at the Prod–ShipLoc level using a combination of NNTS and advanced time-series models (e.g. ARIMA and ARIMAX) created a more consistent and accurate forecast outperforming both the FC-Base and FC-Base+Expert from Lag0–Lag11 with an accuracy of 80.58% on average. A 6% increase as compared to the FC-Base+Expert and a 7% increase compared to the FC-Base weekly forecasts. These performance improvements were completely automated using advanced predicative models without any judgmental overrides—in addition, without the inclusion of POS and customer trade inventory or sales promotions. The next step in the process is the addition of POS and customer trade inventory for their main key account (retail customer).

In terms of forecast bias, both FC-Base and FC-Base+Expert (CDP) have a consistent negative bias across all lags at the Product–Ship Location level, while the FC-Enhanced forecast has a consistent positive bias across Lag4–7, as shown in Figure 5.8. A positive bias indicates that there is a systematic over-forecast of sales order quantities compared to actual sales order quantities, whereas negative bias indicates an under-forecast. A non-zero bias can lead to an over- or under-supply of shipments from ShipLoc DCs to CustLoc DCs. The consistent positive bias using FC-Enhanced forecast, can be attributed to the use of a neural network model. The project team found that the neural network model tended to produce positive non-zero outputs

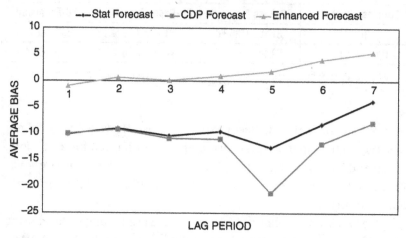

Figure 5.8 Comparison of Forecast Bias Using Three Forecasts at Prod–ShipLoc Level

for zero-valued inputs. Also, both the FC-Base and FC-Base + Expert forecasts for week Lag5 are very negative (–10% and –23%) indicating significant under-forecasts which could cause backorders, thus affecting customer service levels. While the FC-Enhanced forecast for week Lag5 has a positive bias (2%). Given the current COVID-19 crisis, the consumer goods company was in a much better inventory position based on the FC-Enhanced forecast, given the abnormal increase in sales for those products.

In Figure 5.9, the results compare the forecast accuracy with the addition of POS and customer trade inventory data as explanatory variables, along with sales order historical and future forecast data. Both forecasts were generated using the NNTS method. Given the limited POS and customer trade inventory data for the current year the project team was limited to only one key customer. Recall that the order history data provided was available for seven years. Thus, to generate comparable forecasts, the project team used sales order history data over the same time period based on where POS and customer trade inventory data was available.

The results clearly demonstrate an incremental improvement in weekly forecast accuracy using the additional POS and customer trade

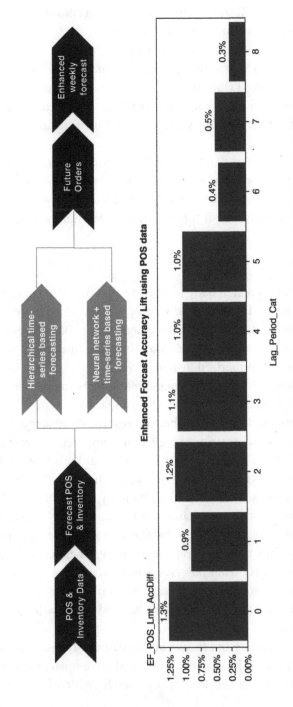

Figure 5.9 Enhanced Customer Weekly Forecast Accuracy Using POS & Customer Trade Inventory as Explanatory Variables

inventory data. For Lags0–5, there is a 1–2% accuracy improvement. However, the improvement is less than 1% for Lags 6–8. Furthermore, there is a sharp dip in accuracy for Lags7–8 forecasts. The consumer goods project team agreed that this incremental improvement in forecast accuracy using POS and customer trade inventory data would have been higher if more data were available. This indicates that POS and customer trade inventory data can enhance the accuracy of the forecasts.

It should be noted that the forecast performance (accuracy) metrics are at the Prod–ShipLoc–CustLoc level the lowest level of the product hierarchy (execution level). The focus of any forecast accuracy should be measured at the execution level, not the highest level.

Daily Forecast Results

The project team created daily forecast results that were generated by disaggregating the FC-Enhanced weekly forecasts into daily forecasts using three separate models, as discussed earlier. Daily forecast accuracy and bias over Lag30 (lags 30 days into the future) are shown in Figure 5.10 and summarized in Table 5.2.

As mentioned earlier, the demand planning team did not have the resources to create daily forecasts for comparison; hence the project team had presented only FC-Enhanced results. Comparing Tables 5.1 and 5.2, the project team observed that compared to weekly forecasts, there is a dip in daily forecast accuracy at both Prod and Prod–ShipLoc levels. This is to be expected because they were breaking down weekly forecasts into daily forecasts. At both Prod and Prod–ShipLoc levels there is a noticeable cyclical pattern in the daily forecast accuracy which repeats every seven days. For most of the lags, the Prod level forecasts are more accurate than the Prod–ShipLoc level forecasts, but the project team observed some exceptions, for example at Lags5, 12, 19, 26. In terms of forecast bias, on average, the Prod level forecasts had a positive bias, whereas the Prod–ShipLoc level forecasts had a negative bias.

To truly appreciate the results of this case study, we need to compare the daily Prod–ShipLoc advanced predictive model forecast accuracy and bias to a Naïve forecasting model, which is the accepted

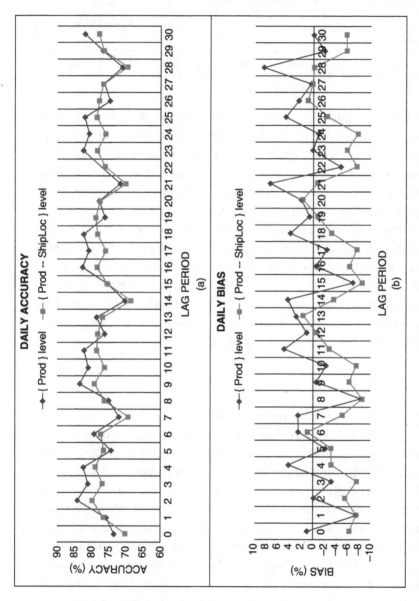

Figure 5.10 Daily Forecasting Accuracy at Prod and Prod–ShipLoc Level (a) and Daily Bias (b)

Source: Roger Baldridge, Kedar Prabhudesai, Varunraj Valsaraj, Dan Woo, and Jinzin Yi, *"Using Machine Learning and Demand Sensing to Enhance Short-Term Forecasting,"* SAS White Paper 2020.

Table 5.2 Summary of Enhanced Daily Forecast Accuracy and Bias at Prod and Prod–ShipLoc Levels Summarized Using Mean ± Standard Deviation

Forecast level	FC-Enhanced Accuracy	FC-Enhanced Bias
{Prod}	78.13 ± 3.97 %	0.30 ± 3.91 %
{Prod - ShipLoc}	70.39 ± 3.09 %	-4.06 ± 3.28 %

Source: Roger Baldridge, Kedar Prabhudesai, Varunraj Valsaraj, Dan Woo, and Jinzin Yi, "Using Machine Learning and Demand Sensing to Enhance Short-Term Forecasting," SAS White Paper 2020, pp. 1–12.

benchmark. Figure 5.11 compares the daily FC-Enhanced forecast accuracy to a Naïve model. The FC-Enhanced Forecast at the Prod–ShipLoc level is 76.39% accuracy on average across 30 days versus the Naïve model at 46.45%. Most companies don't have a 70% forecast accuracy at the monthly total product level or weekly level, let alone at the product ship-to-location daily level.

What is even more incredible is the bias between the FC-Enhanced daily Prod–ShipLoc versus the Naïve model. The FC-Enhanced model has a positive bias of less than 1%, versus the Naïve model with a negative 5% bias. (See Figure 5.12.) More advanced predictive models tend to be more stable over time with less bias. Also, the bias tends to be positive, which, given the current climate, benefits many grocery retailers and consumer goods companies.

Conclusions

The use of machine learning clearly demonstrates how this technique can be used effectively to enhance short-term weekly and daily product ship-to-location demand forecasts. This new weekly forecasting methodology uses a combination of segmentation, traditional time-series models, and machine learning methods to automatically choose the best model for each Prod–ShipLoc–CustLoc combination. This new approach using machine learning establishes the efficacy of these methods by improving short-term forecasts for a large consumer goods company. At the weekly level, there was a significant improvement in forecast accuracy over existing forecasting procedures across multiple lag periods. The results also demonstrate that POS and customer inventory data clearly further improve the daily and weekly forecast

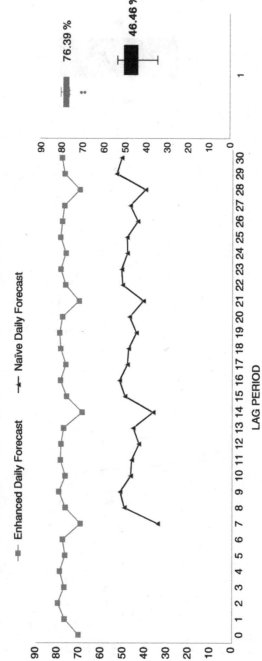

Figure 5.11 Daily Forecasting Accuracy at Prod and Prod–ShipLoc Level Versus a Naïve Model

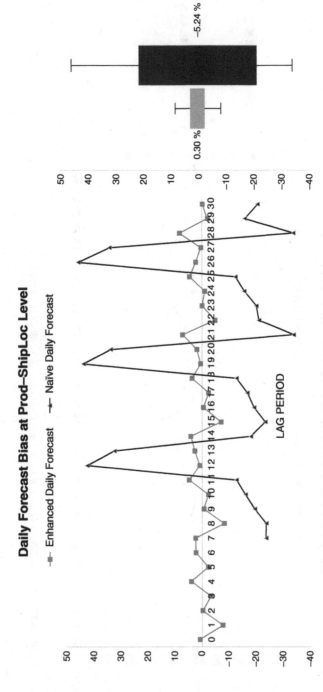

Figure 5.12 Daily Forecasting Bias at Prod and Prod–ShipLoc Level Versus a Naïve Model

accuracy. It is believed that these new methods provide a flexible, transparent, and scalable solution for effective demand management for consumer goods companies, and can also be used by retailers.

CASE STUDY 2: USING ADVANCED ANALYTICS TO ADAPT TO CHANGING CONSUMER DEMAND PATTERNS

Retailers and consumer goods companies are urgently trying to determine how changes in consumer behavior are affecting their regions, channels, categories, brands, and products during and beyond the COVID-19 crisis, and what actions they can take now. They are desperately looking to find new ways to adapt to the shifting consumer demand patterns in response to the pandemic. They are being forced to find quick, creative ways to adjust their business strategies to improve business performance while preparing for the new normal. The length of time it takes for the demand forecasting process to incorporate rapid changes or short-term spikes in demand is a challenge for most companies. Short-term spikes can occur with retail store promotions, sudden changes in weather conditions, social media activity, and, of course, disruptions like pandemics.

The concept of rapid demand response (RDR) forecasting is based on updating demand forecasts to reflect real and rapid changes in demand, both during and between planning cycles. In this case, reacting to a pandemic, companies can use it to effectively respond, recover and imagine the new normal. Another challenge is enabling RDR forecasting, which is not easy given the explosion of digital data and the enormous amount of information available regarding the automated consumer engagement. Data has been increasing drastically because of the Internet of Things (IoT) and the mass of incoming data from devices is making it difficult to separate demand signals from the noise. In many cases, these short-term spikes exceed the projected baseline demand, and are not always a result of planned sales promotions or marketing events but rather an unforeseen event—such as a disruption. The following is a case study of how a regional European online grocer implemented an RDR forecasting process using advanced analytics and machine learning to solve its short-term demand-sensing challenges.

Situation

As a result of COVID-19, normal consumer demand patterns have changed, to say the least. Activities like a trip to the grocery store or dining out with friends are difficult at best, or even prohibited. While the hospitality industry has been hit hard, online shopping doesn't appear to be slowing down as we move from preliminary to outbreak, stabilization, recovery, and finally to identifying the new normal. In several places around the world, grocers are among the few businesses that remain open. This has resulted in unprecedented increases in sales. According to *Progressive Grocer*, e-commerce grocery sales for home delivery and/or store pickup reached $5.3 billion in April 2020, a 37% increase over March sales, which were already at record highs.[15] As a result, meeting today's demand will require online retail grocers to understand their customers and anticipate their buying patterns at the point of purchase if they want to meet and exceed their customers' expectations more quickly and efficiently.

COVID-19 thrust online retail grocers into the position of trying to fulfill urgent demand, meeting customers' needs on the fly. The estimated percentages vary, but more consumers are turning to online grocery purchases as they stay at home out of fear of the coronavirus. Due to this situation, a regional online grocer experienced an increase in online grocery purchases of more than 200%, virtually overnight. This generated substantial supply chain bottlenecks and product substitution challenges, creating order cancellations as consumers turned to digital channels to purchase food and other goods. It's likely that this shift in consumer demand will continue, even after the coronavirus subsides. Companies that act quickly and modernize their delivery models to help consumers navigate the pandemic safely and effectively will have an advantage over their competitors.

Approach to Short-Term Demand Sensing

Continuing shifts in consumer spending on groceries has forced this regional online grocer to work carefully in applying historical sales data to forecast future demand and accurately align products and categories with shoppers' needs. Understanding true demand, and those disruptive events that have an impact on each product and location, is critically important. Sales orders alone will not account for the changing demand patterns resulting from the COVID-19 pandemic. It will require investing in new data, advanced analytics, and technology to make the necessary adjustments, both now and in the future. Grocers that adapt to meet online consumer demand will rise above the crisis as community lifelines, ready for a larger shift in online sales.

If we understand the business processes at an organization, we can identify its challenges and ultimately determine the best possible solution. This requires an understanding of affected KPIs, categories, products, and departments, and identification of the data necessary to solve the problem. The best approach is to implement a short-term forecasting process using advanced analytics and machine learning (ML) utilizing internal and external data to predict weekly demand across the online grocer's product portfolio. In this case, this was necessary as consumer demand trends and seasonality were no longer valid due to the disruptions caused by COVID-19. Figure 5.13 is a summary of the process flow and data used in the models.

Data Investigation

Demand increased as consumers fearing shortages loaded their pantries. Rising exchange rates and government stimulus to fight the economic impact of COVID-19 had an inflationary effect and contributed to further increases in consumption for the region, a trend that will likely continue into recovery. Subsequently, the availability of goods decreased, creating low availability across many product categories. Consumers reacted to the fear of a shortage by initially purchasing more of certain goods, such as pet food and toilet paper. However, consumption eventually returned to previous levels, resulting in post-crisis volume declines. Work-from-home and self-isolation policies forced consumers to shift from visiting food-service outlets to ordering from online retailers. The result is increased consumption of these products during and potentially after the crisis. (See Figure 5.14.)

Understand a Customer's Needs → **Understand the Customer's Business Processes** → **Understand Data** → **Understand Which Methods to Use** → **Understand How to Estimate the Result** → **Understand How to Apply in PROD**

Sources

No	Data	Source	Region	Fields	Apply in PROD
1	Epidemic Data	John Hopkins University	Country/State/Province	Cases, Recovered, Deaths	Epidemic
2	Macroeconomic Data	Federal Reserve Bank of Philadelphia	US	GDP, CPI, Unemployment etc.	Cases
3	Google Trend	Google library (Open source code in R)	Country/State/Province/City	keyword search trend Online Grocery, Covid trends	Recovery
4	Covid Sentiments	Twitter API (Open source code in Python)	Country/State/Province/City	keyword search tweets	Deaths
5	Forex	Python based module (Open source code)	Country	Forex	Forex

Variables

Orders	Google Trends
Total Orders Qty	Rice
Stock Availability	Pasta
New Clients Qty	Covid
Total Clients Qty	Isolation
Price Regular	Product Delivery
Price Promotion	

Summary

Data Time Frame	2018 -2020
Region	Europe
Lowest Level	SKUs
Total Levels	5
Frequency	Daily
Total SKUs	665
Total Obs	295K

Figure 5.13 Process Flow and Data Used to Model Shifting Short-term Demand Patterns

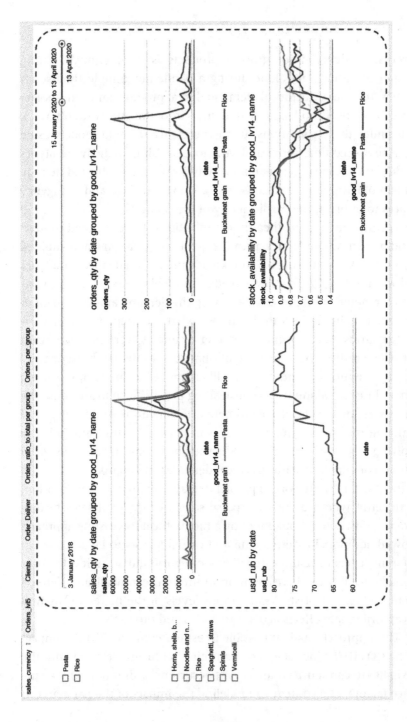

Figure 5.14 Uncovering Insights from the Data Using Advanced Analytics

Analytics Approach

Forecasting demand for grocery products is hard enough during normal conditions, let alone during a pandemic. Simple time-series models that take historical demand for a product and extrapolate those patterns (trend and seasonality) into the future don't work well under these conditions. It was necessary to build models using more advanced time-series and ML models. Using predictive analytics models, the online grocer demand analytics team was able to integrate epidemiological data, exchange rates, Google trends, and stringency indices to improve the predictability of the models.

Fortunately, public health organizations have a good understanding of how pandemics spread, and this information was combined with other key data sources to take advantage of advanced analytics and ML models. The data was readily available to estimate the various parameters in the models, allowing the demand analytics team to run what-if simulations to determine what will happen under various scenarios. Some of the parameter estimates were not significant but allowed the grocer to test what happens to demand forecasts by varying the future values within a likely range. A simple model using demand history alone will be misleading unless it can incorporate the various actions by local governments, the medical community, and changing consumer demand patterns in reaction to the pandemic. By applying machine learning to product attribute data and other external data in combination with historical demand, the approach proved to be the most accurate way to predict demand by product and location, particularly where there was sparse sales history, or if sales history had been disrupted. Implementing a hierarchical forecasting approach allowed additional external data and casual factors to be deployed at different levels of data aggregation—category and store levels. Additionally, it allowed the estimation of internal cannibalization effects from product out-of-stocks at various levels of the hierarchy, as well as capturing halo effects across categories and products.

This approach made it possible to estimate and predict the impact of the COVID-19 four stages of disruption on future demand with the flexibility to configure various event occurrences, duration, and recurrence factors. The strategy of modeling the impact of the pandemic at the product and location level, then testing multiple algorithms for best fit, was significantly more accurate than using a one-model-fits-all approach. The demand analytics team was able to estimate event impacts and quantify the unique effects for each product and location, up and down the hierarchy. The demand planners were able to consider multiple scenarios regarding the impact of the disruptive events on future demand using robust real-time what-if capabilities.

Results

Several categories and products were selected to model and forecast including noodles and nests, pasta horns, shells, butterflies, and bows. A four-step process was applied to test the accuracy of the models:

1. Only use internal historical demand data.
2. Include Google Trends.
3. Include epidemiological data.
4. Include exchange rates.

By adding various casual factors, the demand analytics team was able to determine which factors improved the predictability of the models using MAPE (Mean Absolute Percentage Error) as the default performance metric. In other words, the lower the MAPE, the more accurate the model performed with those additional factors incorporated. Starting with just historical demand data, the model's average MAPE was anywhere between 20% and 60%, a very high forecast error. However, as additional causal factors were added, the forecast accuracy improved significantly—the MAPE decreased to 4–9%, resulting in a 91.7% accuracy on average across all the product categories. This translates to an overall 12.3% improvement in forecast accuracy on average across those product categories and SKUs. (See Figure 5.15.)

Demand planners can greatly benefit from real-time feed and automation of data, providing an up-to-date view of global and regional patterns. Plus, it is important to have what-if scenarios to adjust product forecasts based on key consumer sentiment. This advanced analytics approach using ML ensemble models (gradient

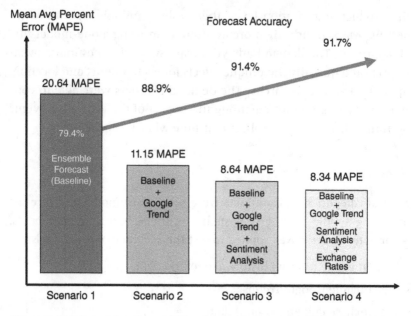

Figure 5.15 Forecast Results as Additional Causal Factors Are Added to the Models

boosting combined with random forest) is a proven methodology and a straightforward solution to adopt and implement across a product portfolio. The end deliverable was a new automated ML capability that was implemented in the company's dedicated cloud environment along with a COVID-19 dashboard delivering real-time intelligent automation to the demand planners, as seen in Figure 5.16.

Delivering Real-Time Results

The demand analysts delivered a real-time feed and automation of data, providing the demand planners with an up-to-date view of global and regional patterns. They also delivered additional what-if scenarios to adjust product forecasts based on key consumer sentiment. Finally, they were able to replicate this capability in the company's dedicated cloud environment and deployed it in days with the help of their technology provider.

Retail and consumer goods executives should plan to rapidly adapt their marketing and demand plans to reflect shifting consumer demand

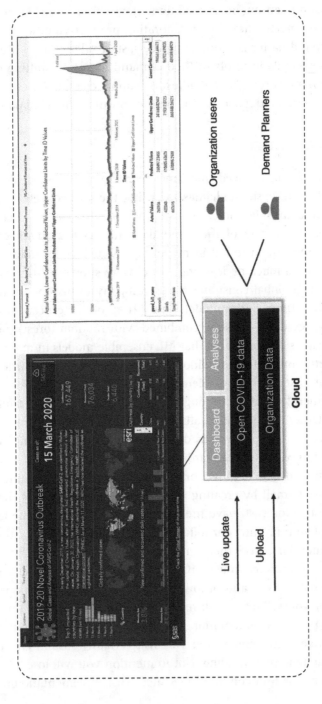

Figure 5.16 Short-term End-to-End Interactive COVID-19 Forecasting Dashboard

patterns and sentiment. In addition, they should quickly optimize their e-commerce channels, recalibrating product volumes with the new demand patterns, prioritizing the fastest-selling SKUs. Retailers should expect daily resets to their demand forecasts, shifting online assortments accordingly, and adjusting supply chain logistics and distribution centers to meet shifting online consumer demand patterns.

CLOSING THOUGHTS

This chapter introduced machine learning (ML) strategies and provided some basic guidelines for using them effectively. It introduced some considerations for using ML for time-series forecasting including structuring of the input data and extraction of features from the input data to aid in modeling. Guidelines for determining when to use a machine learning model were shown in the two case studies: (1) a global consumer goods company using Stacked Neural Networks + Times Series models, and (2) an online grocer using ML ensemble (gradient boosting combined with random forest) models. The examples demonstrated that ML ensemble models in many cases significantly outperform traditional time-series methods, particularly when forecasting product hierarchies, as evidence by MAPE error measurements which were roughly half the size of that for traditional models. Other details and pitfalls were covered, including process and model architecture, as well as data considerations, and compatibility of activation with data standardization techniques.

If you do decide to move forward with AI/machine learning techniques, start small by creating a project for those products that are the easiest to forecast, have the most data, and represent the largest portion of your product portfolio. In many cases, companies either try to introduce ML across their entire product portfolio in a "big bang" approach, or they try to use ML to forecast their most difficult products that have sparse and/or low-quality data. In both situations, you are setting yourself up for failure. If you fail during the initial proof-of-value (POV) or implementation, you will not only lose the confidence of executive management, but you will certainly sustain challenges in gaining additional funding. Not to mention you will lose adoption and trust by the user community. A successful implementation rollout plan that has many small wins will be more successful and will gain trust and adoption across the entire organization.

Also, consider creating a "Center of Analytics Excellence" within your corporate headquarters, particularly if you are a large global company. Staff your center of excellence (COE) with "demand analysts/data scientists" not just demand planners. What is the difference? Demand analysts would be responsible for creating the statistical forecasts for all the regions/divisions. They then pass those statistical forecasts and model results to the regional/divisional demand planners to refine (adjust) the statistical forecasts based on local regional field intelligence, such as pricing actions, sales promotions, and others. Also, they provide the regional demand planners with what-if scenario planning capabilities.

The skill sets of the newly created demand analyst positions are different from the demand planners. The demand analysts should have advanced statistical skills and strong business acumen. They also need strong collaboration skills as they work closely with the regional demand planners. The regional demand planners do not necessarily require a strong statistical skill set but they do work closely with the local commercial business teams to refine the statistical forecasts reflecting regional sales/marketing activities (i.e. pricing actions, sales promotions, marketing events, and others). A question that always surfaces is the ratio of demand analysts to demand planners. Based on experience, it is recommended that there be one demand analyst for every three to four demand planners. This seems to be the optimal mix between demand analysts and demand planners. Once all the statistical models are generated, demand analysts only need to tweak the statistical baseline forecasts on an exception basis requiring fewer resources. The demand analysts can also provide ad hoc analysis in support of the global commercial teams to assess business strategic initiatives and tactics.

If you are implementing an analytics-driven forecasting and planning process, those statistical forecasts need to include key performance indicators (KPIs) such as price, sales promotions, and others, which the demand planners can utilize to make adjustments through what-if analysis, not "gut feeling" judgment. POS/Syndicated Scanner data (true demand) needs to be integrated into the demand planning process, which will encourage the commercial teams to engage with the demand planners. The goal is to have demand analysts building statistical models and forecasts that include KPIs, such as sales promotions, price, advertising, in-store merchandising, and more. Then, demand planners working closely with the commercial teams (sales/marketing) running what-if simulations to adjust the forecasts based on data, analytics, and domain knowledge rather than "gut feeling" judgment. The what-if analysis is done at the local divisional/country level for tactical planning but can also be conducted at the corporate (global) level for strategic planning. This is done using cloud-enabled, large-scale hierarchical forecasting technology.

One final thought, before you embark on more advanced modeling algorithms like machine learning: make sure you have exhausted all the traditional time-series methods. Although ML models have proved to be more accurate, they require ample amounts of high-quality data, more advanced statistical skills, and scalable technology—preferably open-source, cloud-enabled capabilities—to operationalize across a company's entire product portfolio. Consider combining models using either a simple averaging or a weighted combined technique. Finally, consider introducing traditional predictive models with causal/explanatory variables before implementing ML models.

NOTES

1. Tim Denman, "Developing and Building Meaningful Artificial Intelligence," *Consumer Goods Technology*, July 31, 2020. https://consumergoods.com/developing-and-building-meaningful-artificial-intelligence

2. Charles W. Chase, "Rapid Demand Response Forecasting Techniques are Helping Companies Adapt During COVID-19," *Journal of Business Forecasting* 39(2), Summer 2020: 21–23, 26–27. https://ibf.org/knowledge/jbf-issues?date=&keywords=&quarter=Summer&year=2020

3. Ibid.

4. Ibid.

5. James Ochiai-Brown, Sherrine Eid, Sudeshna Guhaneogi, Pasi Helenius, Matteo Landro, and Valentina Larina, "Using Advanced Analytics to Model, Predict and Adapt to Changing Consumer Demand Patterns affected by COVID-19," SAS White paper 2020: 1–16. https://www.sas.com/content/dam/SAS/documents/marketing-whitepapers-ebooks/sas-whitepapers/en/ensure-demand-patterns-stability-111475.pdf

6. Spyros Makridakis, Evangelos Spiliotis, and Vassilios Assimakopoulos, "The M5 Accuracy Competition: Results, Findings and Conclusions," Institute for the Future, University of Nicosia, Cyprus Forecasting and Strategy Unit, School of Electrical and Computer Engineering, National Technical University of Athens, Greece, October 6, 2020: 1–45.

7. Spyros Makridakis, Chris Chatfield, Michele Hibon, Michael Lawrence, Terence Mills, Keith Ord, and LeRoy F. Simmons, "The M2-Competition: A Real-time Judgmentally Based Forecasting Study," *International Journal of Forecasting* 9(1), Elsevier, April 1993: 5–22. https://www.sciencedirect.com/science/article/abs/pii/016920709390044N

8. Spyros Makridakis, Evangelos Spiliotis, and Vassilios Assimakopoulos, "The M4 Competition: Results, Findings, Conclusion and Way Forward," *International Journal of Forecasting* 34(4), June 2018: 802–808. https://www.sciencedirect.com/science/article/pii/S0169207019301128?via%3Dihub

9. Spyros Makridakis et al., "The M5 Accuracy Competition: Results, Findings and Conclusions."

10. Ibid.

11. Ibid.

12. Ibid.

13. Spyros Makridakis and Evangelos Spiliotis, "The M5 Competition and the Future of Human Expertise in Forecasting," *Foresight: The International Journal of Applied Forecasting*, Issue 60, Winter 2021: 33–37. https://econpapers.repec.org/article/forijafaa/y_3a2021_3ai_3a60_3ap_3a33-37.htm

14. Roger Baldridge, Kedar Prabhudesai, Varunraj Valsaraj, Dan Woo, and Jinxin Yi, "Using Machine Learning and Demand Sensing to Enhance Short-Term Forecasting," SAS White Paper 2020: 1–12. https://www.sas.com/en/whitepapers/enhance-short-term-forecasting-111335.html

15. Abby Kleckler, "Online Grocery Sales Soar Over March Records," *Progressive Grocer*, April 28, 2020. https://progressivegrocer.com/online-grocery-sales-soar-over-march-records

CHAPTER **6**

Intelligent Automation Is Disrupting Demand Planning

Business leaders are embracing automation not just to take advantage of the breakthrough pace of digital change, but also to create a new digital ecosystem where they hold competitive advantage. Artificial intelligence (AI) is the newest recruit to the workforce, bringing new skills and automation to help people do new jobs, and reinventing what's possible.[1] The impressive advances in AI and machine learning (ML) over the past decade have been supported by supervised deep learning: training ML algorithms to perform narrow, single-domain tasks. The learning is supervised because you're telling the algorithm the correct answer (the label) as it is exposed to many examples using big data. We're now seeing unsupervised learning systems that learn faster, require less data, and achieve impressive performance. These supervised and unsupervised "intelligent automation" techniques can help experts achieve automation while enriching their domain expertise to do their work more effectively—not to eliminate or replace these experts.

The challenge is that people have not yet developed the level of trust in artificial intelligence and machine learning that they have in other technologies that automate tasks. People sometimes confuse automation with autonomy. Intelligent automation (IA) techniques can be applied to all kinds of activities across your organization to reduce the everyday repetitive work while uncovering key insights to improve the effectiveness of your processes, as well as your workforce. Rather than just being considered an add-on, IA now represents a fundamental change in how technology systems are built and implemented. As a new foundational layer of technology architecture, an increasing number of capabilities are being shaped that allow machines to become more sophisticated in how they learn and make decisions. This means that the process of automating these tasks becomes much easier.

WHAT IS "INTELLIGENT AUTOMATION"?

Machine learning refers to the ability of predictive algorithms aided by computer systems to improve their performance by exposure to data without having to follow programmed instructions. Therefore, ML is the process of automatically uncovering patterns in the data.

Upon discovery, the patterns can be used to make predictions. The more data ML processes, the better it can make quality predictions to the point where it can predict situations before they occur. Computing power and in-memory applications now allow algorithms to be applied faster to detect when consumer behaviors deviated from the usual habits.

AI systems work through two phases: (1) the learning phase, and (2) the execution phase, as it learns to uncover patterns and make decisions. These technologies enable organizations to model their processes and let the computer orchestrate making decisions regarding direct workflows during subsequent steps. With these technologies, organizations gain efficiency by having all or part of the process executed by the computer, thus improving speed and productivity. With intelligent automation (IA), processes become increasingly more intelligent. They can adapt to change and become more precise over time, taking advantage of faster data processing to the point where human input is only needed on an exception basis.

Intelligent automation is a real-time learning system that can generalize and optimize from a common set of rules and is aided by artificial intelligence and machine learning. Intelligent automation driven by AI and ML is disrupting the way companies do business. IA can be applied to all kinds of activities across your organization to reduce the everyday repetitive work while uncovering key insights to improve the effectiveness of your processes, allowing your workforce to work smarter and more efficiently.

The rapid deployment of automation is helping companies set new standards of efficiency, speed, and functionality. Instead of being replaced, humans will see unprecedented job creation and new opportunities to add more value. Applications can range from routine to groundbreaking, such as collecting, analyzing, and making decisions about textual information to guiding demand planners to anticipating consumer purchasing behavior. It is already helping companies overcome conventional performance trade-offs to achieve unprecedented levels of efficiency that reduce costs while increasing profitability. The variety of business challenges to which IA can be applied is expanding as technologies for voice recognition, natural language processing and

ML improve. These technologies are becoming increasingly available as IoT devices capture streaming information and open-source cloud-based services become more widespread.

Leading organizations are driving more of their processes into smarter machines. They are rethinking what they do across every area of the enterprise—from their business processes to the customer experience. Some activities where IA is helping companies are:

- Data collection
- Security and systems monitoring
- Transaction management with ERP systems
- Scheduling and staffing
- Accounting and finance
- Business planning
- Customer experience
- Marketing and communications

The levels of automation include:

- Basic automation of frequent repetitive simple tasks
- Advanced automation that orchestrates workflows across departments and applications
- Intelligent automation that mimics complex research and expert decision making

The foundational elements for intelligent automation are:

- Institutionalized business process
- Reducing effort and increasing accuracy
- Centralized application with auditing and instrumentation
- Quantifiable metrics to measure and inform model improvements
- Analytics infrastructure to support machine learning
- APIs to allow software agents to mimic and drive tasks
- Continuous monitoring and automation governance

Intelligent automation is empowering humans with its advanced smart technologies and agile processes to make faster, more intelligent decisions. The key benefits of IA in business include:

- Improved productivity
- Increased process efficiency
- Improved customer experience
- Unprecedented value (ROI)

The advantages of using IA applications can lead to new business strategies that could not have been conceived of previously. Companies who have invested in IA have been able to automate about half of their tasks, reducing process times by as much as 50%. Completing tasks more quickly means companies address more complex tasks without spending additional time and revenue. Depending on the industry, faster job completion with improved precision can mean increased revenue.

HOW CAN INTELLIGENT AUTOMATION ENHANCE EXISTING PROCESSES?

Forecast value added (FVA) has become a standard metric for most companies to improve not only forecast accuracy, but reduce non-value add touch points in the demand planning process, thus improving process efficiency.[2] The challenge is not only to identify overrides that are non-value add, but also those that are value add. In fact, many overrides add very little value. According to prior research, as much as 75% of statistical forecasts are adjusted using judgment each cycle.[3] Also, when raising forecasts there is over-optimism, which leads to bias that makes forecasts substantially worse—that is, less accurate. Furthermore, adjustments that lower statistical forecasts tend to reduce MAPE, making forecasts more accurate. Overall, small adjustments tend to predominate and on average they only slightly lower forecast accuracy. However, the smallest 25% of manual adjustments, or as much as 50%, have little impact on forecast accuracy.[4]

This situation is made more difficult when you have thousands of SKUs across multiple channels including brick-and-mortar, mobile, online, Amazon.com, and other related e-commerce channels in multiple countries requiring millions of forecasts. Using Excel makes it impossible for demand planners to review and manually adjust all those forecasts, and so they rely on aggregate-level adjustments that are disaggregated down their business hierarchies. In many cases, mass aggregation of overrides is not an accurate way of manually adjusting statistical forecasts, even when based on additional sales and marketing activities that were not considered or available during the origination of the statistical forecast.

Consider the challenge of managing all those touch points using Excel. What if we apply IA to boost FVA with machine learning? We can do this with the goal of reducing the complexity of managing all the FVA information through automation, while providing demand planners with targeted intelligence to pinpoint where, when, and by how much to make manual overrides to the statistical forecast. However, before we consider applying IA to improve demand planners' value add, we need to better understand FVA.

WHAT IS FORECAST VALUE ADD?

Companies have been searching for a performance measurement that can effectively measure and improve the demand forecasting process, reduce cycle time, and minimize the number of touch points. The best approach a company can take is to implement a methodology for measuring demand forecasting process performance and accuracy called Forecast Value Add (FVA), or Lean Forecasting.[5] Forecast Value Add is a metric for evaluating the performance of each step and each participant in the forecasting process. FVA is simply the change in forecast accuracy before and after each touch point in the process, based on any specific forecast performance measurement, such as Percentage Error (PE), Absolute Percentage Error (APE), Mean Absolute Percentage Error (MAPE), or Weighted Absolute Percentage Error (WAPE).

FVA is measured by comparing the forecast accuracy before and after each touch point or activity in the demand forecasting and planning process to determine if that activity added any value to the accuracy of the demand forecast. Using the statistical forecast as a standard benchmark or baseline, companies can measure each touch point in the demand forecasting process and compare it to the accuracy of the statistical (baseline) forecast. If the activity increases the accuracy of the statistical baseline forecast, then that activity should remain in the process. However, if the activity does not improve the accuracy of the statistical (baseline) forecast, it should be eliminated or minimized (simplified), to reduce cycle time and resources, thereby improving forecast process efficiency. (See Table 6.1.)

FVA is a commonsense approach that is easy to understand. The idea is simple—it's just basic statistics. What are the results of doing something versus what would have been the results if you hadn't done anything? According to Mike Gilliland, FVA can be either positive or negative, telling you whether your efforts are adding value by making the forecast better, or whether you are making things worse.[6] FVA analysis consists of a variety of methods that have been evolving through industry practitioners' applications around this innovative performance metric. It is the application of fundamental hypothesis testing to business forecasting.

Do Manual Overrides Add Value?

FVA attempts to determine whether forecasting process steps and participants are improving the forecast—or just making it less accurate. It is good practice to compare the statistical forecast to a naïve forecast, such as a random walk or seasonal random walk. Naïve forecasts, in some situations, can be surprisingly difficult to beat; yet it is very important that the software and statistical modeler improve on the naïve model. If the software or modeler is not able to do this—and you aren't able to implement better software or improve the skills of the modeler—then just use the naïve model for the statistical (baseline) forecast. A "naïve forecast" serves as the benchmark in evaluating forecasting process performance. Performance of the naïve model provides a reference standard for comparisons. In other words, is the forecasting process "adding value" by performing better than the naïve model?

FVA is consistent with a "lean" approach identifying and eliminating process waste, or non-value add activities that should be eliminated from the process. Non-value add resources should be redirected to more productive activities that add value to the company. However,

Table 6.1 Performance Metrics Comparisons

Products	FORECASTS			Actual Demand	APE		
	Statistical	Marketing Override	Sr. MGMT Override		Statistical	Marketing Override	Sr. Mgmet Override
	(units)		(units)	(units)			
Product Family X	1831	2030	2675	1993	8.1%	1.9%	34.2%
Product A	1380	1400	1800	1450	4.8%	3.4%	24.1%
Product B	228	320	400	290	21.4%	10.3%	37.9%
Product C	165	230	350	185	10.8%	24.3%	89.2%
Product D	58	80	125	68	14.7%	17.6%	83.8%
WAPE					12.9%	13.9%	58.8%

the flaw is that we don't know whether these observed differences are real (i.e. are they a result of a step in the process?) or simply due to chance. This is another reason why a more rigorous statistical test is needed to identify the "real" differences. Table 6.2 illustrates the results of a typical demand forecasting process using FVA.

According to recent research, FVA and WMAPE (Weighted Mean Absolute Percentage Error) are now the two most popular forecasting performance metrics surpassing MAPE. Many companies, however, still prefer to use MAPE only, but used alone it only tracks and reports forecast performance. MAPE and WMAPE explain the magnitude of the forecast error, but they do not tell you anything about whether demand is forecastable. Subsequently, both MAPE and WMAPE provide no indication of the efficiency of your forecasting and planning process. To understand these things, you need to use FVA analysis. FVA can also be used as a basis for performance comparison. Suppose you are a forecasting manager and have the authority to provide a bonus for outstanding performance to your best demand planner. The traditional way to determine which analyst is best, the manager needs to compare their forecast errors. Table 6.3 is based on this traditional

Table 6.2 An Example of an FVA Report

Process Step (1)	MAPE (2)	Naïve (3)	Statistical (4)	Override (5)	Consensus (6)
Naïve	50%	–	–	–	–
Statistical Forecast	45%	5%	–	–	–
Planner Override	40%	10%	5%	–	–
Consensus Forecast	35%	15%	10%	5%	–
Approved Forecast	40%	5%	5%	0%	-5%

Notes 1. Column 2 gives MAPE of each set of forecast. For example 50% MAPE is of Naïve Forecasts, 45% of Statistical Forecasts, and so on.
2. Other columns give percentage point improvement made by one set of forecast over the other. For example, Statistical Forecasts improved over the Analyst Override by 5 percentage point, and 10% over the Consensus Forecasts.
Source: Michael Gilliland, *The Business Forecasting Deal: Exposing Myths, Eliminating Bad Practices, Providing Practical Solutions*, Wiley, June 8, 2010.

Table 6.3 Which Demand Forecasting Is More Accurate?

Planner	MAPE
A	20%
B	30%
C	40%

Source: Michael Gilliland, *The Business Forecasting Deal: Exposing Myths, Eliminating Bad Practices, Providing Practical Solutions*, Wiley, June 8, 2010.

analysis, which clearly indicates that Planner A is the best demand planner and deserves the bonus. But is this traditional analysis the correct analysis?

What if we consider additional information about each demand planner and the types of products they are assigned to forecast? Although, Planner A had the lowest MAPE, the types of products that were assigned to this planner were steady state (long-established mature) items, with some trend and seasonality, no promotional activity, no new items, and low demand variability. In fact, an FVA analysis might reveal that a naïve model could have forecast this type of demand with a MAPE of only 10%, but FVA reveals that Planner A made the forecast less accurate. See Table 6.4.

Planner B, however, had more difficult demand to forecast with some added dynamics of promotional activities and new items that make forecasting even more challenging. FVA analysis reveals that Planner B added no value as compared to a naïve model, but did not make the forecast less accurate. Based on the FVA analysis, Planner C deserves the bonus. Even though Planner C had the highest MAPE of 40%, they had very difficult items to forecast—short-life-cycle perishable food items with lots of promotional activity and high demand variability. Only Planner C added value as compared to the naïve model by improving the accuracy.

This simple example reveals another factor to be wary of in published performance benchmarks—not all companies and products are the same, nor do they consider FVA. As such, it is not advised to compare yourself or your company to what others are doing. If a company achieves best-in-class forecast accuracy, it may be because they have demand data which are easier to forecast, not because their process is

Table 6.4 Performance Metrics Comparisons with Naïve Forecast

| Planner | Item Life | | | | | Demand | | | |
	Item Type	Cycle	Seasonality	Promotions	New Items	Volatility	MAPE	MAPE (Naïve Forecast)	FVA
A	Basic	Long	No	None	None	Low	20%	10%	-10%
B	Basic	Long	Some	Few	Few	Medium	30%	30%	0%
C	Perishable Foods	Short	High	Many	Many	High	40%	50%	10%

Source: Michael Gilliland, *The Business Forecasting Deal: Exposing Myths, Eliminating Bad Practices, Providing Practical Solutions,* Wiley, June 8, 2010.

worthy of admiration. Also, you can't compare model fit indices for models based on different underlying data. The proper comparison is your performance versus a naïve model. If you are doing better than a naïve model, then that is good. And if you or your process is doing worse than a naïve model, then you have some challenges to overcome.

The FVA approach is meant to be objective and analytical, so you must be careful not to draw conclusions unwarranted by the data. For example, measuring FVA over one week or one month is just not enough data to draw any valid conclusions. Period to period, FVA will go up and down, and over short periods of time FVA may be particularly high or low due to randomness and/or variability of the data. When you express the results in a table, as shown in Table 6.4, be sure to indicate the time frame reported, and make sure that the time range has enough historical points to provide meaningful results.

The best results would occur with a full year of data from which to draw conclusions. If you've been thoroughly tracking inputs to the forecasting process already, then you probably have the data you need to do the analysis immediately. You should consider computing FVA with the last year of statistical forecasts, planner overrides, consensus forecasts, executive approved forecasts, and actuals. Naïve models are always easy to reconstruct for the past, so you can measure how well a naïve model would have done with your data from the past year. Graphical presentation of the data, using methods from statistical process control, can be a big help in getting started with FVA. A thorough and ongoing FVA analysis will require, however, the ability to capture the forecast of each participant in the process at every touch point (or step) for your entire item, as well as for location combinations for every period. This will quickly grow into a very large amount of data to store and maintain, so companies will need software with enough scalability along with automation. This is not something you can do in Excel spreadsheets.

Only by documenting the design, specifications, and assumptions that went into the forecast can we begin to learn the dynamics associated with the item(s) we are trying to predict. Forecast measurement should be a learning process, not just a tool to evaluate performance. You cannot improve forecast accuracy unless you measure it. You must establish a benchmark by measuring current forecast performance before you can establish a target for improvement. However, tracking forecast error alone is not the solution. Instead of only asking the question "What is this month's forecast error?" we also need to ask, "Why has forecast error been tracking so high (or low) and is the process improving?"

FVA is truly an innovation in business forecasting that is being widely accepted as part of a company's standard performance metrics. The FVA performance metrics are a proven way to identify waste in the forecasting process, thus improving efficiency and reducing cycle time. By identifying and eliminating the non-value add activities, FVA provides the means and justification for streamlining the forecasting process, thereby making the forecast more accurate.

CASE STUDY: USING INTELLIGENT AUTOMATION TO IMPROVE DEMAND PLANNERS' FVA

During each forecast cycle demand planners at a large consumer goods company engage in a weeklong, multistep process that includes an array of manual workflow processes. The workflow starts with a review of the latest statistical forecast created by manually cleansing the demand history (sales orders or shipments) by removing outliers and removing promotion volumes, then using the most effective statistical models to forecast the baseline volume. The promotional volumes that were removed from the demand history are manually reviewed and revised by the commercial team (sales and marketing), and then manually blended back into the baseline forecast to create the final demand plan. (See Figure 6.1.)

This is a manually intensive workflow during the first week of each monthly forecast cycle. The demand planners typically develop the statistical baseline forecasts, who may be regional or centrally located. They work under the guidance of the demand planning manager. Statistical baseline forecasts are communicated to members of the demand management team by the demand planners. This usually includes regional sales leaders, brand managers, and product managers. Additional manual adjustments are made throughout the process because of changes in marketing programming, new

Monday	Tuesday	Wednesday	Thursday	Friday
Generate and review forecast exceptions from previous week.	Import and apply promotion uplifts created by sales/marketing.	Review forecasting parameters for A class and strategic items.	Lead consensus planning meeting with sales and marketing.	Gather inputs from S&OP meeting.
Manually run data cleansing routines (separate historical demand into baseline and promoted volumes).	Apply new product volumes where needed.	Review forecast at higher aggregations.	Apply any changes arising from the consensus planning meeting to the forecast.	Apply any changes arising from the pre-S&OP and/or S&OP meeting to the forecast.
Resolve any issues related to last forecast submitted to supply.	Review statistical baseline/promoted forecasts generated on exception basis.	Coordinate with sales and marketing to capture any changes to targets.	Prepare and submit reports for pre-S&OP (weekly) and S&OP (monthly) meetings.	Last-minute checks at the aggregate level.
Generate/review performance metrics (MAPE, WMAPE, FVA) report for previous week.	Manually, blend promotion uplifts into the baseline statistical forecast.	Reconcile top-down forecast changes (apply mass aggregations) to lower levels.		Approve and submit forecast to supply plan.
Run and review statistical baseline forecast generated based on new history on exception basis.		Manually, tune lower levels based on sales/marketing input.		

Demand Planner's Workload

40% Data Issues/Setup/Cleansing

30% Forecast Management/Tuning

20% Coordinate/Achieve Consensus

10% Reports/KPIs and Learning

Figure 6.1 Demand Planner Weekly Activities

corporate strategies, and changing market dynamics along with changing consumer preferences and behavior. This adds additional complexities as demand planners try to manually incorporate these changes into the demand plan.

As a result, more than 40% of the demand planner's time is spent managing information and data. Another 30–40% is spent managing and fine-tuning the demand forecast based on new market and customer information, changes in marketing programming (tactics), and coordinating the consensus forecast (supply plan). Finally, creating and updating KPI reports represents about 10% of the demand planner's time. With the introduction of intelligent automation (IA) using machine learning (ML), a large portion of the manual, repetitive activities can be automated (see the highlighted activities in Figure 6.1), allowing demand planners to be more productive, adding real value to the overall process.

The demand planners have been tracking their FVA for over two years. However, the process is very cumbersome as the company has expanded its presence across more geographic areas, regions, markets, and channels while expanding their product offerings and product facings on shelf. Meanwhile, they automated many of the data collection and processing repetitive activities and installed a more advanced statistical forecasting engine that includes machine learning (ML) capabilities. The company currently has over 200 demand planners globally. Now that they have automated the data collection and processing, and installed a more robust predictive analytics engine, the company decided to determine how they could further automate and improve the demand planning process using Intelligent Automation supported by machine learning.

A New IA Approach Called "Assisted Demand Planning"

Recently, the global consumer goods company ran a pilot to test a new IA technology that uses ML to improve their demand planners' FVA. This new capability uses ML to learn from past demand planners' manual overrides, and then becomes a digital assistant to the demand planners, guiding them up/down the product hierarchy and suggesting where to make forecast value add overrides. The pilot/proof-of-concept (POC) focused on two main objectives:

1. Identify entities that need overrides.
2. Provide demand planners with the direction and range of overrides (as to the need to raise or lower statistical forecasts) at various levels of the business hierarchy.

ML analyzes past statistical and consensus forecast overrides to learn from successful and unsuccessful forecast adjustments to identify the best periods to review candidate products for overrides. It then provides guidance to the demand planners regarding where, and by how much, to adjust the business hierarchical forecasts by either raising or lowering the statistical forecast. (See Figure 6.2.)

Process Approach

In Figure 6.3, a minimum of two and a half years of historical overrides based on an 18-month rolling forecast were collected for five product categories in two geographic areas for more than 700 items. A 60-day future forecast was used for FVA purposes. In-sample and out-of-sample training and validation periods were used in comparison to the FVA analysis to choose the appropriate ML model. A three-step approach was implemented:

1. Enrich;
2. Model; and
3. Assess.

Process Steps

Step 1: Enrich the process by identifying value-add and non-value-add overrides made by several demand planners and add any other attributes that are available.

Step 2: Build ML models using neural networks, gradient boosting, and ensemble random forest training models in a competition to determine the champion model.

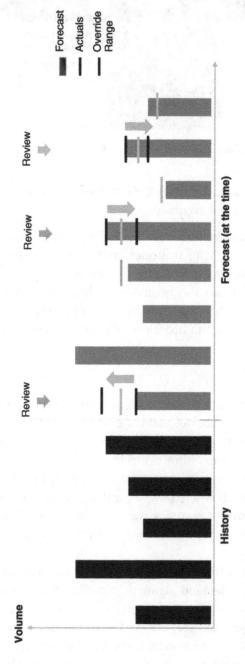

Figure 6.2 Override Only If the Forecast Can Be Improved

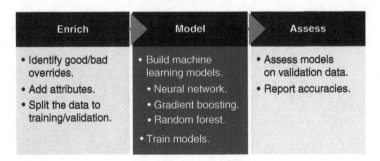

Figure 6.3 Intelligent Automation Process Approach

Step 3: Assess models using the out-of-sample validation data and report the levels of accuracy.[7]

These steps can be enhanced by adding other causal factors like sales promotions, pricing strategies, and others. In this POC there were no causal factors to enhance the ML models to show proof of value. Smart rules can also be added, such as not making overrides if the MAPE is less than 10%, or that you only consider FVA analysis results if the three-month historical FVA average is greater than 30%.

Results

The assisted demand planning using the intelligent automation process reduced the number of manual overrides by 47%, allowing the demand planners to focus only on those products and periods that would benefit the most from overrides. As a result, it improved the demand planners' overall forecast value add by 6.3%. Also, for those products and periods where IA told the demand planners not to make overrides, the forecast accuracy was 86%, as the statistical forecasts generated by their new predictive analytics engine where much more accurate.

A user interface (UI) utilizing the company's collaborative planning technology guides demand planners in making manual overrides, as to what direction (up or down), and within a volume range. (See Figure 6.4.) As you can see, arrows for March, May, and June indicate the direction of the override. The highlighted cells indicate the lowest volume range and, above the arrow, indicate the maximum

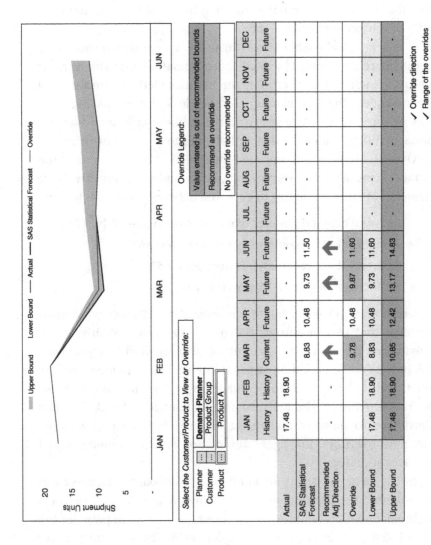

Figure 6.4 User Override Interface

203

overall override volume. For April there is no arrow up or down, indicating no manual overrides are suggested for that month because the statistical forecast is more accurate. Each demand planner can scroll up or down the product hierarchy by planner, customer, and product. Note that there is no limitation to the number of levels in the hierarchy. It is based on available data.

If a demand planner chooses to make a manual override for a month not recommended by intelligent automation, a default warning appears to indicate that overriding the statistical derived forecast is not recommended. Demand planners can be blocked from making overrides in those cells or the system can flag those cells with warning messages but still allow the demand planner to make an override.

Overall, ML helped to improve the statistical model accuracy (on average) across all the product groups, items, and geographies with the champion ML model—in this case, neural network model—as follows:

- Reduced demand planner overrides (touch points) by 47%
- Accuracy if ML recommends no overrides: 86%
- Accuracy if ML recommends overrides: 65%
- An increase in overall FVA accuracy of 6.3%

Given these results, using ML to boost the FVA process has demonstrated that IA can automate demand planners' repetitive work of managing the enormous amounts of data required to support the FVA process while providing targeted intelligence to pinpoint where, when, and by how much to manually adjust the statistical forecast. The real benefits are the ML recommendations to not make manual adjustments to the statistical forecast because it is much more accurate than prior overrides. Intelligent automation reduces complexity and improves accuracy.

In the same way that an automobile's onboard computers can be connected to diagnostic machines, allowing a technician to assess the problem within minutes (versus hours manually) to pinpoint the exact failed part, intelligent automation helps the demand planner to work smarter, but not be replaced by the machine. IA will help demand planners analyze vast amounts of information to boost the FVA process, guiding them with surgical precision to work smarter. Demand planners will be able to ingest and analyze massive amounts of forecast information, respond quickly to complex inquiries, and make overrides with precision across the entire business hierarchy.

> *"The conversation we should have is how machines and algorithms can make us smarter, not how smart we can make the machines."*
>
> —*Tom Gruber, Co-creator of Siri (TED Talk, 2017)*

CLOSING THOUGHTS

This Intelligent Automation example demonstrates how the pace of change is accelerating, but also the pressure that companies are under to reinvent themselves. In fact, most executives agree that organizations are being increasingly pressed to reinvent themselves and evolve their business before they are disrupted from the outside or by their competitors. IA has become a key enabler of the changes required to compete in the digital economy. Businesses will only be able to manage the enormous wave of complexities that arises from this unavoidable digital change. If they can seamlessly harness and integrate, at scale, everything that's disrupting their business, executives can meet those challenges with new skill sets and a very different workforce.

IA is not just about technology systems that create automation that's driving real change. IA is having an effect out in the physical world as well, changing the rules of e-commerce by moving ever closer to same-day delivery, boosting crop yields through precision by using IA to support digital farming, and more. IA isn't an option—it's a requirement. The question is whether you have the capabilities to not just use it but implement it across every aspect of your organization. IA will give companies newfound power to drive change with their organizations. IA will become a core competence providing a pervasive capability to every aspect of your business; however, doing so will require a people-first attitude and approach toward gaining adoption across the entire corporate enterprise—culture, skills, and processes—before experiencing the full benefits.

Several other consumer goods companies have since experienced the benefits of IA by implementing "Assisted Demand Planning," incorporating sale promotions and gaining as much as a 9.6% improvement in FVA. Those companies have embraced automation not just to take advantage of this new breakthrough digital change, but to create a new digital company where they hold competitive advantage over their competitors. They are early adopters who realize that AI/machine learning will be their new recruits to the workforce, bringing new skills to help employees do new jobs and reinventing the possible. Rather than just looking at AI/machine learning as an add-on, they recognize that IA is a new foundation layer of their IT architecture. As a result, these companies are increasing the number of applications being created that allow machines to become more sophisticated in how they learn and make decisions. Essentially, that means the process of automating tasks will become easier, and part of their corporate culture.

Intelligent automation supported by machine learning is changing the game, particularly for demand forecasting and planning. Most executives will tell you that when shaping business plans and strategy, consumption-based forecasting and planning can serve as a great counterweight to gut feelings and biases.

NOTES

1. Paul Daugherty, Marc Carrel-Billiard, and Michael J. Blitz, "Intelligent Automation: The Essential New Co-worker for the Digital Age," *Accenture*, Technology Vision 2016: 1–13.
2. Michael Gilliland, *The Business Forecasting Deal: Exposing Myths, Eliminating Bad Practices, Providing Practical Solutions*, Wiley, June 8, 2010: 1–246.
3. Robert Fildes and Paul Goodwin, "Good and Bad Judgment in Forecasting: Lessons from Four Companies," *Foresight: International Journal of Applied Forecasting*, Issue 8, Fall 2007: 5–10. https://www.ephmra.org/media/2879/6-paul-goodwin-foresight-article-lessons-from-4-companies.pdf
4. Ibid.
5. Michael Gilliland, *The Business Forecasting Deal*.
6. Ibid.
7. Roger Baldridge and Varunraj Valsaraj, "Assisted Demand Planning Using Machine Learning for CPG and Retail," SAS White Paper, September 18, 2018: 1–12. https://www.sas.com/en/whitepapers/assisted-demand-planning-109971.html

CHAPTER 7

The Future Is Cloud Analytics and Analytics at the Edge

Cloud computing is the technology of the future, particularly for predictive and anticipatory analytics. Given that demand forecasting and planning has been cited as the area that will deliver the most benefits from predictive analytics, we can assume that cloud computing would also be the preferred technology platform. As this technology continues to grow, there will be debate surrounding the best approaches to utilizing cloud computing due to the high demand for advanced analytics skills. The cloud computing market has been growing fast and shows no signs of slowing down. As a result, spending on public cloud services now accounts for more than half of worldwide software, server, and storage spending growth, according to recent research conducted by several analytics firms. In addition, there is growing demand for certified cloud professionals, as well as basic cloud computing skills.

WHY CLOUD ANALYTICS?

Many companies are still running their applications on their internal networks, having made previous investments in the necessary hardware, software, and IT infrastructure. It can be costly and complex, however, to maintain such technology deployments, which require regular upgrades and special technical expertise to keep pace with changing demands. This is why companies are moving portions if not all of their applications to the cloud. It is not just core business systems like finance, HR, and supply chain that are suited to the cloud, but also analytics applications. There are three key benefits:

1. **Increased agility.** With the ability to scale analytics capabilities up and down as required, a company can pivot faster than ever before.

2. **Increased innovation.** The flexibility of the cloud enables a company to act quickly, fail fast, and share learnings and new skills across the different departments and analyst teams.

3. **Reduced costs.** By moving infrastructure services to a pay-per-use model, companies cut on-premise costs by roughly a third.

There are frequent debates about on-premise versus cloud. People cite security concerns, connectivity issues, and network speed as good reasons to keep their data on-site. As companies gain more experience running applications in the cloud, they will become more confident in migrating their mission-critical services, including analytics. Although there were initial concerns over data security, there's now a growing recognition that applications in the cloud can be more secure than on-premise. Today, cloud security includes a broad set of policies, technologies, applications, and controls utilized to protect virtualized IP, data, applications, services, and the associated infrastructure of cloud computing. It is a sub-domain of computer security, network security, and, more broadly, information security. In fact, cloud security and governance are in many cases more secure than on-premise applications.

WHAT ARE THE DIFFERENCES BETWEEN CONTAINERS AND VIRTUAL MACHINES?

Most cloud deployments are based on virtual machines (VMs), but it is becoming clear that containers can offer significant benefits. Consequently, before choosing one cloud technology over another, it is important to understand the key differences between them. The corporate IT strategy, and purpose of the application deployment will determine if VMs or containers are beneficial in the public, private, or hybrid cloud. The answer will depend on three primary factors:

1. The functionality differences between VMs and containers;
2. The level of interdependence between private and public cloud components; and
3. Users' willingness to customize their own cloud performance.

VMs and containers run applications differently to create virtual resources. VMs' special software solution, known as a hypervisor, partitions a server from the operating system (OS), creating a true virtual machine to share only the hardware. While containers virtualize the operating system, the OS and some middleware are shared. VMs are functionally more flexible because the guest environment where the applications run is like a server. A company can pick its own operating system and middleware independent of what other VMs are using on the same server. Containers require a company to accommodate a common OS and middleware when they choose applications, as each container uses the core server platform and shares it with other containers. (See Figure 7.1.)

Organizations with a variety of software platforms may have difficulties using containers because of the need to standardize on a single hosting platform. Although everything runs on a single OS, they may need to harmonize it all to use a single version of some or all the middleware applications. This can be difficult to do if the software is dependent on a specific version. Conversely, containers have less overhead because there is no duplication of the platform software for every application or component deployed. This lowers overhead and makes it possible to run more components per server using container technology. In addition, deployment and redeployment of applications and components run much faster in containers. It is also generally easier to operationalize containers than VMs when applications are more varied.

Virtual machines and containers differ in many ways, but the primary difference is that containers provide a means to virtualize an OS so that multiple workloads can run on a single OS instance. With VMs, the hardware is being virtualized to run multiple OS instances. Containers' speed, agility, and portability make them a more practical technology to help streamline software development.

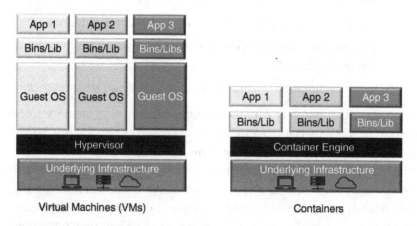

Figure 7.1 VMs Versus Container Architectures

WHY CLOUD ANALYTICS?

Many companies are still developing foundational technology capabilities that are key to realizing the benefits of AI/machine learning, such as cloud/data center infrastructure, cybersecurity, data management, and development processes and workflows. As companies move up the analytics maturity curve, they are likely to report mature capabilities in these areas. These are clear indications that CIOs and C-level business leaders are planning to increase these new capabilities; however, if the cloud isn't there, they are not going to do this very well.

Cloud services is particularly critical for AI/machine learning. Paying for on-demand cloud computing resources is more cost effective than buying and operating a computer infrastructure to support predictive analytics.[1] It also offers more flexibility to serve different business units with their individual needs and access to the latest technologies. Having an infrastructure in the cloud allows companies to provide for the different needs of each business unit without having to buy the entire technology platform. In addition, the cloud enables the use of the latest and best-in-breed technology. Cloud computing shifts management of the technology to the cloud provider, thus improving time to value from months to days—moving to cloud means someone else is doing all the heavy lifting from development to deployment.

PREDICTIVE ANALYTICS ARE CREATING IT DISRUPTIONS

AI/machine learning experts are putting high demands on IT—more demand in terms of speed and agility. The differences between IT that works and IT that doesn't work for ML are significant. Whether it's computing resources, DevOps, or new technologies for experimenting with different algorithms and data, analytics practitioners are pressing IT to respond. AI/machine learning is driving significant and, in many cases, dramatic changes to software development and deployment processes. As a result, those who have already implemented AI/machine learning are likely to report a strong impact on both software development and deployment in the cloud.

AI/machine learning brings significant change as compared to traditional technology implementations because the deployment process is dynamic, requiring continuous monitoring and retraining. Managing these systems requires ongoing management of the AI/ machine learning models, not just before but also after they have been deployed. It means being ready to make improvements and corrections to the models in real time. Those companies who have deployed ML are always collecting data and refining the models, as the models are not static. It also requires making sure that once a model is trained, it can be "unlearned." It may require corrective action if a pattern assumed to be correct has changed and is no longer significant, thus requiring new data and/or corrective actions. ML algorithms are designed to improve results as additional informative data is collected and entered into the models. Although a predictive model works well, it still requires ongoing maintenance, as well as the most relevant information and data. When you start to deploy ML models, things may change as a result, and over time may no longer work as well. This is where ML is different from a typical software development process. The training and testing processes should continue as the environment or operating conditions change. This works best using cloud-based containers.

The main reason for the need to constantly reevaluate predictive models is that the initial model is unlikely to incorporate all the variables influencing demand to predict all the patterns or account for how consumers are interacting in the marketplace. A good example is COVID-19, which has disrupted the trend and seasonal patterns for essential products and eating out at restaurants. Those past trends and seasonal patterns are no longer valid due to the disruptions caused by the pandemic. So, demand analysts need to find other data sources that can be used as leading indicators, and are representative to the situation at hand, such as POS, epidemiological, Google trends, economic, and other data. In other words, the demand analysts serve as backup operators who recalibrate and retrain the models with the new information and data. This illustrates the human factor involved. It is a little different from a typical software project in that, once it's deployed, the human interaction with it can change, as the models originally deployed may become outdated due to disruptions.

DATA IS INFLUENCING SOFTWARE DEVELOPMENT

The demands that AI/machine learning places on an organization mandates the need to manage data holistically and proactively. This has influenced software development practices and increased the need for IT collaboration regarding architectural strategies, and interaction with experts and practitioners. There is a need for more awareness regarding how data flows throughout the company, and how data applies to all software development, not just the development of AI and machine learning models. As organizations plan their use of the data they collect and generate, a shift in attitude and approach also influences IT. The people who design applications in IT don't just need to think about hardware and applications; they also need to think about the data. It is becoming more and more apparent that the applications they're creating or designing create data that is going to be used later in the process. This just wasn't true a decade ago. So, whether it's an application process or a website design, data quality is now a core part of that design principle.

Storing data in the cloud has clear advantages. Cloud's elastic provisioning capabilities give companies access to additional storage space when they need it. What companies choose to store in the cloud, versus on their local servers, does make a difference. The following types of data are good fits for public cloud storage.

- **Customer-facing data.** If a company has large amounts of customer-facing data, such as catalogs of merchandise, it may make sense to host that data in the cloud where it can be copied redundantly as needed, geographically distributed, or provisioned up or down according to customer demand. This puts the data closest to the people who need it.

- **Distributed data access.** Data that can be accessed from several locations, particularly read-only data or data that is synchronized periodically from a central source, are good fits for the cloud. The public cloud has fewer physical constraints on storage, which gives companies the ability to provision out as much as they need and as budget allows, but IT administrators must take into consideration bandwidth requirements and possible latency challenges.

- **Data backups.** Backing up data from a local system such as a desktop or an enterprise data warehouse to a cloud host is a good example of an instance where cloud-based storage makes sense. Bandwidth and storage space are two limiting factors. The more of each that a company has at their disposal, the easier it is to mirror local data in the cloud. However, a cloud-based backup can become tricky if dealing with terabytes of data. If siphoning that data from the cloud over the network isn't prohibitive, ask the cloud provider to send a physical copy of the data.[2]

In many cases, particular types of data are best kept in a local data center or private cloud. Here are a few examples of data that should be kept on-premise.

- **Mirrored data.** Mirrored refers to the real-time operation of copying data, as an exact copy, from one location to a local or remote storage medium. In computing, a mirror is an exact copy of a data set. Most commonly, data mirroring is used when multiple exact copies of data are required in multiple locations. Copies of data stored in the cloud are synchronized passively to one or multiple hosts. There are services that use a VMware-hosted appliance to perform local synchronization with a company's private cloud.
- **Sensitive data.** Some companies choose to keep sensitive customer data local because of security concerns or to adhere to certain regulatory guidelines, such as health care information. From a practical standpoint, at-rest and in-transit encryption, more comprehensive service-level agreements (SLAs), and other safeguards have helped restore companies' trust in hosting sensitive data in the cloud. But security is as much about perceptions as it is about actual procedures, and some organizations are simply more comfortable keeping sensitive data local.
- **Synchronized data.** Although it is becoming possible to ensure multiple copies of a piece of synchronized data, sometimes the only way to guarantee it is to keep one copy where it is consumed most often, which is usually local.

Often, companies keep some data in the cloud and related data on-premise. If they must keep data synchronized, one major consideration is application-aware synchronization. If the data exists as files, then it is not complicated. However, more sophisticated databases must be synchronized according to the application. Live-mounted databases need to be synchronized to and from the cloud via attendant applications. In many cases, those apps must be able to see the sync target as a conventional file system; otherwise, the apps would need an extension that allows them to easily transfer data in and out of the cloud.[3]

It is not always practical to remotely host instances of data, as there may be no business advantages. For example, a company may not need to mirror a large database that only a select number of people access in several locations. On the other hand, housing "big data" in the cloud is a good fit for data that requires broad access, whether as a public resource, for data analytics, or for business intelligence (BI) purposes.

WHY CLOUD-NATIVE SOLUTIONS?

AI/machine learning development requires more, and earlier, collaboration between IT and the user community than traditional application development. Choices about aspects of ML such as computing architecture, how the data will flow in a particular application, how the new AI/machine learning system will change business processes in various parts of the company, and how people will interact with the system through user interfaces now become part of the early-stage decisions. It has raised the stakes on the up-front alignment between the organization and IT regarding technology architecture, data, and API strategies. It creates a lot of complexity early in the project development process. In fact, one of the things companies have found is that projects slowed down significantly in the beginning because there is a lot of alignment required. Many questions arise that never would have come up before. When it's time to use the data, they quickly realize the data structure needs to be accelerated because a lot of the earlier questions were not raised regarding data requirements.

This means that domain experts need to understand more about how the technology works, just as technology experts need to be smarter about the business when discussing AI/machine learning projects. This cultural shift requires IT leaders to be comfortable with business colleagues' questions about details, down to the technology functions, data, and computing architecture that support them. Historically, business leaders have not been concerned about whether data is in an enterprise data warehouse or a local data mart supporting the applications, but now they do, and it all matters for a successful AI/machine learning deployment.

So, what are the advantages of cloud-native AI/machine learning applications? Most importantly, the cloud environment is "elastic." This is the most significant advantage for most businesses because the ability to customize how much data and where it's stored without later implementing costly upgrades and system changes is the most important benefit. The environment grows or pivots as the development expands. No matter what kind of hardware and software a company buys, they will always be working towards obsolescence. This is the norm and has been for decades, but with the advent of big data and AI/machine learning, companies are moving faster toward obsolescence.

The introduction of the cloud has democratized computing capabilities. Companies can deploy applications at scale using massive cloud computing and storage capabilities. Cloud-native apps never settle into in-house systems. Instead, they run in the elastic computing environment, delivering reusable features through containers that are agile. You can deploy programs faster, even progressively bigger programs, and with fewer burdens on a company's limited computing resources. In addition, the cloud can package applications into a container, allowing the ability to replicate the results across multiple technology platforms.

WHY DOES ALL THIS MATTER?

Machine learning requires data sets for training models to perform tasks. For example, the ML algorithm learns to identify how consumers react to different sales and marketing tactics by consuming raw training data and comparing it via various programming vehicles, such as sales promotions, pricing actions, in-store merchandising, and others. Accessing the type of data needed for training more complex tasks can be frustrating when there is no human or processing power available. The lone data scientist can't go through thousands of pieces of data to train the machine to recognize those sales and marketing tactics. Instead, by deploying those tools in the cloud, a company can use intelligent automaton supported by machine learning to automate and operate at scale. The cloud allows organizations to use automated or managed machine learning algorithms to remove the burden of limited human resources. It removes limitations on access to data, allowing all stakeholders to access the application and insights. In short, everyone gets to know which sales and marketing tactics influence consumers to buy their products, and at what magnitude. It also opens the door for citizen data scientists to deploy applications without having experience writing code. The cloud uses automation to train and deliver the results from the models. The user can evaluate the model, debug, and replicate results from the cloud directly.

Intelligent automation on the cloud supported by ML is becoming the driver of cloud computing. Companies can deploy ML models and deep learning to the elastic and scalable environment of the cloud. Cloud native is less of a new technology and more of a paradigm shift. Businesses can use the cloud to deploy microservices to find data lakes for the better, more in-depth training required for deep learning. The cloud is beyond uncovering consumer insights and more of how to influence consumers to buy your products. Cloud intelligent automation gives companies the ability to deploy services without having to deploy native apps. Organizations can leverage the cloud for their existing applications, access data sources, and perform big data pulls. Building a culture of continuous innovation can be difficult without proper infrastructure. For the first time, companies have access to software and services that go far beyond their in-house capabilities.

CLOUD-NATIVE FORECASTING AND PLANNING SOLUTIONS

Although spreadsheets have always been the preferred technology for demand forecasting and planning, many businesses are now pivoting away from them for many reasons. In addition to being tedious, spreadsheets are difficult to manage, prone to inaccuracy, not scalable, and create islands of fragmented information. This makes it difficult for companies to have confidence in their demand forecasts and plans, resulting in misinformed, skewed business decisions. A cloud-native forecasting and planning platform is much easier to organize and manage than spreadsheets, while providing greater governance and control over the numerous what-if scenarios that are created on a weekly basis to evaluate and ultimately make accurate business decisions. The cloud also makes it easy to integrate commercial, financial, and operational data, which increases accuracy and ensures forecasts are aligned with company goals and objectives.

Each organization requires varying levels of detail in their analytics models, and the dimensions differ between organizations. For example, sales, marketing, and demand planning will all require different dimensions, and therefore, the modeling tactics utilized may differ depending on the strategic, operational, and tactical processes. Creating analytical models on a granular level will allow businesses to maintain an agile supply plan that can be altered quickly, giving dynamic organizations the versatility they need to execute the plan.

WHY MOVE TO A CLOUD-NATIVE DEMAND PLANNING PLATFORM?

With a cloud-native platform, a company's data can be accessed from anywhere. Commercial, operational, and market data integration is essential for successful demand forecasting, but it relies on the use of open and agile technology platforms. The cloud can eliminate the need for on-premise proprietary technology solutions while decreasing the costs of ownership and providing an integrated consolidated view of all data. Thus, providing a single source of truth for the company. Cloud-native enterprise platforms offer:

- **A normalized and harmonized data repository.** The cloud technology accesses the data stored in a centrally maintained repository (data lake, DRS, or other), and each functional area can build from that data to create analytics models that rely directly on the most up-to-date downstream and transactional information. This results in greater cohesion and collaboration among functional areas, resulting in enhanced demand and supply planning.

- **Collaboration across the organization.** The cloud can be accessed from anywhere with a cloud-native data repository, thus allowing every functional area in the organization to constantly stay up to date with new industry, sales, marketing, and financial information. More importantly, they have the ability to share information across all functional areas. Cloud-native analytics technology offers additional collaborative real-time capabilities providing alerts, comments, drilldown capabilities, and others, facilitating communication across the demand forecasting and planning process. The software retains all previous versions of analytics models and plans, so participants can refer to prior versions as needed.

- **Reduction in time and improved process efficiencies.** Managing analytics in the cloud is easier and more efficient than managing numerous spreadsheets. With enhanced collaboration across the demand planning process, companies can reduce the time spent in meetings while improving office workflow.

- **Enhanced Scalability.** The cloud makes it easier to scale analytics, particularly AI/machine learning algorithms, by enabling multidimensional modeling. It also accommodates the scaling needs of the business by seamlessly accommodating the increased number of users and product proliferation without technical challenges or the need to add additional licenses. The cloud can handle large volumes of data easily, as your data needs increase, and storage capacity grows.

- **Improved technology deployment.** With the cloud, deployment is much easier and cheaper than with on-premises technology. It eliminates installation and software updates, offers spreadsheet functions for an effortless transition reducing the learning curve making it easy to upload and consolidate data and information.

Cloud-native technology can help to improve efficiency and the accuracy of the demand forecasting and planning process. With cloud-native analytics applications, companies can deploy predictive analytics capabilities and increase collaboration while lowering the cost of ownership, and they can fast-track deployment. A cloud-native technology platform is highly scalable, allowing companies to increase their usage requirements without the need to purchase additional technology.

WHY "ANALYTICS AT THE EDGE"?

Analytics at the edge is a technology approach to data collection and analysis where an automated analytical calculation is performed on data at a sensor, network switch, or other device instead of waiting for the data to be sent back to a centralized data repository. It is a distributed information technology architecture in which client data is processed at the edge of the network, as close to the initial source as possible. In its simplistic terms, edge computing moves portions of storage and computing resources out of the central data warehouse, or the DSR closer to the source of the data itself. As discussed in earlier chapters, data is the lifeblood of the digital economy and those companies who have embarked on digital transformation will benefit the most by becoming data driven. Data provides valuable business insights and supports real-time delivery of critical information to support business processes and operations. Today's businesses are overflowing in a tidal wave of information, as huge amounts of data are routinely collected from sensors and IoT devices operating in real time from remote locations operating globally.

However, the flood of data is changing the way businesses handle data storage, processing, and calculating the results. The traditional computing paradigm built on a centralized data warehouse with normal Internet connectivity is not well suited for transferring reams of near real-time data. Bandwidth limitations, latency issues, and unpredictable system disruptions all contribute to network bottlenecks. Companies are responding to such data challenges related to the new digital economy by deploying edge computing applications. Rather than transmitting raw data to a central data warehouse for processing (and where analysis work is performed), the data is captured, whether it's from a retail store, the factory floor, a sprawling warehouse facility, or across mobile devices. Only the results of the computing work at the edge, such as real-time business insights and prediction results, are sent back to the data center for review and human interactions. As a result, edge computing is reshaping technology architectures and business computing. (See Figure 7.2.)

Traditional enterprise computing produces data at a client endpoint, such as a user's computer or laptop. That data is moved across a wide area network (WAN) such as the Internet, or a corporate local area network (LAN) where the data is stored and processed by an ERP (Enterprise Resource Planning, or transactional system) application. The result of that processing is then conveyed back to the client via endpoint devices. This has been a proven and time-tested approach to client-server computing for most typical business applications for the past several decades. However, the number of devices connected to the Internet, and the volume of data being produced by embedded devices, is growing far too quickly for traditional enterprise data center infrastructures to accommodate.

The process of moving all this newly captured data and information takes time and is disruptive, as it puts an incredible strain on the global Internet, causing congestion and bottlenecks. Rather than transmitting raw data to an enterprise data center for processing and analysis,

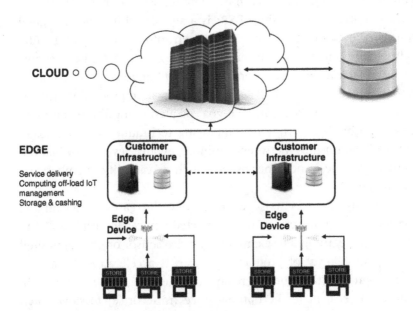

Figure 7.2 Edge Computing and Analytics Architecture

edge computing puts the processing work where the data is generated, whether at the retail store, the factory floor, or a sprawling utility network. Only the result of that computing work at the edge, such as real-time business insights, equipment maintenance predictions, or other actionable answers, is sent back to the enterprise data center for review and other activities. Edge analytics is an analysis process where an automated analytical algorithm is performed at a sensor, network switch, or other device (data collection point). As a result, edge computing is restructuring business computing.

Edge analytics has gained attention as the IoT-connected devices have been embedded to collect and analyze real-time information. In many organizations, streaming data from store beacons, smart shelf, computer vision, or cold chain logistics on board transportation trucks and other remote devices connected to the IoT creates an enormous amount of consumer rich information and data, which can be difficult and expensive to manage. By capturing the data using event stream processing and applying predictive analytics at the edge of a corporate network, companies can set parameters on what information is worth sending to the cloud or on-premises data repositories like a DSR.

Event stream processing (ESP) is a set of technologies designed to assist the construction of event-driven information systems. ESP technologies include event visualization, event databases, event-driven middleware, and event processing languages, or complex event processing (CEP). ESP deals with the task of processing streams of real-time event data with the goal of identifying the meaningful pattern within those streams, employing techniques such as detection of relationships between multiple events, event correlation, event hierarchies, and other aspects such as causality, membership, and timing.

Analyzing data as it is generated will decrease latency in the decision-making process on the connected devices by using ESP and AI/machine learning. For example, if a price sensor on the retail shelf detects the velocity of product purchases is accelerating, it can (1) send a signal to the store merchandising team to restock the shelf, and/or (2) recalculate the optimal price (raise price) to slow down sales until inventory can be ordered from the central warehouse to replenished store inventory before the product is out of stock. This can save time as compared to transmitting the data to a central data warehouse for processing and analysis, potentially enabling organizations to reduce or avoid out-of-stocks on shelf. Another primary benefit of edge analytics is scalability. Pushing analytics algorithms to sensors and network devices alleviates the processing strain on enterprise data management and analytics systems, even as the number of connected devices being deployed by organizations and the amount of data being generated and collected accelerates.

The most common use cases for edge analytics is monitoring edge devices. This is particularly true for IoT devices. A data analytics platform can be deployed for the purpose of monitoring a large collection of devices for the purpose of making sure that the devices are performing normally. If a problem does occur, an edge analytics platform would be able to take corrective action automatically. If automatic remediation is not possible, then the solution platform will inform the appropriate area via an alert with actionable insights that will help them address the situation.

EDGE ANALYTICS BENEFITS

Edge analytics delivers several compelling benefits:

- **Near real-time analysis of data.** Because analysis is performed at the point of data collection, often on the device itself, the data can be analyzed in near real time. This would simply not be the case if the device had to transmit the data to a back-end server in the cloud or in a remote data center for processing.
- **Scalability.** Edge analytics is by its very nature scalable, because each device analyzes its own data, and the computational workload is distributed across devices from retailer back to consumer goods supplier if necessary.
- **Possible reduction of costs.** Significant costs are associated with traditional big data analytics collection, processing, and storage. Regardless of whether the data is processed in a public cloud or in an organization's own data center, there

are costs tied to data storage, data processing, and consumption. Some edge analytics platforms for IoT devices use that device's hardware to perform the data analytics eliminating the need for back-end processing.

- **Improved security.** If data is analyzed on the device that captured it, then it is not necessary to transmit the full data set across the network. This can help improve security because the raw data never leaves the device that captured it.

EDGE ANALYTICS LIMITATIONS

Edge analytics is a relatively new technology, and as such not all the hardware is currently capable of storing data or performing complex processing and analytics. However, those devices capturing real-time data can be complemented with existing ESP and AI/machine learning technology. Like any other technology, edge analytics has its limits. Those limitations include:

- **Not all hardware supports it.** Simply put, not every IoT device has the memory, CPU, and storage hardware required to perform deep analytics onboard the device.
- **Companies may have to identify the technology stack to assemble creating their own edge analytics platform.** Although there are off-the-shelf standard capability platforms available, it is possible that an organization might have to develop its own edge analytics platform based on the devices that it wants to analyze.

FORECASTING AT THE EDGE

Access to ever-larger data sets continues to complicate the forecasting process, leading to even more variety in how forecasts are developed. According to recent research, as many as 40% of companies are not particularly happy with the accuracy of their forecasting and planning process that takes far too much time to develop each business cycle. Using analytic algorithms as data is generated, at the edge of the corporate network, companies can set constraints to determine what information is worth sending to the cloud, to a demand signal repository, or other data repositories for later use. Companies can process data continuously, on the move, in-memory with high speed and low latency to sense demand, understand what's influencing demand, and act to anticipate future demand. Thus, enhancing the customer/consumer experience while ensuring supply chain efficiencies at the retail store, channel, and/or mobile device purchase point.

The key benefit for retailers and consumer goods companies using edge analytics is the ability to analyze data as it is generated, which decreases latency in the decision-making process as the data is collected through connected devices. For example, if sensor data from mobile devices indicate that product purchases of a product are trending upward, business rules built into the algorithms interpreting the data at the network edge can automatically alert consumer goods suppliers to increase production for that product to meet demand. Using event stream processing combined with AI/machine learning, that information can save time and lower costs as compared with transmitting the data to a central hub for processing and analysis, potentially enabling companies to minimize or eliminate back orders.

Rather than designing consolidated data systems where all the data is sent back to an enterprise data warehouse, data lake, or DSR in a raw state, where it has to be cleaned and analyzed before being of any value, why not do everything at the edge of the system, including demand forecasting using predictive analytics and/or machine learning? Understanding and filtering out the noise from the useful information and navigating down to the individual device (or node), retailers can anticipate future demand to eliminate out-of-stocks on shelf and optimize store-level promotions. Combining nodes across the store (and/or mobile devices) can help identify increases in demand as a result of sales promotions, thus improving promotion effectiveness and driving inventory policy. Another key benefit of forecasting at the edge is scalability. Pushing analytics algorithms to sensors and network devices alleviates the processing strain on enterprise data and analytics systems. Instead of demand planning, we can accomplish real-time demand execution across the supply chain. This offers the first step toward the autonomous supply chain.

Forecasting at the edge will allow companies to apply predictive analytics across devices to enhance the customer journey. This has an impact on not just how retailers market to the consumer, but also how they drive the ideal product assortment within each store, channel, or location, including e-commerce. Forecasting at the edge also enhances the ability to make decisions as to whether the optimal inventory should be held locally or in regional distribution centers or customer warehouses closer to the customer ordering point; thus providing the analytics and insights to make those decisions end-to-end across the supply chain. Companies can use these insights to improve the effectiveness of marketing campaigns, product assortment and merchandising decisions, distribution, and operations across all channels of business using predictive analytics and machine learning.

Today, the technology exists to support forecasting at the edge. There are no longer any data or technology hurdles to overcome. Only our own inhibitions and the desire to take the leap toward achieving the end goal of an autonomous supply chain are stopping us. The multitude of forces affecting the relationship between demand and supply are set to expand their influence. Smart leaders will take advantage of the flood of digital data to better understand those forces to make more accurate and predictive supply chain decisions.

So, are you stuck in a vicious cycle of planning demand, using 2- to 4-week-old data, or are you conducting real-time demand execution anticipating demand at the edge?

CLOUD ANALYTICS VERSUS EDGE ANALYTICS

Cloud analytics and edge analytics are techniques for gathering relevant data and then using that data to perform analysis. The key difference between the two is that cloud analytics requires raw data to be transmitted to the cloud for analysis. Although cloud analytics has its place, edge analytics has two main advantages. First, edge analytics incurs far lower latency than cloud analytics because data is analyzed on-site in many cases, often within the device itself, in real time, as the data is created. The second advantage is that edge analytics doesn't require network connectivity to the cloud. This means that edge analytics can be used in bandwidth-constrained environments, or in locations where cloud connectivity simply isn't available.

Edge analytics is still evolving as new technologies and practices are being developed to enhance its capabilities and performance. Perhaps the most remarkable trend is that edge computing and services will continue to become more widely available over the next decade. It is apparent that COVID-19 has called the attention to possibilities of edge analytics. Although edge analytics is only being considered a possibility today, the technology will certainly be expected to become more ubiquitous shifting the way the Internet is viewed, bringing more ideas and potential use cases for edge technology.

CLOSING THOUGHTS

While cloud computing has firmly established itself as the "new normal" for corporate IT organizations, the cloud is becoming a key component for a successful digital transformation. Consequently, CIOs will need to update their processes and upskill their staff to maintain the necessary control while the cloud rapidly flourishes. Open-source, cloud-ready point solutions now allow companies to monitor consumer demand on a daily and/or weekly basis providing real-time updates regarding shifting consumer demand patterns based on current market conditions related to unforeseen disruptions.

The shift to multicloud environments has been an ad hoc transition for many organizations, often born out of necessity rather than a well-thought-out strategy. The ease of buying and utilizing public cloud services is leading many business managers to create new teams to support migration to the public cloud without necessarily including IT. These so-called "shadow IT" initiatives have been fine as quick stop-gap solutions to support specific business needs, but they have created huge challenges. The most common challenges are increased complexity, silos of information and applications, plus increased security risk.

In the highly competitive digital transformation environment, an ad hoc public cloud strategy is not a strategy at all. IT must be part of the solution or else organizations will face too much complexity and uncertainty. According to recent research, there is a range of potential challenges that include:

- Legacy IT infrastructure without a planned strategy for modernization.
- Ad hoc collection of point specific applications for managing cloud environments.
- Management is in-house with no external assistance.
- IT investments are heavily biased to capital expenditures.[4]

With the expansion of multicloud environments and organizations using cloud services from different providers to avoid vendor lock-in or use of best-of-breed solutions, the public cloud is not a simple matter of choosing a service, connecting to the data source, and you're ready to go. The notion of public cloud simplicity is becoming something of an oxymoron in today's multicloud environments. IT teams face growing complexity in cost management, governance, app and data portability, performance, security, compliance, and data control. None of those challenges are simple to solve. However, they can be addressed with hybrid cloud solutions that allow IT teams to use consistent tools, processes, and procedures that stretch across all platforms, including multiple public clouds, on-premise data centers, and edge locations. With hybrid cloud computing, the IT teams can reduce complexity through centralized management, increased automation, improved security, and consistent tools, technologies, and processes. In many cases, the hybrid cloud is becoming the most effective architecture for enterprise cloud adoption.

Many companies are now investing in "cloud centers of excellence" (CCoE) to address the governance challenges that differ from their on-premise experiences. A CCoE is a multidisciplinary team of IT and a cloud team of domain experts who develop and lead the strategy to support successful, standardized cloud adoption. The purpose of the CCoE is to help business units implement cloud technologies that are secure, efficient, and cost-effective. The CCoE's core objective is to mitigate undesirable cloud outcomes by assembling an experienced, interdisciplinary, and collaborative team of domain experts. There are three core CCoE benefits:

- **Uniformity.** Establish best practices, guidelines, security, and governance for every business unit to adopt. A well-planned and standardized cloud strategy supporting regulatory compliance.

- **Acceleration.** "Quick start" cloud projects with greater speed and success than independent trial-and-error efforts. The CCoE provides guidance, answers questions, and helps departments complete projects faster than individual business units attempting to learn cloud technologies from the ground up.

- **Efficiency.** Minimize cloud usage through optimized utilization and costs. Adhere to common guidelines and practices to make cloud deployments easier to understand, improve, and troubleshoot.[5]

The CCoE team members reflect a broad cross-section of complementary skills and experiences. Domain experts should include representatives from the business side as well as IT staff with expertise in operations, infrastructure, security, and applications. A CCoE should also include business stakeholders who can align the goals and objectives for adoption with overall business plans.

Analytics at the edge is still in the early phases of deployment. The evolution to a distributed cloud architecture at the edge should not be thought of as a specific data center location, but will reside at any number of locations, depending on the expectations and resource requirements/availability for a given application. The location of an application could shift to different edge data centers during its life cycle, driving the need to intelligently scale infrastructure both within and between edge data centers and to the central cloud, while automating workloads between locations at the edge of the network.

An additional implication for analytics at the edge is the value of processing the vast amounts of data generated locally by devices and reducing traffic back to the central cloud. The goal is to reduce the latency and amount of traffic between distributed sites to the central cloud and effectively serve the large-scale analytics required to push extrapolations and predictions to the devices at the edge, thus improving performance. Analytics at the edge is an extension of cloud computing, which relies heavily on intelligent automation through interpretation of massive KPI streams from underlying resources. Automation will depend significantly on the collection and analysis using AI/machine learning on the network edge and virtualized (container) resources, as well as on the ability to anticipate trends by turning mountains of data into actionable insights and predictions. Leveraging these insights will sense and adapt to edge applications' needs securely, and in real time.

The rapid expansion of the digital economy is having an unforeseen impact in our lives across multiple business sectors worldwide. Companies in almost every industry are being forced to rethink all aspects of their business to keep up with the pace of change. The speed of commerce is accelerating so quickly that real-time business, the ability to access up-to-date information and interact with consumers and machines across a business network in real-time, is now the goal for many companies. Meanwhile, technology has become the backbone that makes real-time business decisions possible. It involves the complex process of receiving, processing, retrieving, and delivering data instantly as changes or transactions occur. The potential for real-time analytics is raising expectations across the entire business landscape as e-commerce is replacing traditional brick-and-mortar shopping. Business networks are quickly transforming into digital ecosystems, as multiple organizations across entire industries begin to transform to achieve the goal of real-time consumer interaction.

The unparalleled speed of technological change has made it challenging for many business leaders to grasp all the implications and the full potential of the digital economy. While companies grapple with the decisions over how, when, and on which areas to focus in their digital transformation journey, the marketplace around them continues to forge ahead with new digital formats at record-breaking speed. As barriers to entry fall, more agile lateral competitors will take advantage of the latest digital innovations and opportunities, further blurring industry lines. This growth has the potential to quickly take the industry in a completely new direction, leaving traditional business leaders shaking their heads and asking, "What do we do now?"

NOTES

1. "How AI Changes the Rules: New Imperatives for the Intelligent Organization," MIT SMR Connections Custom Research Report, 2020: 1–24. https://www.sas.com/content/dam/SAS/documents/marketing-whitepapers-ebooks/third-party-whitepapers/en/mit-how-ai-changes-rules-111222.pdf
2. Serdar Yegulalp, "The Basics of Cloud-based Data Storage," *Tech Target*, May 6, 2012. https://searchcloudcomputing.techtarget.com/tip/The-basics-of-cloud-based-data-storage
3. Janette Kosior, "Using the Cloud to Enhance Modeling and Forecasting," *Planful*, 2020. https://planful.com/blog/using-the-cloud-to-enhance-modeling-and-forecasting/
4. "What Is Edge Computing? Everything You Need to Know," *Tech Target E-Guide*, 2020: 1–28. https://searchdatacenter.techtarget.com/pro/What-is-Edge-Computing-Everything-You-Need-to-Know?offer=Content_OTHR-PillarPage_Whatisedgecomputing?Everythingyouneedtoknow
5. Stephen J. Bigelow, "How to Build a Cloud Center of Excellence," *Tech Target*, January 8, 2021. https://searchcloudcomputing.techtarget.com/tip/How-to-build-a-cloud-center-of-excellence

Index

Page numbers followed by *f* and *t* refer to figures and tables, respectively.